ALSO BY JOAN BISKUPIC

American Original: The Life and Constitution of
Supreme Court Justice Antonin Scalia

Sandra Day O'Connor: How the First Woman on
the Supreme Court Became Its Most Influential Justice

Breaking In

Breaking In

*The Rise of Sonia Sotomayor
and the Politics of Justice*

Joan Biskupic

Sarah Crichton Books

Farrar, Straus and Giroux

New York

Sarah Crichton Books
Farrar, Straus and Giroux
18 West 18th Street, New York 10011

Library of Congress Cataloging-in-Publication Data
Biskupic, Joan, author.
    Breaking in : the rise of Sonia Sotomayor and the politics of justice /
Joan Biskupic.
        pages   cm
    Includes bibliographical references (p.   ) and index.
    ⁻ ISBN 978-0-374-29874-6 (hardback) — ISBN 978-0-374-71241-9
(ebook)
        1. Sotomayor, Sonia, 1954–   2. Hispanic American judges—
Biography.   3. Judges—United States—Biography.   I. Title.

KF8745.S67 B57 2014
347.73'2634—dc23
[B]

                                                        2014016703

Designed by Jonathan D. Lippincott

www.fsgbooks.com
www.twitter.com/fsgbooks • www.facebook.com/fsgbooks

1   3   5   7   9   10   8   6   4   2

For Clay and Elizabeth

I spent countless hours of my childhood looking at the passing subway cars that streaked by my grandmother's windows . . . With some frequency, my cousins and I would make faces at the passing people. Other times, I would stare at the faces at the subway doors and wonder who those people were and what kinds of lives they lived . . . I wonder now if any of those passing subway riders on the Number 5 trains ever saw us in the window of Grandma's apartment. I wonder if they ever wondered who we were and what we would become.

—Sonia Sotomayor, in 2007

I stepped into a moment of history.

—Sonia Sotomayor, in 2010, one year after her
Supreme Court appointment

Contents

Breaking In

ONE

Life of the Party

This party celebrating the end of the Supreme Court's annual term is an exclusive affair that bears all the trappings of a staid, cultured institution and its privileged occupants. Festivities are staged in two majestic rooms that face each other across a red-carpeted hallway. Oil portraits of the nation's chief justices, all men in dark formal garb, line the oak-paneled walls. Crystal chandeliers hang from the high, gold-glazed ceilings. The large elegant room on the east side of the corridor holds a gleaming grand piano. This is where the entertainment takes place. Across the hall, food and drink are laid out on silver trays and white linen–covered tables. As the end-of-term party for June 2010 was approaching, Chief Justice John G. Roberts, Jr., sent invitations to the staff. He mentioned the customary platters of hors d'oeuvres that would be offered and the law clerks' musical parodies that would be presented. He also reminded invitees that the party was open only to full-time Court employees, not to part-time workers, interns, or contractors—another sign of the special nature of this event at this elite place.

Justice Sonia Sotomayor, a Bronx-born Puerto Rican, was about to attend her first such party. The nation's first Hispanic justice had joined the Supreme Court the previous August, a 2009 appointee of the nation's first African American president.[*]

---

[*]The term "Hispanic" refers to people who trace their family's origins to the Spanish-speaking countries of Latin America or to Spain. The author uses the terms "Hispanic"

Sotomayor had already shown herself to be a different kind of justice. She was more social than the others, kicking up her heels at parties that made the gossip columns. When she danced with actor Esai Morales at a National Hispanic Foundation for the Arts gala, pictures of her in a shiny black jacket and pants went viral; ditto when she donned a New York Yankees jersey and threw out a first pitch for her adored home team. She reveled in the attention.

A few weeks earlier, in June 2010, she had returned to the Bronx as the guest of New York City officials who had renamed the housing project where she grew up. The Bronxdale Houses had become the Justice Sonia Sotomayor Houses.[1] As she stood before three hundred cheering people, Sotomayor recalled how hopeful the Bronxdale Houses had seemed in the late 1950s when she moved there from a run-down tenement. Mayor Michael Bloomberg called her an inspiration to millions of New Yorkers. Later she sang and danced onstage with the choir from her high school. Wearing a bright red jacket, she was loose, at ease, seemingly all confidence.

Now she was back at the Supreme Court for the culmination of her first term and the end-of-term party.[2] After the justices and staff heaped their plates with food, they took seats for the entertainment. Sotomayor sat near the front. So did Justice Ruth Bader Ginsburg, whose husband, Martin, had died three days earlier after a long illness. Ginsburg, a survivor of two serious bouts with cancer, had prided herself on not missing a single day of Court business during her husband's illness. She was exhausted but not about to skip this celebration. Her close friend Justice Antonin Scalia, always an easy target in the law clerks' parodies because of his exaggerated mannerisms, secured a spot along a back wall of the room. As the rows of wooden chairs quickly filled, other people began to line the walls, too. About two hundred employees crowded in.

---

and "Latino" interchangeably, following the practice of the U.S. Census Bureau, the Pew Research Center's Hispanic Trends Project, and other research and academic authorities. Sotomayor has adopted such usage, too, describing herself on various occasions as Hispanic, as Latina, and as a Puerto Rican.

Chief Justice Roberts began the festivities with a *Jeopardy*-like trivia contest. The three-clerk teams, named Life, Liberty, and the Pursuit of Happiness, fielded his queries as an aide kept score on a whiteboard. Next, the musical spoofs began. Law clerks—the young, mostly Ivy League–trained attorneys who assist the Court—assumed the roles of the nine justices and poked fun at their foibles. The clerks kept these parodies tame. Certain expectations of decorum permeated the Marble Palace, as it has been called. Precedent and consistency were valued in the justices' relationships as well as in the law.

Justice Sotomayor was about to upset those expectations. As the skits were ending, she sprang from her chair, turned to the law clerks, and declared that although their musical numbers were all fine enough, they lacked a certain something. With that, a law clerk cued salsa music on a small portable player, and Sotomayor began dancing. She took quick steps forward, then back, and turned, then went forward, back again. The Cuban- and Puerto Rican–inspired rhythms were as new to this setting as the justice who was dancing. For her salsa partners, Sotomayor first grabbed a few law clerks, who, it became clear, had arranged this diversion with her. Then she beckoned the justices, starting with Chief Justice Roberts. A buttoned-down man who rarely shed his suit jacket at the Court, Roberts was reluctant, looking terribly uncomfortable. The audience was apprehensive. By tradition, this was an event where the law clerks performed and the justices watched. Roberts decided to be a good sport. He got up and danced with her. Briefly.

Sotomayor's barrel-ahead style clashed with the usual order and predictability at the Supreme Court. The institution operates on a down-to-the-minute schedule. Everyone knows his or her place, which corridors are open, which are closed. Steady, quiet rhythms control, for better or worse, reflecting the ideal of consistency in the law. But now a justice was dancing salsa in a room where portraits of former chief justices set the stodgy tone. Sotomayor's hips swayed to the beat of the distinctive drums and horns, and as her thick, curly black hair fell into her face, she brushed it away with her hand. As she sought out partners, nervous colleagues danced a bit, one by one, then retreated to their chairs. Justice Anthony Kennedy, six foot two and favoring dark suits with coordinated tie and pocket handkerchief, did a jitterbug-style move. Justice John Paul Stevens, at age ninety the eldest, got up, too, but he felt as if he had two left feet and quickly sat down, happy to watch Sotomayor move on to other partners.

"Where's Nino?" she shouted toward the back. Scalia, his thinning black hair slicked back, started to shake his head. There was no way he was going to dance. But then he did, sort of. Justice Samuel Alito, tall and shy, looked even more awkward when Sotomayor got to him. He resisted. But the rest of the audience was into the spectacle now. People were standing up, laughing and whooping. So Alito stood and danced a little bit. Then Sotomayor went toward Ginsburg, who had just endured some of the most difficult days of her life. She did not want to rise from her chair, but Sotomayor whispered to her that her late husband would have wanted her to dance. Ginsburg relented and followed Sotomayor in a few steps. Ginsburg put her hands up to Sotomayor's face. Holding her two cheeks in her palms, Ginsburg said, "Thank you."

As the program closed and people began leaving the room, emotions were strong. It had been a difficult term, and Sotomayor's enthusiasm was catching. Scalia, who could shake things up in his own way, joked as people passed him near the doorway, saying, "I knew she'd be trouble."

But some people were not as amused, and the episode increased their skepticism of Justice Sotomayor. They thought she was calling too much attention to herself, revealing a self-regard that challenged more than the Court's decorum. One justice and one top court officer said separately that it was just too much blurring of the lines between the clerks, who traditionally took the stage at the party, and the justices, who sat in judgment in the audience.

But that was Sotomayor. She had spent a lifetime challenging boundaries and disrupting the norm. And this episode as she was ending her first term testified to why it was she who became the historic *first* at the Supreme Court.[3] She was not one to wait her turn.

If she had waited, or held herself back at crucial junctures, she would not have been there. And once there, she believed it should be in her own hands to define her presence. Before this first end-of-term party, in fact, she had lined up a book agent and begun negotiating a publishing contract to write her autobiography.[4]

This book tells a different story. Rather than biography, it examines the cultural and political shifts that merged with Sotomayor's life and led to her appointment. It is a tale of how the timing of her generation helped lift up the daughter of a nurse and factory worker. While Hispanics were emerging as a political force in America, Sotomayor was overcoming her own hurdles and walking the narrow line between identity and assimilation. She had the intelligence and perseverance to do what no other Hispanic had done.

A child of housing projects who graduated from Princeton University and Yale Law School, Sotomayor, through her life story, tracked the ascent of Latinos in America, with their growing numbers and influence.[5] She was born in 1954, the year of *Brown v. Board of Education*, which ended the doctrine of "separate but equal" and opened schools to blacks and Hispanics. It was also the year of *Hernandez v. Texas*, which marked the first time the Supreme Court held that the Constitution protected Hispanics from discrimination with the same force as it protected blacks.

Sotomayor's formative years in the 1960s and 1970s coincided with the civil rights efforts of Puerto Ricans and other Latinos. Her life and career paralleled the activism and progress of her people. She went from a timid schoolgirl who kept her head down to an assertive woman who learned to maneuver in a predominantly white male world, gaining admission to Princeton and Yale partly through racial and ethnic preferences. "I am the perfect affirmative action baby," she said early in her career.[6] Once she became a lawyer and set her sights on the federal judiciary, she won lower court nominations, in part, because of her ethnicity, and she was approved only after close calls and fortuitous timing. Patrons such as Senator Daniel Patrick Moynihan, who amassed and wisely used his political cards, played a recurring role in her story. Those connections and

her own savvy helped her navigate a system known for ravaging
nominees, especially when race or ethnicity was an element of the
nomination.

Sotomayor watched in the 1990s and early 2000s as advocacy
groups tried to position other lawyers to be the first Hispanic on the
Supreme Court. Among them were federal judge José Cabranes,
who was born in Puerto Rico and came to the mainland with his
family at age five, and Washington lawyer Miguel Estrada, a Honduran who immigrated as a teenager. Only after they and others fell
out of contention because of the politics of the day did Sotomayor
represent an obvious choice when President Barack Obama—whose
own 2008 victory went against the odds—sought to choose the first
Hispanic justice.

Yet Obama's choice for the Supreme Court might not have been
this Puerto Rican daughter of the Bronx. One of his mentors from
his Harvard Law School days was against it. "Bluntly put, she's not
nearly as smart as she seems to think she is, and her reputation for
being something of a bully could well make her liberal impulses
backfire and simply add to the firepower of the [conservative] wing
of the Court," wrote Harvard law professor Laurence Tribe, an important liberal voice in American jurisprudence.[7] Tribe, who later
altered his opinion of Sotomayor, had been Obama's professor at
Harvard and an early supporter of his bid for the presidency.

Obama himself was ambivalent as he faced the 2009 vacancy
after the retirement of Justice David Souter. Obama saw the political value, certainly, of naming the first Hispanic justice. But the man
who, as a student, had held the top editorship on the *Harvard Law
Review* and then taught at the University of Chicago Law School had
his own elite interests. He was attracted to other candidates he
knew from Chicago's academic enclave of Hyde Park. His preliminary list, right after the 2008 election, was topped by three names:
Diane Wood, a judge on the U.S. Court of Appeals for the Seventh
Circuit who lectured at the University of Chicago; Cass Sunstein, a
Harvard law professor who earlier had taught at the University of
Chicago; and Elena Kagan, a former University of Chicago professor
who had become dean of Harvard Law School.[8]

Sotomayor's inclusion on Obama's expanded list arose from her education, experience, and connections, as well as the diversity she would offer. Her appointment might perhaps be compared to that of the first African American justice, Thurgood Marshall, the civil rights giant who developed the strategy leading up to *Brown v. Board of Education*. President Lyndon B. Johnson had chosen Marshall in 1967 as part of the president's broader civil rights efforts. Johnson, who had been the force behind the 1964 Civil Rights Act and the 1965 Voting Rights Act, sensed that public attitudes about race were changing. His nomination of Marshall was a principled move, to be sure, yet not one without political calculation.[9]

But any comparison between Marshall, a first-generation civil rights advocate, and Sotomayor, heir to the Latino pioneers who came earlier, goes only so far. What's more, while Johnson was on the cutting edge, Obama's choice of the first Latina felt overdue. For years, decades even, presidential candidates had been vowing to appoint a Hispanic justice. In 2009, when it finally happened, Hispanics represented 16 percent of the United States population. During the 2000s, the Hispanic population grew four times faster than the overall U.S. population.[10]

Opposition to Sotomayor at the time of her nomination came not in the form of the outright racism that Southern senators had shown Marshall in 1967, but in the subtle bias of commentators that she was not up to the job. Such criticism portrayed her as an intellectually inferior jurist and offered a narrative that competed with her personal story of success. She would later say, "It was very, very painful both on the court of appeals and on the Supreme Court nomination process that people kept accusing me of not being smart enough. Now, could someone explain to me, other than that I'm Hispanic, why that would be?"[11]

Such bluntness separated Sotomayor from others who jockeyed for position in the nation's capital. She spoke candidly of cultivating the necessary skills, building the networks, and overcoming personal setbacks. Her Supreme Court appointment was the culmination of an ambition stoked early on. In law school, she said, she realized the role individual judges could play in social justice—to protect voting rights or reduce segregation. "The idea that a single person could make such a difference in the cause of justice was nothing less than electrifying," Sotomayor wrote in her memoir, "and having more or less accepted the primacy of career in my life, I saw no reason to stint on ambition."[12]

Having achieved appointments to lower federal courts in the 1990s, she was careful to avoid controversy and continued to build alliances. She also did not tamp down her heritage or personality. She was not someone who "happened" to be Puerto Rican. She talked of eating such island specialties as pig intestines. And when it came time for her to administer her regular shot of insulin to care for her diabetes, she did not retreat to the ladies' room. Even at fancy dinners she took out the kit she always carried and injected herself at the table. Her unvarnished approach sometimes discombobulated associates, but it also conveyed an authenticity, even a vulnerability, that drew people to her.

In her early years at the Supreme Court, she elicited intense admiration alternating with annoyance for her garrulous, forceful style. She was a different model at an institution where justices, as a group, have been relatively bland and socially conforming, even as they differed radically on the law. What passed for flamboyance at the Court would generate a yawn in other venues. When Roberts's predecessor as chief justice, William Rehnquist, put gold stripes on the sleeves of his black robe in 1995, mimicking a character from Gilbert and Sullivan, it made national news.[13]

What follows is, first, a story of fortuitous timing and alignment with national events for a woman who was determined—as seen at her first Supreme Court end-of-term party—to stand out. Her ethnic identity helped her get ahead, but only after she surmounted hurdles that stopped most of her Latina cohort and, in point of fact, stopped almost everyone else seeking great stature in the judiciary.

Sotomayor's voice has been heard in a memoir that has earned her millions of dollars and sold hundreds of thousands of copies. She connects with people beyond the Washington Beltway as no other justice has. People reach out to hug her. She is a magnet, especially, for children. When Pew Research polled Hispanics on community leaders in 2013, Sotomayor and U.S. senator Marco Rubio, a Florida Republican, topped the list of those named.[14]

She attests to the dreams and aspirations of America. It is in the national fiber to believe someone can come from nothing, work hard, and become something. But Sotomayor's rise has not been without adverse reactions. The justice appointed for life still has her doubters, and it remains to be seen how she will answer them over time. She has played up her ethnicity and celebrity status as a "first," in contrast to the man who put her where she is today. President Obama rarely gives voice to his experience as the child of a black father and a white mother, and in political Washington, only on the most exceptional occasions does he speak about race in a personal way.[15]

This book offers an early look at how Sotomayor is publicly defining herself and compares her with other groundbreaking justices and her contemporary colleagues. The contrast with Elena Kagan, President Obama's second appointee, offers one measure. Justice Kagan has become known as a shrewd tactician among her colleagues. She has been held up by White House officials as a model for Obama appointees to all federal courts—a judge who has the "potential to persuade" conservative colleagues.[16] Kagan's pattern on the bench and in opinions indicates that she sees herself operating strategically as one of nine justices. Sotomayor, in contrast, is more of a solo operator, engrossed in her own determinations on a case, less interested and adept in getting others to adopt them.

As she challenges presumptions about how justices act and enlarges their place in the American mind, it may be that the personal characteristics that propelled her to this moment in history prevent her from being most effective. It is not clear that the popularity she has achieved outside the Court can be matched by a persuasive ability within its marble walls.

She has begun to make her mark, primarily by seeking fairer procedures for criminal defendants. Her writings reflect the knowledge earned in a big-city prosecutor's office and years presiding over trials, as well as the more personal experience of being a Latina.

As surprising as her salsa dancing was at the first end-of-term party, some justices say it now seems to have reflected the core of her character. She shakes up the proceedings and confronts her colleagues in their private discussions of cases.

When she asked them to dance, they did. On the law, they may be less likely to follow.

TWO

"Life Is All Right in America . . . If You're All White in America"

By the time Sonia Sotomayor was a teenager, in the late 1960s, the Puerto Rican Day Parade in New York City had grown from a procession through Spanish Harlem into an annual spectacle that ran for hours up Manhattan's Fifth Avenue. Big bands played brass, and smaller ensembles strummed Latin rhythms on guitars. Majorettes with batons strutted along the street. Beauty queens threw flowers from floats, and men in colorful shirts flipped straw hats in the air. Amid the pageantry, mayors from Puerto Rico's cities flashed broad smiles as they rode the route, while New York dignitaries and often the governor himself presided at the reviewing stand.[1]

As hundreds of thousands of people watched along the avenue and on local television, the parade—initiated in 1958—offered a platform for Puerto Ricans to show their flag, literally, and to flaunt their island past and deepening connection to mainland America. The event attracted state and national politicians, including Democratic U.S. senator Robert F. Kennedy in 1966 and 1967, before his presidential run. The parade also became a venue for political agitation, as in 1971, when hundreds of the nationalist Young Lords and other demonstrators supporting Puerto Rican independence threw bottles and bricks.[2] Even when the event was not marred by violence, it became increasingly raucous in the late 1960s and early 1970s.

Once, when Sonia Sotomayor was watching the parade on television at the home of a friend, her friend's father made a remark that startled and stuck with her. She remembered him saying, "Aren't those disgusting people?"[3] References to "those people" were not new to this Puerto Rican growing up in the Bronx. She had heard bigoted comments before, sometimes whispered, sometimes spoken loudly, as at this moment.

Sotomayor stood up and turned to her friend's father. "Those people? They're my people. I'm Puerto Rican," she said as she walked out.

Even as a girl, she had a way of declaring her identity in the bluntest terms. If people got in her face, she got in theirs. When whites taunted this Latina who sometimes traversed their neighborhood, she fought back with her fists. As she grew, she remembered the slights by people who doubted her classroom ability because of her ethnicity. Sometimes she raged quietly when she felt the sting of prejudice. Other times, in more formal academic settings, she went public with her complaints.

As Sotomayor established her place, beginning with the conflicts she navigated with her mother and father and then with classmates and teachers, she developed strategies for taking on a world that might have dismissed her as one of "those people."

She was headstrong from an early age: if she did not like what she was being fed, she would purse her lips together, puff out her cheeks, and make it nearly impossible for her mother to get a spoonful of food into her mouth. When misbehavior landed her in a "time-out corner," her mother would be the first to give in. Recounted Sotomayor: "She would say, 'Come out when you've reconsidered.' And I never would . . . She would have to call me out" from the corner.[4] Sotomayor excelled in the high school debate club, and when a Yale classmate told her she argued "like a guy," she had to admit to herself that from an early age she was defined by an aggressiveness not usually seen in females of her day.

She was determined to avoid the failures of some relatives— cousins who married young or turned to illegal drugs. The worst was the experience of her father, who was depressed, alcoholic, and unable to overcome the vicissitudes of his difficult life. With little formal education and often unemployed, he would sit in a chair, stare out the window, and simmer in anger at his perceived exile in New York. Young Sonia would eventually see the drained Seagram's 7 bottles in his dresser drawers and under his mattress. It was a bed he rarely shared with Sonia's mother.

As Sotomayor was standing up to her personal trials, the nation's civil rights movement was expanding beyond African American concerns to Latino interests, particularly in the Mexican American hubs of Texas and California. Her assertion of her own identity coincided with increasing Latino visibility across America in the 1960s.

The political activities of the era provided the scaffolding that would lift Sotomayor from the Bronx, through the precincts of the Ivy League, and ultimately onto the federal bench. Her childhood experience was distinctly Puerto Rican. Yet when she was appointed to the Supreme Court in 2009, she was a symbol for all Hispanics.

◆

Puerto Ricans were relative newcomers to the mainland. But great numbers of Mexican Americans had been living in the West for more than a century and, throughout the 1900s, asserting claims for equal rights in California, Texas, and other states. In the 1960s, as Sotomayor was coming of age in the Bronx, Mexican American civil rights activist Cesar Chavez was organizing farmworkers and seeking better conditions for laborers in California. His escalating boycotts and strikes, which triggered violent attacks on picket lines, made constant headlines.

The struggles of Puerto Ricans—for jobs, housing, and good schools—increasingly made the news, too, as the great postwar migration from the island intersected with the financial crises that gripped New York and other cities. Their plight would become grist for sociologists, including in the seminal study by Nathan Glazer and Daniel Patrick Moynihan, *Beyond the Melting Pot*, first published in 1963. Popular culture also captured the simmering social tensions. In *West Side Story*, Leonard Bernstein's adaptation of the

Romeo and Juliet tale featuring a star-crossed Puerto Rican girl and Polish American boy, New York Puerto Ricans sing, "Life is all right in America . . . if you're all white in America." The 1957 Broadway musical, turned into a 1961 Academy Award–winning movie, may have stigmatized Puerto Ricans more than any other twentieth-century work, but it captured the reality of the opportunities many Puerto Ricans found on the mainland. As the lyrics from the song "America" went on, "Free to be anything you choose . . . free to wait tables and shine shoes."

So, as the "Puerto Rican problem," as it sometimes was called, emerged in the news of the day, in sociological studies, and even onstage, Sonia Sotomayor was living it.

◆

Puerto Ricans had been migrating to New York for decades in search of jobs and a better life, but the period from the mid-1940s to the mid-1960s produced the most consequential surge of people escaping the Caribbean island for the mainland. It was during this massive migration that Sonia Sotomayor's mother and father arrived. Her parents were on separate journeys and did not know each other when they and other relatives left a place scarred by centuries of colonial tutelage and economic struggle.

Puerto Rico's history of colonization began when Christopher Columbus discovered the island in 1493, on his second major voyage, and Spain took control. The land produced abundant coffee and sugarcane and provided Spain with a western fortress. Yet its small size and dearth of minerals offered little opportunity for wealth. Spain failed to develop the island's agricultural potential and saw Puerto Rico primarily as a military bastion. It remained an island of heartbreaking contrasts: a lush terrain and malnourished people. Diseases—malaria, tuberculosis, and cholera—were rampant.

Puerto Rico sat on the sidelines during the struggle for trade and power among emerging countries. It failed to catch the revolutionary, separatist spirit that took hold in Latin American countries in the late 1700s and early 1800s. José Cabranes, a loyal son of Puerto

Rico who would become a legal scholar, federal judge, and Sotomayor mentor, wrote in a 1974 essay that "a certain docility before more powerful economic and political forces is a notable characteristic of a people who were Spain's last and most loyal colony in the New World."[5] Cabranes would later say that when he first met Sotomayor, which happened to be shortly after he penned that essay, he was struck by how she countered the stereotypes. Nothing about her was docile.

During the Spanish-American War, in 1898, U.S. military troops invaded Puerto Rico. The United States officially took control from Spain with the Treaty of Paris that year. In 1917, with the Jones Act, Congress granted U.S. citizenship to all persons born in Puerto Rico, yet it did not accord Puerto Rico full rights as a territory. This action and the persistent ambivalence regarding political status—belonging to the United States but not being completely a part of it—would infect the island, sparking sporadic violence and feeding bitterness about how its people fit into American culture. A single, nonvoting delegate, known as a resident commissioner, represented Puerto Rico in the U.S. Congress. Puerto Ricans on the island could not cast ballots in elections for U.S. presidents or members of Congress. Puerto Rico was racially mixed, with people having indigenous Taíno, African, and Spanish and other European roots. Native-born Puerto Ricans were U.S. citizens, but when they came to the mainland, they often were treated as foreigners and forced to navigate obstacles arising from America's tragically durable racial hierarchy.

The first major exodus of Puerto Ricans followed twin catastrophes: Hurricane San Felipe Segundo and the Great Depression. In 1928, Felipe cut a swath across the island, destroying 250,000 homes, one-third of the sugarcane crop, and half of the coffee trees. In those early years, most of the Puerto Ricans who migrated north came from rural parts of the island; they had little education and were unable to speak English, which made it difficult for them to find jobs. They were relegated to squalid living conditions, creating the so-called Puerto Rican problem in New York City. The backlash, according to a *CENTRO Journal* study, was fueled by newspapers and magazines across the ideological spectrum.[6] In a 1947 story entitled "Sugar-Bowl Migrants," *Time* magazine compared Puerto Ricans to "Okies" who had fled to California during the Dust Bowl. The article lamented that the majority of Puerto Ricans arriving in New York were "beggar-poor, had no prospects of jobs or any training." *Time* added that the Puerto Rican economy simply could not support most of its population. The average family wage on the island was twenty dollars a month.[7] It meant that people like Sotomayor's relatives would continue to migrate to the mainland in search of a life, even if it was only a bit better than what they left behind.

In their examination of Puerto Ricans in *Beyond the Melting Pot*, Glazer and Moynihan pointed out the economic roots of the Puerto Rican migration to the mainland United States: "The island lived off a cash crop—sugar—that had collapsed with the depression; it had almost no industry; in any case even in the best of times the agricultural workers who make up the majority of the population lived under incredibly primitive conditions."[8]

◆

Sonia Sotomayor's mother, Celina, made the decisions essential to breaking the family's cycle of poverty. Celina Baez was born in Puerto Rico in 1927—the year before the San Felipe Segundo hurricane hit—and grew up in Lajas, a small farming community on the southwestern coast. She was the youngest of five children, and after her birth, her mother became sick and delusional. She died when Celina was nine. Celina's father had already abandoned the family, leaving the youngest to be raised by the older siblings. It was a dismal existence. They had no running water and little money. Celina's older brother beat her regularly with a belt. For food, she often ate fruit that fell from trees.[9]

Yet on an island permeated by poverty, illiteracy, and disease, Celina managed to develop a love of learning. As her daughter Sonia would recall in speeches with a decidedly optimistic gloss, "Although my mother had no money for books or pencils, she found a way around those problems by memorizing her school lessons. Each day, she would run home after school to spend an hour among the trees behind her home. There, she would line up her towering friends in her imagination and use a stick as a pointer to teach the trees the lessons she had learned for that day."[10] Later, in her 2013 memoir, Sotomayor acknowledged her mother's grimmer existence and sense of abandonment. She said that Celina accepted her lot in life: "With their mother helpless and their father missing, it was kids raising kids and just her bad luck to have been the youngest. At least they sent her to school."[11]

During World War II, when Celina was barely seventeen, she lied about her age and joined the U.S. military so she could leave the island. She enlisted in the Women's Army Corps and shipped out to Georgia for training at Fort Oglethorpe as a telephone operator. After training, she was assigned to the New York City Port of Embarkation. She met Juan "Juli" Sotomayor, who was born in 1921 and grew up near the capital city of San Juan. He had migrated to the mainland with his family during the war. Juan's father died on the island when he was thirteen, and his mother, Mercedes, raised five children on her own. Juan's father's death deeply disturbed him; his daughter Sonia would later say it may have been the root of his problems with alcohol.

When Celina first met Juan, she was struck by his youthful exuberance. He told her she was beautiful. He taught her to dance and paid attention to her as no one had ever done. They were a handsome couple. Celina was trim, with delicate features. She tweezed her eyebrows into sharp arches above her dark eyes and favored fashionable dresses that fit tightly at the waist. Like Celina, Juan was on the shorter side, but he had broad shoulders and a dynamic presence. He had thick black hair and looked dapper in the suit and tie he wore when he went out on the town.

Juan's mother, Mercedes, welcomed Celina into the Sotomayor circle, and Celina and Juan were married in 1946, just as Celina completed her service in the Women's Army Corps. In the tenement apartment the couple rented in the Bronx, Juan painted the walls with bright colors and laid beautiful tiles. He had an artistic flair and an eye for details. When he decorated the Christmas tree, his daughter recalled decades later, he varied the arrangement of colored lights and ornaments and carefully hung the strands of silver tinsel.

Celina used her GI benefits to earn a high school equivalency diploma through a GED program. She found a job as a telephone operator at Prospect Hospital, on the southwest side of the Bronx. Juan, who had only a third-grade education and spoke no English, landed a job at a mannequin factory.

Sonia was born on June 25, 1954, nearly eight years into their marriage. Celina returned to work as a telephone operator soon after her daughter's birth and decided to begin classes to prepare for a practical nurse's license. Juan, known into adulthood as "Junior," was born three and a half years later.

◆

Sonia Sotomayor's birth fell shortly after the Supreme Court's landmark ruling in *Brown v. Board of Education*. That May 17, 1954, decision would begin desegregation and eventually clear the way for African Americans and other children of color to attend the same schools as whites. Equally significant for Hispanics, the Supreme Court issued *Hernandez v. Texas* two weeks before *Brown*, declaring for the first time that Hispanics merited constitutional protection from discrimination. Until then, lower court judges had issued conflicting opinions on whether Mexican Americans and other minorities who were not black should be protected from bias under the Constitution's Fourteenth Amendment equality guarantee.

Writing for a unanimous Court, Chief Justice Earl Warren said that the guarantee of equal protection of the law could be invoked by Hispanics—not just by blacks—with civil rights claims. The case had been brought by Pete Hernandez, a Mexican American convicted of murder by a jury from which people of Mexican descent had been systematically excluded. In the quarter century leading up to Hernandez's challenge, no person of Mexican or Latin American descent had served on any Jackson County jury, although the county's population was 10 percent Mexican American.[12] "The state of Texas would have us hold that there are only two classes of people—white and Negro—within the contemplation of the Fourteenth Amendment," Chief Justice Warren wrote in *Hernandez v. Texas*. But "community prejudices are not static," Warren said, and over time new groups could deserve constitutional protection because of newly developed prejudices in America.

Warren, a former California governor who understood the anti-Mexican segregation that permeated Texas, wrote that Hernandez met his legal burden of proving "that persons of Mexican descent constitute a separate class in Jackson County, distinct from 'whites.'" Warren cited evidence that lawyers for Hernandez had gathered regarding community attitudes. "The participation of persons of Mexican descent in business and community groups was shown to be slight," the chief justice wrote. "Until very recent times, children of Mexican descent were required to attend a segregated school for the first four grades. At least one restaurant in town prominently displayed a sign announcing 'No Mexicans Served.' On the courthouse grounds at the time of the hearing, there were two men's toilets, one unmarked, and the other marked 'Colored Men' and 'Hombres Aqui' ('Men Here')."[13]

Such evidence helped to demonstrate that although no Texas statute mandated official discrimination, local custom and practice had led to such bias. "It taxes our credulity to say that mere chance resulted in there being no members of this class among the over six thousand jurors called in the past 25 years," Warren wrote as the Court overturned Pete Hernandez's conviction.

People of Mexican ancestry had a deep connection to the United States that put them at the center of early legal cases involving Latino rights. They had lived in what became the states of California, Texas, and other southwestern lands for hundreds of years,[14] but they would long be seen as outsiders and face decades of prejudice and violence, including lynchings in the late 1800s and early 1900s. As late as 1943, Los Angeles was wracked by the "Zoot Suit Riots," during which U.S. sailors beat scores of Mexican American boys and men and left them naked in the streets.[15]

Thus, the *Hernandez* decision in the year of Sotomayor's birth
gave Latinos a tool for fighting bias and seeking equality. "With the
Hernandez ruling," observed Roberto Suro in *Strangers Among Us:
Latino Lives in a Changing America*, "the Supreme Court affirmed
that being nonwhite, being a minority, need not emerge from the
unique experience of African-Americans as slaves and as victims of
de jure segregation . . . *Hernandez* opened a door for the Mexicans
of South Texas, and eventually all other Latinos would pass through
that door."[16]

◆

In 1957, when Sonia Sotomayor was three years old, Celina arranged for the family's move to the Bronxdale Houses, a low-rent,
city-run housing project. The complex would, when finished a few
years later, consist of twenty-eight seven-story redbrick buildings.
In the 1950s the "projects" did not have the stigma they gained in the
1960s. When the Sotomayors moved into their unit on Bruckner
Boulevard, New York's public housing offered clean stairwells and
neat lawns, not broken elevators, mounds of debris, and illegal drug
trafficking. Many of the first residents, including the Sotomayors,
had come from small, decrepit tenements. Their new homes evoked
a sense of prosperity.

But her father felt something different. Juan had not wanted to
move away from the neighborhood of his mother and the rest of the
Sotomayor clan. He would sit for hours looking out the Bronxdale
windows. "My dad would . . . point to the empty lots that surrounded
the projects," Sotomayor said wistfully in one speech, "and tell me
about the kinds of stores that would eventually be built on that land.
One night, as we sat by the window, my dad pointed at the sky and
told me that a man would someday land on the moon. He did not
live long enough to see the stores built or to hear about the moon
landing."[17]

Sotomayor later revealed the extent of her father's detachment
and alcoholism. As he sat at the window of their Bronxdale apartment, she wrote, he "stared in silence at the vacant lots, at the high-

ways and the brick walls, at a city and a life that slowly strangled him."[18] She recalled the shame of hearing relatives talk about the dirty dishes in the sink and no toilet paper in the bathroom. Her mother was working and her father too drunk to manage the household.

Juan's drinking got worse when the mannequin factory where he worked closed, and he had trouble finding a new job. Eventually he was hired at a radiator factory. Celina, meanwhile, took on longer hours at the hospital. Mercedes and other relatives said that if Celina were not gone so much, maybe Juan would not drink so much.

For her own compensation, young Sonia developed a deep relationship with grandmother Mercedes, who offered the kind of unconditional love she did not experience with her mother. "She was my childhood savior," Sotomayor said years later, adding that although she often drove her parents crazy with her shenanigans, she "could do no wrong" with her grandmother.[19] Mercedes—who loved music and poetry, conducted séances, and could make a party out of any occasion—allowed Sonia and her cousins to stay overnight at her apartment on weekends.

Her walk-up apartment faced the tracks of the elevated train. Young Sonia would often gaze out the window and look at passengers' faces as train cars rumbled by. She wondered about their lives and what kinds of jobs they were heading to in Manhattan. She later said that she also wondered whether any of the passing riders noticed her and her cousins at the window of her grandmother's apartment and considered what *they* might become.[20]

In Sonia Sotomayor's early renditions of her family life, she featured her mother as an inspiring force. Only in the 2013 telling did Celina emerge as a woman who was also detached and so interested in projecting a "movie star" glamour that she resisted playing on the floor with her children or even picking them up for fear of mussing her clothes. Sonia felt clumsy and ill-attired in her mother's eyes. She said that feeling of never being "put together" extended into her adulthood.

"Even though my mother and I shared the same bed every

night . . . she might as well have been a log, lying there with her back to me," Sotomayor wrote. "My father's neglect made me sad, but I intuitively understood that he could not help himself; my mother's neglect made me angry at her. She was beautiful, always elegantly dressed, seemingly strong and decisive . . . Unfairly perhaps, because I knew nothing then of my mother's own story, I expected more from her."[21]

Sotomayor learned early on to depend on herself. Before she was a teenager, two other experiences further shaped her character. Just as she was about to turn eight, she discovered that she was a diabetic. "I was always, always thirsty," she told a group of schoolchildren decades later. "Then I started to do something that mortified me. I started urinating in my bed." Her parents took her to the hospital for tests. When a lab technician pulled out his needle to draw blood, she panicked. She jumped from her chair and ran out of the hospital and hid under a parked car. "I kept trying to get into a little ball," she recalled.[22]

The worst part of the diabetes diagnosis, she said, was seeing her mother cry for the first time and—at least for that moment— appear helpless. Celina was aware of the prognosis for a child with diabetes in the early 1960s. She feared amputations and blindness. But Celina soon confronted her fears and brought her young daughter to the Jacobi Medical Center, a public hospital in the Bronx with a juvenile diabetes specialty, where her daughter learned to manage her condition.

It fell to Sotomayor to give herself insulin shots before she left for school. In the early morning, her mother was working at the hospital and her alcoholic father's hands were too jittery. "When my father made his first attempt at giving me the insulin shot," Sotomayor later wrote, ". . . his hands were shaking so much I was afraid he would miss my arm entirely and stab me in the face. He had to jab hard just to steady his aim." Along with causing her pain, the incident accelerated her mother's recriminations toward the father: "'Whose fault is it your hands tremble?'"[23]

Each morning before school Sotomayor sterilized her glass syringes and metal needles. She would use a pot of water her mother had set on the stove before leaving for the hospital. She would turn on the burner, wait for the water to boil, and then climb up on a chair and drop in her equipment. She learned to extract blood with a little razor and to test her urine for her sugar count. She also quickly figured out that if she failed to check her blood sugar and take her insulin, she could become sick.

Physicians warned that her career options would be limited, and she believed she had to abandon a dream of becoming a detective, born of her interest in the Nancy Drew mystery book series. Intrigued by the character of Perry Mason, played by Raymond Burr, on the television show that ran from the mid-1950s to mid-1960s, she decided to set her sights on becoming a lawyer instead. It is a testament to her mental strength that this child of the Bronx believed nothing could interfere with her becoming a lawyer. But the diabetes also gave her a sense of urgency about her goals. She had heard the family whispers that she could die young.

The second shock of her childhood came when she was nine years old. Her father died of complications from his alcoholism. For Sotomayor it was one more shove out of childhood into adulthood. She adopted her mother's stoicism. Celina, at age nine, had coped with her mother's death. Now daughter Sonia had to do the same with her father's passing. Celina moved the family into a smaller apartment in the Bronxdale Houses and decided the only way to ensure her economic independence was to become a registered nurse. It meant taking out loans for college classes and spending even less time with the children.

Also motivated by the circumstances, young Sonia started working harder at Blessed Sacrament, the grammar school she and Junior attended. The Sotomayor children were sent there for the education and discipline, not because a crucifix hung in every classroom. The family was not particularly religious, Sotomayor would say later. In her effort to become a better student and win the gold stars the nuns doled out, she approached one of the smarter girls in the class and asked about her study techniques. The girl taught her how to underline important information and take notes. Sotomayor said later that in that moment she received not only study tips but the lifelong lesson that she could get help if she asked for it.

She also learned in these years how to handle the bitterness she felt when she was excluded. She desperately wanted to be part of the group of Blessed Sacrament students chosen to see Pope Paul VI in 1965 as he made a historic one-day visit to New York City. But she was not picked, she believed, because her family did not attend regular Sunday Mass at Blessed Sacrament. She watched the event on television and told herself that she was seeing much more than the students among the crowd of a million people on the streets. When she graduated from Blessed Sacrament, a nun wrote in her yearbook, "This girl's ambitions, odd as they may seem, are to become an attorney and someday marry."[24]

It would become clear that Sotomayor defied low expectations.

◆

Her growth coincided with the progress of Puerto Ricans and other Latinos as a political force. One of the nation's early voting rights claims came from another determined Puerto Rican mother, Martha Cardona, who lived with her children in the Bronx. Cardona had moved from Puerto Rico to New York in 1948, raised three children, and become active in her community. In the summer of 1963, state election officials refused to let her register to vote, because she could not satisfy the state's English literacy requirement. She sued, saying that the Board of Elections should either register her as a qualified voter or provide the literacy test in Spanish. She was helped in her lawsuit by local politicians eager to tap into the votes of thousands of Puerto Ricans in their districts. They would not be the first nor the last politicians who understood the value of wooing Hispanics.

Cardona lost in lower courts, but when the Supreme Court took up her appeal in 1966, it endorsed her right to vote. The Cardona decision followed the lead of that June day's ruling in *Katzenbach v. Morgan*, which upheld a provision of the 1965 Voting Rights Act that abolished English literacy tests and said that no one who had completed the sixth grade in an accredited Puerto Rican school could be barred from voting. In Cardona's case, Justice William J. Brennan, Jr., noted that *Katzenbach v. Morgan* endorsed federal power to prevent discrimination in voting rights. In the new *Katzenbach* case, the Court, which earlier had permitted state literacy tests, said Congress's power under the Constitution's supremacy clause gives it particular authority to ban them. So, Brennan said, as long as Cardona, who filed her case before the 1965 act was passed, could show that she had completed a sixth-grade equivalency in Spanish, she would be able to cast a ballot. The paired cases of *Katzenbach v. Morgan* and *Cardona v. Power* offered Puerto Ricans greater access to the voting booth and with other voting rights rulings of the era set Latinos on a course to be part of American democracy.[25]

A few years later, in a voting rights case important to minorities in the Southwest, *White v. Regester*, the Supreme Court said that Latinos and blacks in parts of Texas were entitled to a single-member voting district because multimember districts were diluting their voting strength. The justices adopted a lower court finding that the Bexar County Mexican American community, concentrated on the west side of San Antonio, faced discrimination in education, economic life, and politics. Single-member districts, giving minority voters in a distinct region greater potential to elect one of their own, would bring the Mexican American community into the "full stream of political life" by spurring registration and voting, the Court said.[26]

But the daily reality for Latinos through the late 1960s and early 1970s was not full participation, particularly for urban Puerto Ricans who faced poverty, dead-end jobs, and police brutality. The Supreme Court's *Katzenbach* and *Cardona* voting rights decisions happened to come on June 13, 1966, as a major riot—one of many involving Puerto Ricans during the 1960s—erupted in Chicago, another city that drew Puerto Rican migrants. After World War II, large numbers of Puerto Rican workers had moved to the great manufacturing hub in the Midwest. Migrants in Chicago, however, had a generally low public presence, and just a year before the June

1966 rioting, *The Chicago Daily News* published a story headlined
"Chicago's Proud Puerto Ricans." The article characterized Puerto
Ricans there as the "upbeat West Side Story" and described the local
migrants as "peaceful and furiously ambitious," compared with New
York counterparts "wielding knives in gang fights."[27] The story failed
to capture the conflict on the horizon.

The Chicago riot of June 1966 began when a white police officer shot a twenty-year-old Puerto Rican man after a Puerto Rican
Day Parade celebration in the Humboldt Park neighborhood on
the city's West Side. Youths began burning businesses along Division Street, the spine of the neighborhood. More than fifty buildings were destroyed and dozens of people arrested.[28] The riot was
typical of the Puerto Rican–initiated disturbances in major cities
throughout the decade. On the surface, it was a response to perceived police brutality, yet it more deeply reflected conditions of
poverty and lack of jobs. This was the economic despair and violence from which Celina Sotomayor labored to protect her two
children.

In New York, one of the earliest riots involving Puerto Ricans
occurred in August 1964, on the Lower East Side, ignited by a brawl
with blacks.[29] More deadly rioting by Puerto Ricans broke out three
years later, in the summer of 1967. At least ten people were killed
and several homes burned to the ground after three successive
nights of disturbances in East Harlem and the South Bronx, not far
from where the Sotomayor family lived. The rioting, following a series of questionable police arrests of Puerto Rican men, began when
mobs started overturning cars and setting them on fire. Men pelted
police with bricks and bottles.[30]

Newspapers of the day relied on stereotypes of Puerto Ricans as
a "docile" people lacking aspirations, reflecting a complicated image
created by Puerto Rico's long history under Spanish and American
control and the subjugation of its culture. A 1967 *New York Times*
account of Puerto Rican rioting, under the headline "Puerto Rican
Story: A Sensitive People Erupt," observed that "the shock of the
city's first Puerto Rican mass disorders . . . came against a background in which Puerto Ricans have historically been considered

passive." The Reverend James Sugrue, pastor of All Saints Church in Harlem, was quoted as saying, "We never expected this to happen in this part of Harlem. It's not that the Puerto Ricans aren't as bad off as the Negroes, but the Puerto Ricans don't have the Negroes' sense of 'revolution of expectations.' The Puerto Ricans sort of celebrate their own poverty."[31]

Sonia Sotomayor was anything but a submissive child without aspirations, but the statistics for her contemporaries were grim. When she was starting school in the Bronx, Puerto Rican children had the lowest education attainment rates for New York City, about seven school years. The unemployment rate for New York Puerto Ricans in 1960 was 10 percent, compared with 7 percent for blacks and 5 percent for whites.[32]

Such statistics undergirded what New York City officials and the media had been calling "the Puerto Rican problem." Originating in the 1940s, the phrase reinforced the caricature of Puerto Ricans as people who arrived on the mainland with few skills and subsequently overburdened schools and drained social services. During the years of the great island exodus, the actions of extremists fueled the perception that Puerto Ricans could pose a dangerous political threat. In 1954, the year of Sotomayor's birth, four members of the Puerto Rican Nationalist Party protested U.S. control of the island by firing semiautomatic pistols from a visitors' gallery in the chamber of the U.S. House of Representatives, wounding five House members. The four radicals—three men and one woman—shouted for Puerto Rican independence as they fired. Four years earlier, two nationalists had tried to assassinate President Harry Truman.

In *Beyond the Melting Pot*, Glazer and Moynihan helped cement the notion that Puerto Ricans could not assimilate as other immigrants had, and the authors added to the news media stereotype that Puerto Ricans were naturally inclined to be poor and uneducated. Among the many of Glazer and Moynihan's grim assessments: "Nothing—in education, in work experience, work training, work discipline, in family attitudes, in physical health—gave the Puerto Rican migrant an advantage in New York City."[33]

Only in hindsight did Sotomayor understand what she and

people like her were up against. "There were working poor in the projects," she said. "There were poor poor in the projects. There were sick poor in the projects. There were addicts and non-addicts and all sorts of people, every one of them with problems, and each group with a different response, different methods of survival, different reactions to the adversity they were facing. And you saw kids making choices."[34]

At a young age she made more mature choices because of her personal health and family situation. Sotomayor won a scholarship to Cardinal Spellman High School, a majority-white Catholic school operated by the Archdiocese of New York and named for Francis Cardinal Spellman, New York's legendary archbishop from 1939 until 1967. Soon after, Celina moved the family out of the Bronxdale projects, where drugs and gang violence were proliferating, to the new Co-op City, a housing project of thirty-five towers in the northeastern part of the Bronx. It was a safer area, with more middle-class families.

Racial tensions were spreading beyond the Bronx and New York City. In 1968, the year Sonia started high school, the Reverend Martin Luther King, Jr., was assassinated in Memphis, and blacks nationwide rioted. In Washington, D.C., and Chicago, large swaths of businesses were burned, reducing neighborhoods to rubble. At Cardinal Spellman, Sotomayor became aware of herself as an individual who was part of a larger civil rights struggle. She increasingly overheard comments that referred to her as a Puerto Rican or that had the ring of "those people."

"Your parents let you know that you had to look out for each other," said Charles Auffant, a Puerto Rican classmate of Sotomayor's at Blessed Sacrament. "There was an unwritten rule of camaraderie. Puerto Ricans were still breaking in."[35]

"We were shaped by those extraordinary times and by the communities from which we came, for better or worse," said Theodore Shaw, an African American who attended Spellman High School with Sotomayor and went on to lead the NAACP Legal Defense Fund. Shaw said that Sotomayor could not be pigeonholed: "If you came from Bronxdale and performed academically as she did . . . you were in your own category."[36]

She mingled with white and black students, and her new Co-op City apartment became a welcoming place—like the apartment of grandmother Mercedes—for classmates to gather after school and on weekends. Young Sonia loved to cook and entertain, to be at the center of a party—a pattern that would continue well into her career years and even after she was on the bench.

Dating presented a trickier social challenge. "It had been established that Sonia Sotomayor was not much to look at," she wrote years later with unusual candor. "I had a pudgy nose. I was gawky and ungraceful. I barreled down the halls of Cardinal Spellman, headfirst, unlike those who knew how to amble with a sexy sashay. My own mother told me that I had terrible taste in clothes."[37] Sotomayor said it seemed she was always "everybody's second choice" for dates.

Yet Kevin Noonan, who came from an Irish American home, took an interest in his energetic classmate who moved easily among racial groups. Once she introduced him to her grandmother, Sotomayor's family and friends began presuming the young couple would marry. But her family's warmth was not reciprocated by his. "We didn't go over to his house much," Sotomayor recalled, "because his mother had a hard time accepting me. She wouldn't say it to my face, but the message came through with a tightening of the lips, a slant of the eyebrow, a slam of the door. She would have been happier if I were Irish, or at least not Puerto Rican."[38]

Sotomayor was undaunted, and she pursued the relationship with Noonan. Around this same time, as she was applying to colleges, she also ignored teachers who tried to dissuade her from considering Ivy League schools. A visit to Radcliffe College, however, briefly sapped her confidence as nothing else had. It played to fundamental insecurities, perhaps originally planted by Celina, about her appearance and style.

Sotomayor applied to Radcliffe partly out of her fascination with the 1970 romantic movie *Love Story*, written by Erich Segal, and partly out of her interest in winning acceptance to the best colleges.

Yet in the admissions office on the Cambridge, Massachusetts, campus, she was confronted with everything that she was not. The woman who greeted her was flawlessly coiffed and classically dressed in a black dress and pearls. An Oriental rug, the first Sotomayor had ever seen, and a pristine white couch defined the office. Beside the woman were two small dogs, and the assault on Sotomayor's sensibilities only increased when they began barking at her. The woman called to the dogs, and all three then sat on the couch staring at the awkward student from the Bronx. Sotomayor felt trapped in a world of ornamentation and pretense.[39]

As she recalled the episode, she said she did something she had never done before. She fled. After about fifteen minutes of awkward conversation, she left the room and told the receptionist that she would not be able to meet with the students who were to escort her around campus.

"What's wrong?" her mother asked when she returned to their apartment in Co-op City. "You were supposed to be away for a couple of days." Sotomayor said only that she realized she did not belong there. Neither mother nor daughter said another word about it. Perhaps Celina sensed the rejection in her daughter that she, Celina, had known in her own young life. The story would eventually become part of Sonia Sotomayor's repertoire, marking the only time, she said, that she ran away from a challenge.

As searing as the Radcliffe experience had been, she continued to believe she could fit in at an elite campus. She visited Yale in 1972, and although it felt better than Radcliffe, she was uncomfortable with her student guides, who were consumed with antiwar protests, the revolutionary tactics of Che Guevara, and "down with whitey" attitudes. "Whether it was due to the indeterminate color of my skin or my very determined personality, I moved easily between different worlds" of color, Sotomayor wrote.[40] She was also remarkably positive about her people and own place, so much so that when, as a student, she read Oscar Lewis's classic *La Vida,* tracing one family from San Juan to New York and describing the despair of its circumstances, Sotomayor said she was turned off by the pessimism.

On the advice of a Chinese American friend who was a year ahead of her in high school and had gone to Princeton, she visited the school, which was about an hour south in New Jersey. The students seemed smart but easygoing, she said later, and to the surprise of this Bronx native, she was captivated by the Collegiate Gothic architecture and sweeping green lawns. The promise of a full financial scholarship was the final inducement.

Soon after she applied, Sotomayor received word that she likely would be admitted. She became aware that white students with better grades were not getting in. Others noticed, too, and the reaction of the high school nurse particularly stung. She remarked to Sotomayor that these high-ranking white students were not being admitted. "They're ahead of you. Why aren't they getting in—and you are?" Sotomayor recalled the nurse saying. "The question was loaded with a lot of suggestion that I understood." Sotomayor later wrote in her memoir of the school nurse's accusatory tone toward her, "My perplexed discomfort under her baleful gaze was clearly not enough; shame was the response she seemed to want from me."[41]

Before she left for college, Sotomayor saw a movie that similarly touched her sense of identity: *12 Angry Men*, the Sidney Lumet classic depicting tensions among jurors as they decide the fate of a young Latino murder defendant. More than a decade after the original 1957 release of the film, she watched it with her boyfriend Kevin Noonan.

Set at a time when men wore white shirts and thin ties and often had a cigarette between their fingers, the movie opens with the trial judge's charge to the twelve-man jury in the case of a youth accused of stabbing his father to death. The jurors learn that if the kid from the slums is found guilty, he will get the electric chair. In the jury room, the first vote is 11–1 to convict, with only the juror played by Henry Fonda saying he is not sure the youth did it. "We're talking about somebody's life here," he says, imploring the rest of the jurors to discuss what they've seen and heard rather than vote quickly, try to get it all over with, and go on with their lives. Over the course of the next ninety minutes the audience sees how prejudices play out and what "reasonable doubt" means. As the discussion in the stifling-hot jury room continues and doubts are raised, the men who want to convict make remarks such as "You know how these people lie," "These people are dangerous," and "Slums are breeding grounds for criminals." The film ends when the remaining holdout for conviction, played angrily by Lee J. Cobb, changes his mind and votes for acquittal.

When Sotomayor watched the movie as a young woman, she said she was struck by the idea that justice could prevail, and it would reinforce her choice of a career in the law. Yet she was also deeply affected by the references to "those people." Such words, she said, made her flinch.

"You have to flinch," she said years later after she had seen the movie again. "Those [references] are personal. They were personal when I saw it the first time. I had heard about 'those people' in my life so often."[42]

THREE

"I Am the Perfect Affirmative Action Baby"

Sonia Sotomayor suspected that Princeton University would be challenging, but she had no idea what she would face when she arrived on campus in 1972. Her admittance to the Ivy League school changed the way people regarded her and her family. "I have to tell you, Sonia," her mother had confided, "at the hospital I'm being treated like a queen right now. Doctors who have never once had a nice word for me, who have never spoken to me at all, have come up to congratulate me." Celina presciently added, "What you got yourself into, daughter, I don't know. But we're going to find out."[1]

Sotomayor had graduated near the top of her class at the competitive Cardinal Spellman High School, had smoothed out some of the rougher edges of childhood, and thought she was ready for Princeton. She was wrong. During the first weeks of school she spent most of her time in her dorm room and reverted to the shyness and doubt of her early grade school years. But in what would become an enduring pattern, she confronted her shortcomings, kindled her ambitions, and developed a strategy to get where she wanted to go.

When she discovered the holes in her Bronx education, she turned to professors for help. She made friends and built networks. By the time she graduated, she had earned some of Princeton's top honors, but she never tried to emulate the polish or personal reserve of her more advantaged classmates.

Years later, when the magazine *Mademoiselle* looked at what had become of women who excelled at top colleges in the mid-1970s, it opened the feature story with Sotomayor. The reporter describes her telephone interview on a Friday night, minutes before midnight, just as Sotomayor has gotten home from the office. "Do you mind terribly if I eat my dinner while we talk?" Sotomayor asks. "I'm a diabetic, and I haven't eaten since noon." Later in the conversation, she reveals that she has just given herself an insulin shot. "I work hard and I play hard," she says. "That's the way I am."[2]

Sotomayor worked hard to overcome her deficiencies, the doubts of others, and her own insecurities. Decades later she would be defensive about her achievements as some critics asserted that she succeeded only because of affirmative action. Such attitudes reflected the enduring dilemma of race and ethnicity in America, and the stigma was real.

In the early 1970s it was remarkable that this child of Puerto Rican parents had even enrolled in college, let alone at an Ivy League school. When she started her studies at Princeton, only about 10 percent of all Hispanics between the ages of eighteen and twenty were attending college.[3] But she was riding a wave of change. The civil rights upheaval of the 1960s that she witnessed in the Bronx had raised awareness among government officials nationwide. They perceived the needs of racial minorities as well as the political potential in cultivating a Latino constituency.

President John F. Kennedy launched federal initiatives giving minorities a boost in 1961 with an executive order requiring government contractors to take "affirmative action" to ensure that they did not discriminate on the basis of race, creed, color, or national origin. President Lyndon B. Johnson pushed further by seeking passage of the Civil Rights Act of 1964 and mandating that federal contractors recruit, hire, and promote more minorities.

In 1965, as Johnson was about to sign the historic Executive Order 11246 implementing affirmative action, he laid out his views in a commencement speech at Howard University in Washington, D.C. "Freedom is not enough," he said in the June address to the predominantly black graduating class.

You do not wipe away the scars of centuries by saying: Now you are free to go where you want, and do as you desire, and choose the leaders you please. You do not take a person who, for years, has been hobbled by chains and liberate him, bring him up to the starting line of a race and then say, "you are free to compete with all the others," and still justly believe that you have been completely fair. Thus it is not enough just to open the gates of opportunity. All our citizens must have the ability to walk through those gates.[4]

President Johnson was speaking of the black experience, yet his words could easily have applied to Sotomayor and other Hispanics. "Equal opportunity is essential, but not enough, not enough," he said. "Men and women of all races are born with the same range of abilities. But ability is not just the product of birth. Ability is stretched or stunted by the family that you live with, and the neighborhood you live in—by the school you go to and the poverty or the richness of your surroundings. It is the product of a hundred unseen forces playing upon the little infant, the child, and finally the man."[5]

President Richard Nixon picked up where the Johnson administration left off. In 1972, the year Sotomayor entered Princeton, the U.S. secretary of labor ordered an increase in the representation of racial and ethnic minorities on campuses. "Almost all leading colleges and professional schools came to believe that they had a role to play in educating minority students," wrote William Bowen and Derek Bok, former presidents of Princeton and Harvard, in *The Shape of the River*. "Often spurred by student protests on their own campuses, university officials . . . [took] race into account in the admissions process by accepting qualified black students even if they had lower grades and test scores than white students." Bowen and Bok said that administrators adopted the policies for traditionally academic reasons: to enrich the education of all students with diversity and to enhance the ability of minorities to become leaders in business and government.[6]

At the same time, universities and other public entities had to answer to whites who believed they were shut out because of racial policies. Critics argued that affirmative action led to the selection of unprepared minorities and promoted a race consciousness when the country should be moving toward a color-blind society. Sotomayor would experience the backlash, but she would also benefit from affirmative action more often than not.

During Jimmy Carter's presidency, the recruitment of minorities for the federal judiciary became a national priority. Carter selected an unprecedented number of women, blacks, and Hispanics for federal courts.[7] His appointments to the powerful appellate tier of the federal judiciary, directly below the Supreme Court, offered new opportunities to blacks and Latinos in particular: 16.1 percent of his appointees for U.S. courts of appeals were black, and 3.6 percent were Hispanic. Neither Ford nor Nixon had put any blacks or Hispanics on the appeals courts.[8]

Reynaldo Guerra Garza, a Mexican American, was the first Hispanic appointed to a U.S. court at any level. President Kennedy named him to a district court in Texas in 1961. President Carter elevated Garza to the U.S. Court of Appeals for the Fifth Circuit in 1979.

At the Supreme Court, President Johnson had made history in 1967 with the appointment of the first black justice, Thurgood Marshall, a former appeals court judge who was serving as U.S. solicitor general. The great-grandson of a slave, Marshall was known nationally for taking the lead in litigation against school segregation that culminated in the 1954 *Brown v. Board of Education* decision ending the doctrine of "separate but equal." Born and reared in Baltimore, Marshall, the son of a railroad porter and schoolteacher, devoted his life to helping the poor and disenfranchised. He graduated from Howard University School of Law and became the chief counsel for the NAACP Legal Defense and Educational Fund.

Marshall not only steered the litigation strategy that successfully challenged school segregation, he also shepherded cases against racially restrictive housing covenants and whites-only election primaries. In his public interest work and as a government lawyer, he argued thirty-two cases before the Supreme Court. When President Johnson announced the nomination on June 13, 1967, he said of Marshall, "He is the best qualified by training and by very valuable service to the country. I believe it is the right thing to do, the right time to do it, the right man and the right place."[9] For the shrewd Johnson, Marshall's nomination was also the politically right move, and it completed a groundbreaking series of initiatives on behalf of minorities, including the 1964 Civil Rights Act and the 1965 Voting Rights Act. Still, when Marshall appeared before the Senate Judiciary Committee for vetting, he was subjected to racial humiliation, most notably from South Carolina senator Strom Thurmond, who asked Marshall to name the members of Congress who, in 1866, drafted the language for the Fourteenth Amendment guarantee of equal protection of the law.[10] The Senate confirmed Marshall by a 69–11 vote. All those who voted against him were Southerners.[11]

◆

Five years after Marshall's appointment, Sotomayor entered Princeton, behind her classmates both academically and socially. As a high school student, she had rarely strayed from the Bronx, in contrast to her Princeton classmates who attended prep schools and went off on ski trips and traveled Europe for adventure. Princeton, often called the "northernmost college for Southern gentlemen," did not admit women until 1969. It also was known for its exclusive eating clubs, which did not go fully coed until 1991—only after a lawsuit by women students forced the issue.

In her early weeks living in a dormitory among wealthy classmates in tony surroundings, Sotomayor fixed her attention on a cricket: "Every night, I tore that room apart looking for the cricket." When she told her visiting boyfriend, Kevin Noonan, who was earning a degree in science at the State University of New York at Stony Brook, he laughed because she had not realized that the noisy cricket was outside on a tree branch. The young woman who had grown up with unwelcome cockroaches, not crickets, later wrote, "This was all new to me: we didn't have trees brushing up against windows in the South Bronx."[12] In the Bronx, trains clattered, police sirens screamed, car horns blared, and people shouted at one another in cramped apartments.

When Sotomayor registered for classes, she felt even more the outsider. She often recounted an incident involving a woman from Alabama who had followed a succession of relatives to Princeton. As Sotomayor listened to the Alabama native talk of her privileged world, two of Sotomayor's close friends, one Mexican American, one Puerto Rican, approached, laughing and talking loudly. The woman from Alabama eyed them, Sotomayor recalled, and declared "how wonderful" it was that Princeton "had all these strange people." This was a new twist on the "those people" phrase Sotomayor had heard many times growing up.

But the oft-told tale earned a postscript in Sotomayor's memoir, as she revealed that rather than greet her approaching friends with the English they usually used, she began speaking in Spanish. "I meant no malice toward the girl from Alabama," Sotomayor wrote, "but my pulse was speeding with a sense of purpose. Nothing more needed to be said."[13] It was her way to even the score.

When she was admitted to Princeton, only three years after it had allowed women on campus, she did not realize how much her sex or ethnicity had mattered. But several months later the advantage began to dawn on her as she became involved in outreach efforts for other minority students. She recalled her visit to Yale, where she thought it was just a coincidence that two Hispanic students had been assigned to welcome her to the New Haven, Connecticut, campus. In time, she would embrace her experiences with affirmative action and the boost it gave her. She would not find it stigmatizing, as it was to Clarence Thomas, the other minority justice she joined at the Supreme Court. Affirmative action would become central to her success in navigating her way out of the Bronx and passing through the stately buildings of Princeton on her way to the federal bench.

And she set out to prove she deserved the break she got.

But first she had to face the fact that, as educationally nurturing as her mother and high school teachers had been, they had not prepared her for Princeton. The Spanish language that dominated her early years stymied her ability to write fluid English. The *Encyclopaedia Britannica* in her apartment in the Bronxdale Houses could not compare with the well-stocked libraries in the homes of many of her Princeton classmates. She knew nothing of the classics of literature.

Sotomayor went to a Manhattan bookstore the summer after her first year in search of elementary-grade grammar books and vocabulary builders. "I spent two years, every day, memorizing five new words," she said, "because I just felt deficient compared to my classmates in my mastery of English. These were things I did just to start feeling as if I belonged a little bit."[14] She read *Alice's Adventures in Wonderland*, *Huckleberry Finn*, and *Pride and Prejudice*. An English literature professor had taken points off her grade on an essay because Sotomayor had not understood a reference to Lewis Carroll's classic.

"Who's Alice?" she found herself saying.[15]

Sotomayor looked for mentors, and she found one in a history professor, Peter Winn, who in her first semester had returned a paper covered with red marks. "He spent the next four years being my tutor," she recalled. "Every paper I did, he would correct it and teach me something new about what I was doing wrong." She said he taught her to shed Spanish conventions that had stuck with her. She had to learn to write, for example, "cotton shirt" rather than "shirt of cotton" and "dictatorial authority" rather than "authority of dictatorship."[16]

She did not retreat in humiliation. She did not turn bitter. She developed her own mantra: "How am I *not* going to let this beat me?" In later years she would tell students, "You have to get up and try again. That's sometimes really hard to do, when you get embarrassed over failure."[17]

Sotomayor would take five courses with Winn, who later wrote, "She did not radiate charm or magnetism, nor was she polished or cool. But she had an appealing sincerity and directness, and there was something centered about her that was unusual among first-year minority students at Princeton." Over the years, Winn said, he saw "a tentative teenager—so intimidated that she never spoke in class during her first semester—become a poised young woman who negotiated successfully with top university administrators on contentious issues such as minority hiring practices."[18]

Such activism on behalf of minority employees at Princeton grew out of Sotomayor's involvement with Acción Puertorriqueña (Puerto Rican Action) and the Third World Center, two groups that attracted like-minded minority students. Established in 1971 in the old Osborn Field House, the homey Third World Center offered newly recruited blacks and Hispanics a refuge from the eating-club culture.

Sotomayor's efforts on behalf of minority employees at the university brought her attention beyond campus. When she was a sophomore, and cochairman of the Acción Puertorriqueña, she and other Puerto Rican and Chicano students filed a complaint with the U.S. Department of Health, Education and Welfare alleging that the university discriminated against its staff. In an essay for *The Daily Princetonian*, Sotomayor wrote that there were no Puerto Rican or Chicano administrators or faculty members on campus. This, she said, reflected a "total absence of regard, concern, and respect for an entire people and their culture" and "an attempt—a successful attempt so far—to relegate an important cultural sector of the population to oblivion."[19]

The New York Times published a story of its own at the time, quoting Sotomayor as saying, "Princeton is following a policy of benign neutrality and is not making substantive efforts to change."[20] Sotomayor learned early on the importance of being visible when she raised complaints. A month after the first news stories, a representative of the Department of Health, Education and Welfare's Civil Rights Division met with the students and an associate provost about the alleged discrimination.[21]

Sotomayor was a product of the rough-and-tumble Bronx, yet she was also her mother's studious daughter and a creation of the strict

Catholic school structure. She believed in process. She went through channels. She did not demonstrate. She did not walk out, as other minorities of her generation did, including some who would one day become friends and allies.

While Sotomayor was at Princeton typing up complaints, Charles Ogletree, an African American who would become a Harvard law professor and one of those friends, was organizing a graduation walkout at Stanford University. Ogletree was raised in the California Central Valley town of Merced by parents who had grown up in the Jim Crow South and never finished high school. A year before Sotomayor entered Princeton, Ogletree was admitted to Stanford, where he was itching to challenge authority. He described the sixty-eight African American students among the fifteen hundred freshmen in 1971 as standing out and speaking up: "We wore our hair in Afros the size of small planets and donned bell-bottom pants for every occasion. We danced to the music of Earth, Wind and Fire and enjoyed the mellow sounds of Barry White, Isaac Hayes, and Aretha Franklin. We were also in constant search of reasons to protest."[22] In his senior year, Ogletree helped stage a graduation walkout after he and other black students discovered that the commencement speaker would be Daniel Patrick Moynihan, coauthor of *Beyond the Melting Pot*, a former economic adviser to President Nixon, and then U.S. ambassador to India.

Ogletree was deeply troubled by *Beyond the Melting Pot*, which documented the breakup of the black family: "we were the products of the very family structure that they described as a formula for failure."[23]

For Sotomayor, the grounds of a prestigious school were not a place to be defiant, but a place to prove she could rise to the challenge of an academically rigorous curriculum. In her senior year, she shared with another student the M. Taylor Pyne Honor Prize, the highest distinction Princeton conferred on an undergraduate. It was based on academics and community service.[24] Sotomayor had the raw grades to back up the honor—she graduated in the top 10 percent of her class and earned a Phi Beta Kappa key.

Princeton gave her a seal of approval to counteract people who would stereotype her as inferior. Years later, when Senator Moynihan, a recurring figure in her trajectory, was writing about her qualifications to be a judge, he would highlight the Pyne Prize and that Phi Beta Kappa key. President Obama, in his nationally televised announcement of her nomination to the Supreme Court, would also tout her Princeton record. She had gotten her ticket stamped, and she knew it. She would later advise young people to spend money on college, to take out loans, to do whatever was necessary to get a first-rate education and a prestigious degree.

Supreme Court justice Clarence Thomas, who often complained about the weight of his academic loans, would deliver the opposite message and become one of the strongest public critics of affirmative action. Six years older than Sotomayor, Thomas was embittered by his experience on a similar path from hardship to opportunity. He received a bachelor's degree from Holy Cross and a law degree from Yale, and he recalled particularly his Yale experience with cynicism. He believed people thought he was admitted only because of his race. "It was futile for me to suppose that I could escape the stigmatizing effects of racial preference, and I began to fear that it would be used forever after to discount my achievements," wrote Thomas, who had trouble finding a job after he graduated from Yale in 1974.[25] He said he met a black graduate of the University of Michigan Law School who made a point of not referring to his race on applications. "I wished with all my heart that I'd done the same," Thomas wrote in his 2007 memoir.

> By then I knew I'd made a mistake in going to Yale. I felt as though I'd been tricked, that some of the people who claimed to be helping me were in fact hurting me . . . At least southerners were up front about their bigotry: you knew exactly where they were coming from, just like the Georgia rattlesnakes that always let you know when they were ready to strike. Not so the paternalistic big-city whites who offered you a helping hand so long as you were careful

to agree with them, but slapped you down if you started acting as if you didn't know your place.[26]

Thomas said he was treated dismissively by a succession of high-
priced lawyers at big firms. "Now I knew what a law degree from
Yale was worth when it bore the taint of racial preference," he wrote.
"I was humiliated—and desperate. The snake had struck."[27]

Sotomayor's experience at Yale Law School was not without humiliation and second-guessing because of her ethnicity. She had set
her sights on law school, first as a preteen enthralled by the fictional
defense lawyer Perry Mason, then as a college student inspired by
notions of social justice. Her personal choice came down to Harvard
or Yale because, she said, once she had experienced the Ivy League,
she would not accept a lesser-ranked alternative. She said she
chose Yale over Harvard because the students at the New Haven
campus seemed more relaxed and content.

But, she said, nothing could have prepared "a kid from the South
Bronx" for the atmosphere at a law school housed in the Sterling
Law Building, an ornate stone structure topped with turrets. She
described her Yale classmates as "a different breed of smart." In
her first year, she never raised her hand: "I was too embarrassed and
too intimidated to ask questions."[28] She knew that the only way to
understand the material was to put in the time with her studies. She
gained confidence by participating in mock trials, which drew on
her debate-team background from high school.

She might have felt timid, but she made an immediate impression
as gutsy. Professor Guido Calabresi, who later became a federal judge,
said she was not the usual "take no chances" first-year law student.
"Every once in a while you get a student bursting with ideas, who
shows courage. That was Sonia," he said.[29] Reviewing her papers, he
would not have to encourage boldness, as he would for the typical risk-
averse students. He said his comments would have been more along
the lines of "Maybe be a little more careful." Calabresi and Sotomayor
would end up serving on the federal appeals court together, and he
would play a strong role in her nomination to the Supreme Court.

In New Haven, Sotomayor was more comfortable among small groups of friends, and she gravitated toward people with nontraditional backgrounds, whether from housing projects or an Indian reservation. Friends recalled that she became an impromptu bouncer at graduate student parties, keeping out the New Haven locals who wanted to crash their events at the Gypsy Bar. She was tough, and she could handle the door better than the men in their crowd.

But the bouncer qualities sometimes did not play well back at the Sterling Law Building, where a friend told her that she argued "just like a guy." Sotomayor acknowledged in her memoir, "I have always argued like a man, more noticeably in the context of those days, when an apologetic and tentative manner of speech was the norm among women."[30]

Through the years, she would often be criticized for her domineering approach. But she rightly calculated that she did not need to change. In an earlier era, it might have cost her. The two women who preceded her at the Supreme Court—Sandra Day O'Connor and Ruth Bader Ginsburg—projected femininity, in their skirts, jewelry, and other accessories. They were born in the 1930s and attended law school in the 1950s, when it was easier to navigate the system by following conventions of the day.

While she was at Yale, Sotomayor and her law school friends wondered how long it would take for a woman to reach the Supreme Court. "There were bets being taken whether it would happen in our lifetime [and] . . . the fact that it was still something we weren't sure of bespeaks how historic it became that only two years later [O'Connor] was appointed," Sotomayor recalled of the 1981 milestone. "The doors were opening, but they were very, very small openings."[31]

At Yale, Sotomayor made a crucial connection with José Cabranes, then the university's general counsel and a lecturer. Fourteen years older than Sotomayor, Cabranes was a Puerto Rican success story. A polished dresser with an intellectual air, he also had street smarts. The son of two educators, he had come to the mainland with his family when he was five, had grown up in the South

Bronx and Queens, and had graduated from Columbia College and Yale Law School. Cabranes spoke proudly of his heritage and the importance of Puerto Ricans becoming active players in their new home. "Those of us who migrated in the modern era to the continental United States did so because we or our parents or our grandparents sought to become a part of American society—most particularly to become part of the mainstream of American society," he wrote. "We did not uproot ourselves from our native lands and come to America in search of a permanent place at the margins."[32] In 1979 he would become the first Puerto Rican appointed to a federal trial court within the continental United States.

Sotomayor and Cabranes met shortly before she began classes in New Haven, when she accompanied a Princeton friend who was writing about Puerto Ricans' citizenship and had obtained an interview with Cabranes. During the three-hour luncheon session, Sotomayor and Cabranes did most of the talking. When it was over, he offered her a research job. "I accepted, and José became my first legal employer, then my mentor and career adviser," she said.[33] He liked that she exhibited none of the diffidence associated with the Puerto Rican stereotype. And she liked that he was a successful lawyer who had held on to his identity as a New York City Puerto Rican. He became her model. Years later, when they were equals on the federal bench, their interests would diverge. As she began to displace him as the Hispanic who seemed most likely to be chosen for the Supreme Court, their rivalry would become the subject of intense public curiosity.

Another man in Sotomayor's life, Kevin Noonan, her longtime boyfriend, might at one point have appeared ready to play an enduring role, too. At the start of law school, she married him. She had planned to wait until her late twenties, vowing not to repeat the mistakes of aunts and cousins who married young and saw their marriages sour. But in 1976, when she was twenty-two and about to start law school, she and Noonan decided to live together. In her socially conservative Catholic world, Sotomayor said, that could not happen unless they married. Because her brother, Juan junior, held a

job as a sacristan at St. Patrick's Cathedral on Fifth Avenue, cleaning items used at the altar, they were able to hold the ceremony in
a chapel at the Roman Catholic landmark that was the site of many
grand celebrity nuptials.

She began using the name Sonia Sotomayor de Noonan, following
the Spanish convention. With his science degree from SUNY–Stony
Brook, Noonan obtained a job as a laboratory assistant in Yale's biology
department. Sharing domestic duties, Sotomayor cooked and Noonan
cleaned. As she burrowed into her studies and extracurricular efforts,
he never complained, she said, that she was away too much.

Only later would Sotomayor realize that she was more committed to her work than to him. The marriage would last seven years.

◆

As Sotomayor entered her final year of law school, she began thinking about her career options. During a recruitment dinner in October 1978, an exchange with a partner from a Washington-based law
firm would expose the suspicions that she constantly confronted.
The partner from Shaw, Pittman, Potts & Trowbridge had graduated from Yale in 1965 and joined the firm in 1968. He lured considerable business to the firm and was admired by colleagues, but
he also exuded an air of superiority and was known for making
impolitic remarks. At the recruiting dinner, with about ten people
around the table, he sat across from Sotomayor and grilled her: Do
you believe in affirmative action? Would you have been admitted to
Yale if you were not Puerto Rican? Do law firms do themselves and
young lawyers a disservice by hiring minority students who the firms
believe lack the necessary credentials and whom they likely will have
to fire? His questions reflected the growing opposition to policies
intended to bring diversity to the nation's campuses and workplaces.[34]

Sotomayor, who was twenty-four at the time, wrote later, "I was
stunned, as much by the bald rudeness of the interrogation as by
its implications. I'd heard nothing of the kind so blatant since the
school nurse caught me off guard at Cardinal Spellman." When the
law firm partner asked, "Do you consider yourself culturally deprived?"

she said she wanted to respond, with sarcastic reference to the musical *West Side Story*, "Gee, Officer Krupke, I thought, how do I explain? Shall I talk about my ancestors, the heritage of Spain? About having two languages, two ways of seeing the world? Is there only one culture that counts? I didn't know where to begin answering that one. And an awkward silence descended upon us."[35]

Later that night Sotomayor told friends what had happened. Minority classmates believed she should file a complaint. José Cabranes advised against it. He did not think the partner's offense was that serious, and he also worried that going public would backfire on her. Acting on her own instincts, Sotomayor decided to let the partner know how she felt during the formal interview the next day. She then filed a complaint with the university, challenging Shaw, Pittman's right to recruit on campus. Yale asked a student-faculty tribunal to look into the matter.

The panel determined that the partner had violated the school's antidiscrimination rules and asked the Shaw, Pittman firm to apologize. The firm's first letter was so weak the school asked for another.[36] In the second letter, the firm's senior partner wrote that the partner's remarks were "insensitive and regrettable." Sotomayor recalled that she was most outraged that he would have presumed that she barely got by at Princeton, when she had won its prestigious Pyne Prize and graduated summa cum laude and Phi Beta Kappa.

The recruiting dinner incident made news, including in *The Washington Post*. Such behavior was not unusual toward minorities and women in those days. Sotomayor's classmates had heard such insults and denigrating remarks. "'You're only here because of affirmative action,'" said Carmen Shepard, a Puerto Rican friend of Sotomayor's at Yale. "People looked at you as if you were not deserving. It was pervasive. It was a very difficult and a very painful issue to deal with . . . You get angry. But you don't live angry." Shepard and other classmates said they were not sure they would have been brave enough to challenge a law firm recruiter the way Sotomayor had. "To stop it in its tracks and say that's wrong," Shepard said, "that took courage."[37]

It was a daring move, particularly because of what had happened to Sotomayor a few months earlier while she was a summer associate at the large Manhattan law firm of Paul, Weiss, Rifkind, Wharton & Garrison. Sotomayor failed to do well enough to receive an offer to return after graduation, as was the usual practice, particularly for Yale students.

Paul, Weiss had a sterling reputation and counted among its alumni Supreme Court justice Arthur Goldberg. In the 1970s and '80s, a summer associate job at a large law firm like Paul, Weiss was essentially a guarantee of future employment. Firms rarely refused to invite their summer hires back as full associates, but Sotomayor received no such invitation.

"For this pain of failure—the first real failure since having enrolled in law school—I had only myself to blame, and knowing that, I was profoundly shaken," Sotomayor conceded. After she returned to New Haven for her final year of law school, she sought assistance in writing briefs and signed up for classes that she thought would help her better understand commercial transactions. She tried to remedy her inadequacies. "The unfamiliar taste of utter failure from that summer would stay in my mouth," she wrote. "The memory of this trauma, which I was determined not to repeat, while not suffocating my ambitions, would overhang my every career choice until I became a judge."[38]

It would not be apparent to those watching how much that failure stung. It would be clear, however, that she was motivated, not deflated, by defeat. Sotomayor had a personal resilience that allowed her to survive the system and to work it. As she had done at Princeton, she studied hard to catch up to students from more privileged backgrounds. She served as an editor on *The Yale Law Journal*.

Years later, when she was nominated for the Supreme Court, the *Yale Daily News* interviewed thirty-four of her classmates and concluded that "while she was unquestionably bright, she never emerged as a star—as someone who would one day be nominated to serve on America's highest court." One peer said, "If you had come up with a list of people in our class that would have been named to the Supreme Court, she would not have been on it."[39]

Of course, such a statement could be said about many people who have become justices over the years. But with Sotomayor, it touched a nerve. As she would complain years later, her academic credentials and professional achievements were frequently dismissed. She chalked it up to her being Hispanic. Even as she earned appointments to the federal bench, she said, "It was very, very painful . . . that people kept accusing me of not being smart enough."[40]

The Shaw, Pittman partner had suggested that if a young minority lawyer landed a job she was not ready for, it proved that affirmative action was a failure. Sotomayor disagreed. If that young lawyer could catch up and contribute, she believed, it proved the value of affirmative action. She felt no need to apologize for the policies that had gotten her into Princeton and Yale.

◆

The nation's tensions over affirmative action surfaced in courthouses across the country. In 1978, the same year that Sotomayor was confronted at the recruiting dinner about her qualifications, the Supreme Court took up the landmark case of Allan Bakke, who challenged a race-based admissions policy of the medical school at the University of California, Davis. Blond-haired, Minnesota-born Bakke had served as a naval officer in Vietnam and then worked as an engineer at NASA's Ames Research Center near Palo Alto. At age thirty-four he decided that he wanted to go to medical school, but he was rejected twice. His scores were close to the acceptance cutoff, and a university admissions officer told him that he was squeezed out because of spots reserved for minorities, about sixteen out of a hundred first-year applicants.[41] Bakke sued the university, claiming that the medical school engaged in reverse discrimination by denying him admission while admitting minority applicants he described as "not as qualified."

His case highlighted complex questions of law and fairness—dilemmas that traced back to Sotomayor's formative years and would not subside. Responding to Bakke's claim, University of California president William Saxon said that the school was seeking a mix of students who would best serve the academic and the professional

world, "including the important need of integration." He explained
that for years, selection had been based primarily on the highest
grade point averages and test scores, giving "preference to students
with the best educational opportunities and the most academically
supportive family and cultural backgrounds—in short, middle-
and upper-class white students." Saxon said the result was a short-
age of minority physicians and doctors in poorer, heavily minority
communities.[42]

In a split decision in the *Bakke* case issued on June 28, 1978,
the Supreme Court forbade the use of quotas in the admission of
minority students but allowed schools to take race into account as
one of several factors, based on universities' compelling interest in a
diverse student body. That meant affirmative action would survive,
although not as robustly as civil rights advocates had sought. Justice
Lewis Powell's opinion bridged the gap between two dueling fac-
tions on the Court, and he used as the ideal the flexible Harvard
College admissions policy that allowed for race as a "plus" in an applicant's file as he or she was considered along with other candidates
for the available seats.[43]

The compromise deeply offended Justice Marshall, who said
the universities should be able to use race more directly to increase the number of black doctors. "In declining to so hold,"
Marshall wrote, "today's judgment ignores the fact that for several
hundred years, Negroes have been discriminated against not as individuals, but rather solely because of the color of their skins."[44]
Still, the *Bakke* decision ensured that elite colleges, such as the
ones Sotomayor attended, would continue to encourage minority
applicants.[45]

As battles continued to rage over affirmative action, Sotomayor
talked freely about her own experiences. "I am the perfect affirmative action baby," she declared at a 1994 conference for women
in the law, echoing a phrase popularized by Yale law professor Stephen Carter in his 1992 book. "My test scores were not comparable
to that of my colleagues at Princeton or Yale," Sotomayor acknowledged. "If we had gone through the traditional numbers route of

those institutions it would have been highly questionable whether I would have been accepted." Sotomayor attributed differences in test scores between well-off whites and disadvantaged minorities to the cultural biases built into testing.[46]

She did not retreat in her defense of affirmative action over the decades. Laced throughout her 2013 memoir were statements defending the policy that had launched her. She would observe that even a quarter of a century after the 1978 episode with the Shaw, Pittman recruiter and the *Bakke* Supreme Court ruling, high-achieving minorities still faced doubts. "It is the same prejudice that insists all those destined for success must be cast from the same mold as those who have succeeded before them, a view that experience has already proven a fallacy," she wrote.[47]

Sotomayor was determined to prove her doubters wrong and also motivated by a conversation with a cousin, Nelson, before his death brought on by drug addiction. She told him that he had always seemed the smartest of all the cousins. Nelson responded that she had something better: perseverance. "I know that my competitive spirit—my drive to win, my fear of failure, my desire constantly to outdo myself—bubbles up from very deep within my personality," Sotomayor wrote. "It's rarely directed at others; I compete with myself."[48]

After she graduated from Yale Law School, in 1979, she went to the Manhattan district attorney's office. On the recommendation of Yale's José Cabranes, she was hired by Robert Morgenthau, who, after having served as the United States attorney for the Southern District of New York under Presidents Kennedy, Johnson, and Nixon, had taken the helm of the DA's office in 1975.

Tall and lean, with a commanding presence that earned him the enduring title of "the Boss," Morgenthau was known for his prosecutorial integrity. His roots traced to a world of privilege. President Woodrow Wilson had selected his grandfather as the U.S. ambassador to the Ottoman Empire, and his father became secretary of the treasury under Franklin D. Roosevelt. Morgenthau's relationship with John Kennedy, the first president to appoint him, began when they were teenage boys in New York.

Morgenthau had told Cabranes that he was looking for more Hispanic prosecutors.[49] In the late 1970s and early '80s, the era of Tom Wolfe's *Bonfire of the Vanities*, Manhattan seemed overwhelmed by street crime. The Manhattan district attorney's office had few minority prosecutors, and Morgenthau was constantly under pressure to raise those numbers to build confidence in the system. For decades, Hispanics had found themselves disproportionately pulled into the machinery of the criminal justice process. They were more likely than whites to be crime victims, and a higher percentage of Hispanics were defendants and went to prison.

Being a prosecutor was not exactly what Sotomayor had envisioned for herself. Television's Perry Mason, her childhood idol, was a defense lawyer. When she chose the prosecutor's office, she said, "There was a tremendous amount of pressure from my community. They could not understand why I was taking this job. I'm not sure I've ever resolved that problem."[50] But the DA's office gave her immediate hands-on experience, improved her strategic thinking, and offered her a way to serve victims within her community.

Sotomayor began with misdemeanors, petty thefts, and assaults and moved up to such felonies as racketeering, sex crimes, and eventually murder. This was no law firm setting: her desk was squeezed in with several other prosecutors. Stacks of papers and boxes of evidence loomed over her. In the summer it was so hot that sweat soaked through her clothes. In the winter it was so frigid she wore her coat while she worked.

Challenged in every way, she logged long hours. She would leave the house at 7:00 a.m. and get home at 10:00 p.m. She went into dangerous neighborhoods to interview witnesses and took on difficult child pornography and abuse cases. She was not cowed by defense lawyers, who would sometimes assume that her junior male associates were in charge. When visiting lawyers asked her to get the coffee, she turned her resentment into an "I'll show them" mantra.

Years later she would say that the measure of success in the DA's office in the early 1980s was based on the forceful behavior displayed by her male bosses. For promotion in the felony division, she said, "They picked people who acted as prosecutors as they did. All of the first . . . people selected, myself included, were highly aggressive, very in-your-face prosecutors—because that's the model that they all were."[51]

After her own promotion to the homicide division, she worked on the "Tarzan" murder case. Richard Maddicks was known for swinging into apartment windows on a rope tied to rooftops and shooting anyone who caught him in the act of ransacking apartments. He was charged with murder, attempted murder, robbery, and burglary. Sotomayor persuaded his girlfriend to testify against him, and he was convicted and sentenced to life imprisonment.[52]

But Sotomayor began to wonder whether she was contributing to the greater good. "The one thing I have found is that if you come into the criminal justice system on a prosecutorial or defense level, thinking you can change the ills of society, you're going to be sorely disappointed," she said in a 1983 interview with *The New York Times*. "This is not where those kinds of changes need to be made." Described in the *Times* story about Morgenthau's office as "an imposing woman of 29 who smokes incessantly," Sotomayor spoke candidly of her personal struggles as a Latina from the Bronx. "What I am finding, both statistically and emotionally, is that the worst victims of crimes are not general society—i.e., white folks—but minorities themselves. The violence, the sorrow are perpetrated by minorities on minorities."[53]

Work in the district attorney's office exhausted her. She kept running into the same bad actors over and over. She felt herself becoming uncharacteristically cynical, and the demands, in terms of hours and attitude, spelled the end of her already unraveling marriage to Kevin Noonan.

While she served in Manhattan, Noonan was at Princeton getting a Ph.D. in molecular biology. They drifted apart as they became immersed in their respective professional lives. She said later that she had been so caught up in her career that she barely noticed the distance—real and emotional—between them. They divorced in 1983.[54]

In the years that followed, Sotomayor talked candidly about the miseries of dating, first in the interview with *Mademoiselle* that had followed the path of Ivy League women, and then with ABC's *Good Morning America*. In the TV interview, Sotomayor was direct about how her work was killing her romantic life. "A man who calls you three times and all three times you answer, 'I've got to work late, I'm flying to such and such a place' . . . after the third time, he begins thinking, 'Gee, maybe she's not interested.'"[55]

The year of her divorce was also the year she left the DA's office for the small commercial firm of Pavia & Harcourt. She said she wanted to broaden her experience and was looking for a place where she would not be merely another cog in the machinery. "It became clear that I would need more varied experience if I was going to aim higher than a line attorney in a government bureaucracy," she said, referring to her goal of a judgeship.[56]

At Pavia & Harcourt, which had about thirty lawyers at the time, she began with routine transactions, real estate and consumer warranty disputes. No longer was she in the hard-charging atmosphere of the DA's office. "Within my first couple of days on the job," Sotomayor recalled, "a colleague who sat within earshot of my phone calls let it be known to another litigation associate, who then spread the word, that I was 'one tough bitch,' who could not be pushed around by an adversary." The harsh description surprised her. "Trying case after case by the seat of your pants at the DA's Office, you develop a bravado that can seem abrasive to lawyers who have no acquaintance with that world. It was kind of culture shock in both directions."[57]

In time, she specialized in intellectual property law and represented such high-end European manufacturers as Fendi in copyright and trademark infringement disputes. While at Pavia & Harcourt, Sotomayor also became involved in organizations that worked to advance the economic interests of minorities. Through her Morgenthau connection, she joined the State of New York Mortgage Agency, providing low-rate loans for affordable housing in blighted neighborhoods. Through her Cabranes connection, she became a board member of the Puerto Rican Legal Defense and Education Fund (PRLDEF), founded in 1972 and patterned partly after the NAACP Legal Defense Fund and the newer Mexican American Legal Defense and Educational Fund.[58] PRLDEF's early lawsuits sought bilingual education in public schools, targeted housing bias, and challenged hiring tests that disproportionately excluded minority applicants.

She was serving her community. Yet the ever-savvy Sotomayor realized that her newly formed connections with the legal and business professionals on the PRLDEF board—"the Brahmins of Nuyorican society," she would say—were also a networking bonanza.

"Sometimes, idealistic people are put off by the whole business of networking as something tainted by flattery and the pursuit of selfish advantage," she said as she recounted her years with the Puerto Rican Legal Defense Fund. "But virtue in obscurity is rewarded only in heaven. To succeed in this world, you have to be known to people."[59]

She was proving to have a knack for that.

FOUR

Chance and Connections

Senator Daniel Patrick Moynihan, a former professor and sociologist, had done tours in Washington with four administrations and been in the U.S. Senate since 1977. He was a shrewd operator who usually could get what he wanted. But in the spring of 1991 the tall New York Democrat with an owlish visage and a mop of silver hair had hit a wall with his recommendations to Republican president George H. W. Bush for federal judgeships. Among them was the name of Sonia Sotomayor.

Moynihan needed leverage, and he was considering blocking Senate action on another judicial candidate—Michael Luttig, a Justice Department lawyer and rising Republican star—until the administration acted on his recommendations.

Sotomayor represented much of Moynihan's life's work. As a scholar of demographics and a leading but often controversial voice on racial and ethnic policy, long before he met her in the early 1990s, he had been studying people like her, focusing on ethnic aspiration and assimilation, most notably in *Beyond the Melting Pot*. Now, as a senator, he was seeking diverse candidates such as Sotomayor to recommend for the federal trial court in New York.

Appointments to the federal bench were the president's to make—with, as the Constitution dictates, "the advice and consent of the Senate." For openings on the district courts, home-state senators made recommendations to the president, and they were usually accepted. For the next levels up, the U.S. appeals courts and Supreme Court, presidents jealously guarded and controlled nomination choices.

Soon after Moynihan was elected senator, he sought a more substantive role in the judicial selection process and instituted two new practices for his recommendations for the district court. First, he established a screening committee for nominees.[1] If a panel of lawyers handled suggestions from the legal community and interviewed candidates, he believed, he would have stronger nominees to pass on to the president.

Moynihan also thought that New York's two senators should have a say in judicial recommendations made to the president, regardless of their political party. Traditionally, only a senator from the party controlling the White House made trial judge suggestions to the president. Moynihan, however, thought neither political party should have a monopoly on judicial appointments.[2] Soon after he took office, he developed a plan—distinct to New York—that for every three recommendations he made to Democratic president Jimmy Carter, Moynihan's Republican colleague, Senator Jacob Javits, would receive one. Moynihan thought the arrangement would serve the state's two senators in the long run. Recommending someone for the federal bench was no small privilege. District court judges were appointed for life, and they presided over most of the nation's federal criminal and civil cases.

Moynihan's approach to recommendations for New York–based federal judges continued after Jimmy Carter left office and into the administrations of Republicans Ronald Reagan and George H. W. Bush. But now GOP senator Alfonse D'Amato, who had succeeded Javits in 1980, got three picks to every one that Democrat Moynihan made. That flip of the three-to-one ratio reflected the fact that a Republican White House controlled nominations. The Bush White House did not like giving a Democratic senator any say, which was partly why it was stalling on Sonia Sotomayor and the other U.S. district court candidates Moynihan had recommended in 1991.

Sotomayor's name had first come to Moynihan in late 1990 from his screening committee. On paper, she looked good: Princeton and Yale degrees, a job as a prosecutor in the office of the legendary Bob Morgenthau, now handling copyright and other intellectual property cases for Pavia & Harcourt. At thirty-six, Sotomayor was young for a judgeship, but that did not bother Moynihan, who had joined the Kennedy administration before his thirty-fifth birthday. Her public service credentials—the Puerto Rican Legal Defense and Education Fund and the New York State Mortgage Agency—also impressed Moynihan.

During her five years in the district attorney's office, Sotomayor had developed a reputation as a tough prosecutor, handling all manner of cases, as Morgenthau would say, from turnstile jumping to murder. In her work at the law firm of Pavia & Harcourt she was traveling to Europe to meet with such clients as Fendi and making more money than she had in her life. She was doing so well that she hesitated a bit in the early days of the process. But the federal bench was part of her long-term game plan. And the firm's managing partner, David Botwinik, was a childhood friend of Judah Gribetz, the chairman of Moynihan's screening committee. This was a lucky connection for Sotomayor. Gribetz had worked as counsel to New York governor Hugh Carey and as deputy mayor for governmental relations under New York City mayor Abe Beame. Gribetz's committee had been casting a wide net for applicants who could bring diversity to the bench in order to reflect Moynihan's policy and political interests. Botwinik told Gribetz he thought Sotomayor would be an ideal candidate.

Earlier in 1990 Botwinik had brought an application to her office and told her to fill it out. "He took my work away from me for a week and gave me not only my time and my secretary's time, but the time of a paralegal and even his own secretary, so that together we could fill out those very burdensome application forms," Sotomayor recalled.[3] With Botwinik's endorsement, the committee recommended her.[4]

Then it was time to meet the senator.

The two were separated by a generation but had plenty in common. The Bronx Latina and the Irish street fighter had scrapped

their way up and now appreciated the markers of their elite education and professional status. Moynihan's hard-drinking father had
abandoned the family when he was ten. Moynihan spent part of his
childhood in Hell's Kitchen on New York's West Side, shined shoes,
and worked the docks. He started taking classes at City College of
New York while he was a longshoreman, then joined the navy, serving as a gunnery officer at the end of World War II. When he returned home, he attended Tufts University, earning his bachelor's
degree and eventually a Ph.D. in sociology. Moynihan received a
Fulbright fellowship and attended the London School of Economics.

Robert Peck, a longtime Moynihan chief of staff, said that the
senator struggled to reconcile his past with the present. "He couldn't
decide whether he was down in the dirt Irish or a dandy," Peck said.
"In a working-class [tavern], he could belly up to the bar. But to be
honest, he felt more comfortable sitting in the lounge of the Carlyle
Hotel."[5]

Over the years, Moynihan had developed an extravagant, sometimes exasperating, style of rhetoric that was an amalgam of his Celtic
roots and his high-toned education. Sotomayor had no such affec-
tation; she never lost her Bronx accent.

As she and Moynihan talked in his office, the former scholar
of American demographics delved into her background and traced
her interest in the law. Sotomayor thought she made one of her best
pitches.

Her confidence surprised Moynihan. The man who had lamented
in 1970 "that one-third of the black and more of the Puerto Rican
population are dependent on welfare," knew that the Latina in front
of him could have been doomed by her background.[6] A few bad
choices or rotten luck might have set her on a different path. When
the interview was over, Moynihan was ready to recommend her for
a trial judgeship. And he told her so.

"He loved being able to put up a Puerto Rican, a girl from the
Bronx who went to Yale Law School," Peck said.[7]

◆

Moynihan later asked Gribetz, "Judah, where did you find her?"[8] She was indeed a find. In 1991, when Sotomayor was first being considered, women made up just 12 percent of the federal bench, and minorities constituted about 10 percent. In the entire state of New York, not one federal judge was Hispanic.[9]

With the backing of Republican senator D'Amato, Moynihan sent three names to the Bush White House in March 1991: Sotomayor, Deborah Batts, and David Trager. Batts, an African American, had earned degrees from Radcliffe College and Harvard Law School. A former assistant U.S. attorney, she was teaching at Fordham University School of Law. Trager, who was white and dean of the Brooklyn Law School, held degrees from Columbia College and Harvard Law School and had been an assistant U.S. attorney.

Moynihan made sure the news media knew about his recommendations. He believed that more blacks and Hispanics should be in seats of power, and as a political matter, he knew his support for minorities on the bench would soften some lingering criticism of his earlier racial views.

"He bitterly resented the way he had been accused of racism," Moynihan biographer Godfrey Hodgson wrote, observing that "demons of race" had pursued Moynihan throughout his political life.[10] Moynihan's 1965 report to President Johnson documenting the breakup of the black family, along with his earlier *Beyond the Melting Pot*, could have been interpreted as blaming minorities for their problems. The civil rights community and the liberal establishment were further inflamed by a 1970 Moynihan memorandum to President Richard Nixon that was leaked to the press, in which Moynihan asserted that race relations were being dominated by "hysterics, paranoids and boodlers" on all sides. He advocated a period of "benign neglect." Civil rights leaders called the memo "a flagrant and shameful political document."[11] Moynihan explained that he was not urging neglect of blacks, but rather a cooling-off period for the angry rhetoric on both sides. "It killed me," he said years later. "It won't ever be forgiven; that's all there is to it."[12]

Still sensitive to such complaints, Moynihan was furious with how *The New York Times* displayed—or, to his mind, buried—the story about his recommendation of Sotomayor and the others in its March 2, 1991, edition. The news article, with the headline "3 Recommended for U.S. Court; One Is Hispanic," ran on an inside page in the second section of the newspaper, in what Moynihan regarded as the spot for obituaries.

The senator fired off a letter to the story's author, Wayne King. In his abrupt, iconoclastic style, Moynihan declared, "Good God, they hadn't died! The Obit Page indeed." Moynihan then struck at the heart of his complaint, if cryptically: "My point is this. These are issues involving social tension at profoundly important levels. Have been writing about them all my life. When the paper correctly decides to report the issues, it unavoidably adds to the tension. Hence a certain proportionality suggests that our story be given a comparable weight." Moynihan continued, "You don't have to believe this and won't, but there is nothing political here. From our point of view. Something much deeper and enduring. Pass it on."[13]

What he considered "deeper" was the nation's progress on race. He did not view the Puerto Rican Sotomayor and African American Batts as routine candidates by any measure. They were highly credentialed individuals who knew what it was like to be on society's bottom rungs and face disadvantages because of the color of their skin and their ethnicity.

Yet Moynihan's quarrels with the *Times* were mild compared with his clash with George H. W. Bush's administration. He blamed some delays, particularly when it came to Batts, on racial politics. He outright told his Senate colleague John Danforth, a moderate Republican from Missouri, that if Justice Department lawyers ended up rejecting Batts, "it is because of the color of her skin. They assume black means liberal."[14]

◆

In mid-April 1991 Sotomayor had her first interview with Justice Department aides, including Murray Dickman, an assistant to Attorney General Dick Thornburgh, who was in charge of the department's judicial screening; Timothy Flanigan, an assistant attorney general who had been a law clerk to former chief justice Warren Burger; and John Roberts, then principal deputy U.S. solicitor general.[15]

In the early 1990s John Roberts was a subtler tactician than the aggressive Sotomayor. But neither lacked raw ambition, as would be proven when they ended up together on the High Court more than a decade later. In 2005, Bush's son, President George W. Bush, would nominate Roberts to be chief justice of the United States. In the early 1990s Roberts's work in the U.S. Office of the Solicitor General mainly involved crafting legal positions and writing briefs for that office, which represented the federal government before the Supreme Court. But Roberts was a smart political operator whose judgment was sought throughout the administration.

For her part, Sotomayor quickly learned to work two sides of the nomination process—as a nominee and as a conduit of information. She reported back to the senator's staff that the Justice Department lawyers had called attention to her age. But she was ready: she had checked recent Republican judicial nominees and their ages, discovering that several had been nominated when they were in their early and mid-thirties. She had faxed a copy of her findings to Moynihan's office.[16]

This was the calculating, hands-on Sotomayor. Unlike many lawyers nominated for judicial office, she was accustomed to pushing overtly for what she wanted. She had long put her career ahead of her personal life, and in these chain-smoking, highly caffeinated days she juggled work at Pavia and Harcourt with monitoring the progress of her nomination.

A neophyte when it came to the ways of the nation's capital, Sotomayor nonetheless understood the importance of calling Moynihan's office regularly. Her sense of urgency would set her apart from other nominees. When a month had passed after her interview and there was no word about progress, Sotomayor checked in again with Moynihan's staff. The point man was Joseph Gale, a former corporate lawyer who had joined Moynihan's office in 1985 to work on tax issues. Gale had become a key aide to Moynihan on nominations.

He and Sotomayor had been students at Princeton at the same time, although they did not know each other well. After evaluating Sotomayor's and Deborah Batts's chances, Gale wrote to Moynihan in May 1991 that the Justice Department appeared "to be sitting on" these two district judge recommendations. He said that department lawyers were not returning his calls. He realized that Moynihan needed some leverage.

Gale found it with Michael Luttig, then a thirty-six-year-old assistant attorney general. A few weeks earlier President Bush had nominated Luttig for the U.S. Court of Appeals for the Fourth Circuit, based in Richmond. That powerful regional court handled appeals from trial judges in Maryland, Virginia, North Carolina, South Carolina, and West Virginia. The nomination was a plum for Luttig, a former law clerk to Chief Justice Warren Burger and a law clerk to Justice Antonin Scalia when Scalia was a judge on the U.S. Court of Appeals for the District of Columbia Circuit. In 1991 Luttig was overseeing the Office of Legal Counsel, which produced opinions on the president's constitutional powers. Gale advised Moynihan to put a "hold" on Luttig, thus preventing his nomination from advancing in the Senate.

Moynihan had seen his recommendations stall before. An earlier choice for a U.S. trial court vacancy in New York had been John Carro. Like Sotomayor, Carro was Puerto Rican, but he was twenty-seven years older and part of the vanguard of the Latino civil rights movement.

Carro had moved from Puerto Rico to New York with his family in 1937, when he was ten years old. He grew up in East Harlem and attended Benjamin Franklin High School, also Moynihan's alma mater. Carro went to Fordham University and Brooklyn Law School, served in the administration of Mayor Robert Wagner, and in 1968, after Carro had returned to private practice, Mayor John Lindsay named him to the New York Criminal Court. At that time Carro was one of only a few local Puerto Rican judges, and the first from the Bronx. In 1979 he became a justice in the city appellate division.

Not only was Carro well-known in New York legal circles, he

also had a strong reputation for liberalism and Latino advocacy. He openly lamented the fact that some Hispanic lawyers lost "their identity and commitment" as they moved up in the profession. "I have seen it time and time again where students profess to want to become lawyers to represent their people and right their wrongs, only to come out of law school and seek a safe job in government or in the corporate world, seldom to be seen in their communities again," Carro said in the text of a 1980 speech that Senator Moynihan had saved.[17]

Carro was one of the early leaders of Latino advocacy. Vilma Martínez, president of the Mexican American Legal Defense and Educational Fund, was another. If the president or times had been different, Carro or Martínez might have been in the running for "first Hispanic" at the Supreme Court two decades before it happened.[18]

But in early 1991 Carro asked Moynihan to withdraw his name for a federal judgeship. "As you know it has been almost three years since you first proposed my name to the president," Carro wrote to Moynihan in January 1991, referring to the fact that his name had been raised first in the administration of Ronald Reagan: "Since that time I have been interviewed several times by the Justice Department and the FBI has done what I can only assume to be a thorough background check. Still, the President has not sent my name on to the Senate . . . I can only assume that the President's failure to do so is because he disagrees with the views I have expressed."[19]

Moynihan also was ready to move on. "It is intolerable the way the Justice Department has fiddled with this matter," he wrote to Carro. "It is our loss, of course . . . I do not in the least blame you, considering that you must be caught up with mounds of important and interesting cases. We Benjamin Franklin graduates are not getting any younger, and perhaps do well to stay at our posts."[20]

Now, in late spring 1991, Moynihan did not want a repeat of the Carro episode. He agreed with senior aide Joe Gale that temporarily blocking the nomination of Michael Luttig could help

Sotomayor and Batts. Gale called Jeff Peck, staff director on the Senate Judiciary Committee, chaired by Joseph Biden, a Democrat from Delaware, and asked that no action be taken on Luttig's nomination.[21]

"The Luttig card may work for us," Gale reported back to Moynihan on June 7, 1991. "Jeff Peck advised me that . . . Attorney General Thornburgh called Senator Biden and made a personal appeal to move the Luttig nomination quickly. Biden's reply was, in essence, 'why should I expedite a Justice Department candidate when Justice has been sitting on two of Moynihan's recommendations and won't even return his staff's phone calls?'" Attuned to the trading of favors on Capitol Hill, Gale told Moynihan, "You may want to call Biden to thank him."[22]

The maneuvering occurred behind the scenes and was not the grist of daily news reports. Yet Sotomayor absorbed its meaning. A judicial nomination, particularly of a minority candidate, did not move without some pushing and shoving. She was also seeing how nominees could get caught up in situations that had nothing to do with them. Luttig's nomination for a Richmond-based U.S. appeals court suddenly depended on what happened to a Puerto Rican woman in New York. They were joined, for the time being, because of senators' prerogatives.

Around this time, Attorney General Dick Thornburgh, who oversaw judicial nominations for President Bush, lamented that the process combined "the intricacies of chess and the audacity of old-fashioned hardball."[23] This was part of the age-old politicking over court nominations. But minorities and women, traditionally on the outside looking in, faced greater resistance. The "old boys' club" that controlled the process in the 1990s would continue to flex its muscles as Sotomayor's candidacy moved along.

◆

As Moynihan pressured the Bush administration to act on his recommendation of Sotomayor, a retirement at the Supreme Court reignited the debate over the racial makeup of the nation's highest court. Thurgood Marshall, the first African American justice, announced on June 27, 1991, that he would retire. A few days before his eighty-third birthday, Marshall wrote in a letter to President Bush that "advancing age and medical condition" were forcing him to step down. Marshall was even blunter in a news conference with reporters: "What's wrong with me? . . . I'm old! I'm getting old and coming apart."[24]

Marshall's face was craggy, and his belly pushed out against his white shirt and dark suspenders. He had served as a justice for twenty-four years and watched in frustration as the Court moved to the right in the 1970s and 1980s with Republican appointees who curtailed racial remedies and scaled back defendants' rights. Two days before he announced his retirement, Marshall passionately dissented from a decision that overturned two Supreme Court precedents and allowed the use of "victim impact" statements in death penalty cases, which tended to diminish juror leniency for criminal defendants.[25]

The decision to retire had been difficult for Marshall. A legend in the civil rights movement and the last voice of true liberalism on the Supreme Court, he was not eager to give a Republican president the opportunity to name his successor. But he was sick and weary, and he simply believed his time on the Court was up. At the news conference the day of his retirement, Marshall said that President Bush should strive for the best appointee and that race should not be an overriding factor. He said he did not want the president to select "the wrong Negro" or say "I'm picking him because he is a Negro."[26]

Marshall had put his finger on a recurring issue of how a possible nominee's minority status should affect the selection calculation: Should it be incidental or determinative? And would such an emphasis on race diminish the nominee's credentials?

Immediately after receiving Marshall's retirement letter, President Bush interviewed Clarence Thomas, an African American who had served as chairman of the Equal Employment Opportunity Commission (EEOC) under Ronald Reagan and been named by Bush in 1989 to a powerful federal appeals court in Washington, D.C.

The president liked Thomas, who had a friendly demeanor and a booming laugh. Bush found Thomas's personal story of poverty in segregated Georgia compelling. Still, Bush was concerned that Thomas, at forty-three, had served on the U.S. Court of Appeals for the District of Columbia Circuit for less than two years and might be perceived as inexperienced. Thomas was also controversial because his legal views were exactly the opposite of Marshall's. Thomas opposed programs that encouraged hiring goals or preferences for minorities—programs that had pushed him and Sotomayor up the ladder in Ivy League schools.

Still, the Republican administration had few options. "For that vacancy, it was a very short list," recalled Attorney General Thornburgh. "We knew, even though it was not articulated, that the president wanted a minority. The odds-on choice was Clarence Thomas."[27]

Bush, who before his election had lived in Houston, asked his top lawyers to look for any possible Hispanic candidates. So in 1991, when the Texas-based judge Emilio Garza, the son of Mexican immigrants, was interviewed for the Marshall vacancy, he became the first Hispanic seriously considered for the Supreme Court.

A graduate of the University of Notre Dame and the University of Texas School of Law who had served in the U.S. Marines for three years, Garza was a bachelor with a quiet, studious demeanor. He had been appointed by President Reagan as a trial judge in 1988, and in 1991 Bush had elevated him to the U.S. Court of Appeals for the Fifth Circuit, covering cases from Texas, Louisiana, and Mississippi. His formal commission to the Fifth Circuit was signed in May, barely two months before he, then forty-three, received the call to fly from San Antonio to Washington to interview for Marshall's position.

During the interview with Attorney General Thornburgh and White House counsel Boyden Gray, Garza seemed unprepared for the Supreme Court and the Senate confirmation process. "We felt that he needed more seasoning," Thornburgh said, observing that Gray had been pushing hard for Clarence Thomas and that anyone else would have had to stand out to overcome that preference.[28]

News accounts reported that some top aides to President Bush liked the idea of a Hispanic nominee "on political grounds," and that José Cabranes, then a federal district court judge in Connecticut, was on the administration's list of possible nominees.[29] But no Bush aides reached out to Cabranes, an appointee of Democratic president Carter, for background information or to set up an interview. Thornburgh said later that Cabranes would not have been seriously considered by the GOP administration. "He wouldn't meet our goal for conservatism," Thornburgh said.[30]

There was a natural awkwardness in naming Thomas to succeed Marshall: the black seat going to the only black Republican who would have been considered. White House aides were obviously conflicted. *The Washington Post* reported that an administration official said Thomas prevailed over Judge Garza because of a "semiconscious sense . . . this was a black man to be replaced." The *Post* wrote that the official (unnamed in the story) "then immediately backpedaled, saying: 'Strike that. He was the best person.'"[31]

On July 1 President Bush announced that he had chosen Thomas to succeed Marshall. He called Thomas "the best person at the right time."[32] When reporters questioned how Thomas's race affected the decision, Bush said, "The fact that he is black and a minority has nothing to do with this sense that he is the best qualified at this time. I kept my word to the American people and to the Senate by picking the best man for the job on the merits. And the fact that he's a minority, so much the better." Those presidential references to "best person" and "best man" would exacerbate public cynicism about the process and preoccupy Thomas for years. Writing in his 2007 memoir, Thomas said that five years after his Senate confirmation he asked Boyden Gray, Bush's White House counsel, "Was I picked because I was black?" Thomas suggested that he believed Gray's answer was no. Thomas wrote that he was told that his "race had actually worked against" him because the administration did not want to be perceived as picking someone simply for a "black" seat.[33]

Civil rights groups, including those dominated by Hispanics, were torn over whether to support Thomas, a man who had experienced the discrimination they were fighting but who had spurned their cause in his professional work. Thomas had endured a difficult childhood. His father had abandoned the family, and his mother had few resources to support her three children. After their home in the hamlet of Pin Point, Georgia, burned down, five-year-old Clarence was sent to live with his grandfather, a harsh taskmaster, in Savannah. Thomas often recalled episodes of racial hatred and discrimination from his youth, including what happened on the night of April 4, 1968, when the Reverend Martin Luther King, Jr., was assassinated. Thomas heard a white classmate at the seminary he was attending express great glee at the killing. Thomas said he was losing his interest in the priesthood at the time, and the incident helped prompt him to leave the seminary and transfer to Holy Cross College.

John Lewis, a Georgia Democrat in the U.S. House of Representatives and a respected civil rights leader, opposed Thomas, asserting that a beneficiary of the civil rights movement was now undermining its goals. "Judge Thomas stands poised to deny to others the kind of opportunities that he has enjoyed," said Lewis, who as a young activist was beaten bloody during a March 1965 attack by state troopers in Selma, Alabama. "Of course, I have heard the argument that Clarence Thomas cannot 'forget' where he has come from and, therefore, he will be sensitive to the plight of the disadvantaged. After all, he grew up poor and fatherless in segregated Georgia. My response to that argument is: Look at his record. He has forgotten before."[34]

Just as senators were preparing to vote on the Thomas nomination, Anita Hill, a former employee of Thomas's at the EEOC and the Department of Education, came forward and claimed that he had sexually harassed her. She alleged that he had made sexually charged comments, including some mentions of breasts and penises, which led shocked senators to delay a vote on his nomination and reopen the confirmation hearings. Thomas angrily denied Hill's claims and accused the Senate Judiciary Committee of "a high-tech lynching." He survived, but with the closest Senate vote in more than a century, 52–48. All the Democrats who voted for him were from the South, the opposite of what had happened in 1967, when Southern Democratic senators opposed Marshall. By 1991, blacks had become a core constituency of Southern senators, and Democrats feared alienating them with a vote against Thomas.

◆

During the fight over Thomas's confirmation, most lower court nominations stalled—but not that of GOP favorite Michael Luttig. Moynihan released his "hold" when the Bush administration promised a second round of Justice Department interviews for Sonia Sotomayor. In late July 1991, after Thomas had been nominated but before the confirmation hearings began, the Senate confirmed Luttig, and he was commissioned on August 2. Luttig temporarily remained with administration lawyers behind the scenes, helping to prepare Thomas for his Supreme Court confirmation hearings.[35]

Moynihan vigorously opposed Thomas and was one of the Democrats who insisted on postponing Senate action until after Anita Hill testified. But he also continued to press on Sotomayor's behalf. She could not have asked for a more effective political godfather. "He wasn't the typical horse trader," recalled Moynihan's chief of staff Robert Peck. "He didn't spend a lot of time on the floor. He didn't have a lot of friends in the Senate. But if he wanted something . . . he was prepared to keep banging" on it.[36] The New York Democrat hounded the administration, fellow senators, and his friends in the press on Sotomayor's behalf. Moynihan wrote on August 8, 1991, to Arthur O. "Punch" Sulzberger, publisher of *The New York Times*, "It is absolutely the case that the people we send over to Justice are treated almost as suspects . . . It is degrading. And I wonder that most are willing to go through with it. Out of loyalty I like to think to the committee of New York lawyers that chose them." He complained that Sonia Sotomayor and Deborah Batts "were given the deep freeze."[37]

Sotomayor's nomination moved forward after William Barr succeeded Thornburgh as attorney general in late summer 1991.[38] For extra measure, Moynihan put another "hold" on two other GOP favorites for federal courts of appeals, prompting White House counsel Gray to write to Bush asking him to sign a nomination for Sotomayor—but with a caveat. Gray made sure that Bush knew that Moynihan had been blocking action on the appeals court nominations "to extract a district court judge from us," and he advised the president to sign the Sotomayor nomination but hold off making it official until the administration had gotten word that the two appeals court nominees were confirmed.[39]

The deal satisfied both sides, and Bush nominated Sotomayor on November 27, 1991. For a district court nominee in the 1990s, the hardest part was over. Everything else would be fairly routine. After the White House had submitted her name to the American Bar Association earlier in 1991 for an evaluation, Sotomayor received a "Qualified" rating. (That was above the rarely given "Not Qualified" rating, but not the top "Well Qualified" assessment she would receive in 1997 and 2009 for her respective Second Circuit and Supreme Court nominations.)[40]

When the Senate Judiciary Committee held a hearing on her district court nomination in June 1992, Sotomayor was more than ready. Accompanying her were her mother, Celina; her mother's future husband, Omar Lopez; Sotomayor's brother, Juan, a physician, and his wife and children; a college roommate; and two other friends.

Democratic senator Edward M. Kennedy of Massachusetts presided over the hearing for Sotomayor and two other nominees, also women. It was a first—three women at one hearing—Kennedy said, reminding the audience that in the early 1990s most judicial nominees were men.[41]

New York senators Moynihan and D'Amato appeared before the committee on Sotomayor's behalf. Moynihan introduced her, beginning with her academic credentials from Princeton and Yale. When Senator D'Amato spoke, he referred to her "great, great story of what America can be and is about." There followed an exchange with senior Republican committee member Strom Thurmond, of South Carolina, that revealed the "good ol' boy" tone that permeated hearings:

"Senator, I want to congratulate you on recommending such outstanding ladies," Thurmond said.

"Thank you very much," D'Amato responded.

"I have always known you were a ladies' man, anyway," Thurmond added.

"I'm going to leave that alone," Kennedy said to laughter in the room.

"That is not in the record, I hope," D'Amato quipped.[42]

When Senator Kennedy began the questioning, he said he was impressed by Sotomayor's activities on behalf of the disadvantaged. She responded by talking about her twelve-year membership on the board of the Puerto Rican Legal Defense and Education Fund and its work promoting bilingual education in the public school system. "I . . . believe that those of us who have opportunities in this life must give them back to those who have less," she said. The following week, on June 11, 1992, the Senate Judiciary Committee recommended her nomination to the full Senate. On August 11, eighteen months after Moynihan had recommended her, Sotomayor was confirmed and became the first Latina on a federal court in New York.

Sotomayor's confirmation was a testament to her determination and serendipitous connections. In the 1970s and 1980s she was one of the few Hispanic women within the sphere of such New York power brokers as District Attorney Morgenthau. She earned an appointment to the New York City Campaign Finance Board and witnessed big-city politics, giving her the kind of insight Sandra Day O'Connor developed in statehouse politics in Arizona before being named a state court judge and then a Supreme Court justice in 1981.

When Sotomayor moved from Morgenthau's office to a firm focused on commercial law litigation, she knew it would round out her experience. But, equally important for her goal of a judgeship, that move connected her with partner Botwinik, a friend of the chair of Moynihan's judicial screening committee, when the drive was on for minority and women candidates.

Nearly two decades later President Obama would use this appointment to assert, "It's a measure of her qualities and her qualifications that Judge Sotomayor was nominated to the U.S. District Court by a Republican President, George H. W. Bush."[43] The truth was that the Bush administration really did not want her. She was but one part of multiple deals engineered by Moynihan.

None of the politicking of this first judicial nomination was lost on the street-smart Sotomayor. Less than two years after she was sworn in as a district court judge, she told a conference focused on women in the judiciary, "It is a political appointment. [People] have to make themselves known. You simply do not put in an application."[44]

FIVE

A President and Politics

When Sonia Sotomayor was sworn in as a federal trial judge for the Southern District of New York in the fall of 1992, she asked long-time mentor José Cabranes to administer the oath. It was a role without fanfare. As a federal judge in Connecticut, Cabranes, in fact, had to obtain special court permission to wear the robe and act as a judge in New York's Southern District. He was warned to read just the oath and not say anything more at the district investitures, which were known for their brevity. After a clerk read the district court commission and Cabranes administered the oath, the chief judge asked Sotomayor to sign a piece of paper attesting to her pledge. As protocol dictated, she said, "It is done."

The whole ceremony took less than ten minutes, but Cabranes would not have declined the invitation of Sotomayor, who had continued to tap him for advice as she had run the gauntlet of politics necessary to win President George H. W. Bush's nomination and the Senate confirmation. After a reception, Sotomayor flew to New Orleans for a weekend with girlfriends.

Within two years of that first appointment for Sotomayor, Cabranes appeared to be on deck for a higher court. But he would not find a ready network of political support. And he would face hostility from advocacy groups that would ultimately shift toward Sotomayor.

The events that would surround Cabranes's experience, combined with episodes involving other judicial candidates in the 1990s, made it clear that nominees had to be ready to navigate White

House and Senate politics aggressively. Support and lobbying from key players spelled success; the lack of it could lead to failure. A single crucial backer—at exactly the right place and time—could propel a nominee across the finish line. During the era of President Bill Clinton, key nominations succeeded only because of a late-night call to Attorney General Janet Reno, the persistence of Democratic senator Edward Kennedy of Massachusetts, and a last-minute rescue by Republican senator Alfonse D'Amato of New York.

Presidents understood the power of playing to demographics in nominations, both throughout campaigns and while in office. During his presidential campaign in 1980, Republican Ronald Reagan promised that he would appoint the first woman to the Supreme Court. At the time, in his campaign to unseat Democrat Jimmy Carter, Reagan was not doing well in the polls with women, partly because of his opposition to the Equal Rights Amendment and abortion rights. Three weeks before the election, the former California governor held a news conference to announce that if he had a Supreme Court opening, he would choose a woman.[1] He kept the promise the following year by appointing Sandra Day O'Connor to succeed retiring justice Potter Stewart. Five years after that, Reagan appointed the first Italian American justice, Antonin Scalia.

As a candidate in 1992, Clinton made no pledge with respect to a particular type of appointee, but he strongly suggested that he wanted more diversity on the Court, saying that he wanted a Supreme Court that "looks more like America." He did well with minority voters: 82 percent of African Americans voted for Clinton over incumbent president George H. W. Bush; 61 percent of Latinos voted for him, while only 25 percent cast ballots for Bush and 6 percent for independent candidate Ross Perot.[2]

By the 1990s, the surging Hispanic population made it obvious that an administration could score political points if it were to nominate someone with a Hispanic background.

Clinton's first opportunity came shortly after his January 1993 inauguration. Justice Byron White announced in mid-March that he would be retiring. White, a 1962 appointee of President John F.

Kennedy's, had been a scholar-athlete and a decorated navy officer, who won his Court nomination the way many men had, through a direct connection to the man in the White House.

White first found national fame as an all-American halfback at the University of Colorado in the 1930s. Nicknamed "Whizzer," he went on to play professionally for the Pittsburgh Pirates (renamed the Steelers in 1940) and the Detroit Lions. He was a Rhodes scholar at Oxford University when Kennedy's father, Joseph, was ambassador to the Court of St. James's. He had also earned a law degree at Yale, and when JFK became president, he named White deputy attorney general under his brother, Robert F. Kennedy.

In that number two position at the Justice Department, White played a significant role in the nation's struggle with racial equality. He went to Alabama in 1961 to work with federal marshals to protect the Freedom Riders and other civil rights demonstrators. In one of the most dramatic moments of the turbulent period, White faced down Governor John Patterson, who was allied with the Ku Klux Klan.[3] President Kennedy appointed White to succeed retiring Supreme Court justice Charles Evans Whittaker in 1962. Thirty-one years later White said in his letter to Clinton, "I think that someone else should be permitted to have a like experience."[4]

At the time, the nine-member Court had only one woman, Justice O'Connor, and one black, Justice Clarence Thomas. Clinton's desire for diversity fueled the expectation that the Democrat would take a serious look at racial and ethnic minority candidates.

But Clinton's campaign talk of diversity faded once he was in office. The president initially focused only on white men. He was trying to play it safe and cater to the political middle owing to several controversial efforts on the left in the early weeks of his administration. He lifted the outright ban on gay men and lesbians in the military and had to backpedal on his first two choices for attorney general, Zoë Baird and Kimba Wood, who were eliminated because of questions about their hiring of immigrant workers for household help.[5] In another controversy, Clinton dropped University of Pennsylvania law professor Lani Guinier as the proposed head of the

Justice Department's Civil Rights Division because of conservative complaints about her academic writings related to voting rights.[6]

Clinton dreamed of appointing to the Supreme Court a politician-statesman in the mold of former California governor Earl Warren, who became chief justice in 1953. When the Supreme Court struck down school segregation in the 1954 landmark case *Brown v. Board of Education*, Warren was presiding over a group of justices who had spent much of their careers in political office.

With that ideal in mind, Clinton turned first to New York Democratic governor Mario Cuomo, the only person Clinton, as a candidate, had publicly named as a possible Court nominee. Cuomo was not enamored with the idea of the cloistered life of a justice, yet he did not initially give Clinton a firm no. Instead, he sent conflicting signals to Clinton advisers. George Stephanopoulos, the White House communications director, said that top aides tried to convince the wavering governor—who had a reputation for playing Hamlet—by arguing that it would offer Cuomo a chance to serve his country and enhance his legacy.[7]

As Clinton aides held out hope, advocates for other candidates began to think that their favorites might have a shot. The Hispanic National Bar Association had made public its list of recommendations a few days after Justice White announced his retirement, as they did not want a repeat of what they had heard during George H. W. Bush's presidency, that there was no possible Hispanic contender. In 1991 the White House had been trying to build support for Supreme Court nominee Clarence Thomas, who had alienated minority groups with his opposition to affirmative action as chairman of the EEOC. Bush's White House counsel, Boyden Gray, and his chief of staff, John Sununu, met with a dozen leaders from such groups as the Hispanic National Bar Association, the Mexican American Bar Association, and the Puerto Rican Bar Association of New York. When some of these leaders asked why a Hispanic was not chosen over Thomas, Gray and Sununu said that the president had been open to such a possibility but could not find a suitable candidate.[8]

Carlos Ortiz and Dolores Atencio, leaders of the Hispanic National Bar Association, did not wish any White House in the future
to make such a claim, and they mobilized to develop a slate that
could be turned over to an administration, Democratic or Republican, when an opening occurred on the Court. So when Justice
White announced that he would be retiring, the bar association was
ready with a list of seven contenders: José Cabranes, then a U.S.
district court judge in Connecticut; Joseph Baca, a New Mexico
Supreme Court justice; Fortunato Benavides, a former Texas state
court judge whom Clinton was putting up for the U.S. Court of Appeals for the Fifth Circuit; Vilma Martínez, a former president of
the Mexican American Legal Defense and Educational Fund, who
had returned to private practice in California; Dan Morales, the
Texas attorney general; Cruz Reynoso, a law professor at the University of California at Los Angeles and former California Supreme
Court justice; and Ricardo Urbina, a Washington, D.C., superior
court judge.[9] Sotomayor, who had donned the black robe less than a
year earlier, was not on the list.

None of the seven Hispanic judges and lawyers had reached
the national stature Clinton wanted, and he was blunt about it at
a meeting with Hispanic policy leaders on June 3, in the middle of
his Supreme Court search. Clinton told them he was looking for "a
home run" nominee and that none of the Hispanics on the list came
close to meeting his criteria.[10]

When Cuomo made it clear that he wanted to remain in New
York's world of politics and policy, the momentum for an Earl
Warren–like figure lost its steam. At the urging of Senator Ted Kennedy, the White House turned to Stephen Breyer, who had been a
judge since 1980, when President Jimmy Carter appointed him to
the U.S. Court of Appeals for the First Circuit in Boston. A San
Francisco native who graduated from Stanford University and Harvard Law School, Breyer worked for Senator Kennedy on the Senate
Judiciary Committee staff and helped write legislation to deregulate
the airline industry and establish federal sentencing rules. Senators
of both political parties had high regard for Breyer.

Clinton administration lawyers flew up to Boston in early June to interview Breyer, who happened to be recovering from a bicycle accident. Hit by a car while pedaling around nearby Cambridge, he had suffered broken ribs and a punctured lung. In pain and on prescription medication, he still managed to impress the White House aides. After the session, Richard Berke of *The New York Times* reported, "Several senior White House officials said . . . that they expected Judge Breyer to be selected and that the first face-to-face meeting [with President Clinton] is his final hurdle."[11]

But it didn't happen. After Clinton's luncheon meeting with Breyer at the White House, "Clinton just wasn't enthusiastic," recalled White House counsel Bernard Nussbaum.[12] Breyer's supporters attributed the lack of chemistry between the two men to Breyer's weakened condition from the cycling accident. Making matters more difficult, the White House counsel's office had learned that Breyer had not paid all the taxes for his household help, creating a déjà vu moment for administration officials still smarting from the flubbed nominations of Zöe Baird and Kimba Wood for attorney general. Breyer's situation was not as serious, but the White House did not want another related storm.

By this point, nearly three months had passed since Justice White had told the president he would be stepping down, and Clinton was in a quandary. He asked assistant White House counsel Ronald Klain to call Janet Reno, the new attorney general, for advice. Reno was ready. She chided them for not looking more seriously at Ruth Bader Ginsburg, a pioneering women's rights advocate and a judge on the U.S. Court of Appeals for the District of Columbia Circuit.

It was only then that Clinton began poring over materials that aides had gathered on the sixty-year-old Ginsburg. The result illustrates the serendipity of the Supreme Court nomination process and how diligence can pay off.

While the president and his aides had been looking at other possible candidates, a steady stream of supportive letters from law professors and Clinton allies, elicited in part by Ginsburg's husband, Martin, had arrived at the White House. Senator Daniel Patrick

Moynihan, never far from the stage of an important judicial nomination, also had been pressing Clinton to consider the Brooklyn native.

She was the second child of Nathan Bader, a furrier, and Celia, a homemaker. Her mother died from cervical cancer the day before her high school graduation. That heartbreaking experience, along with her regard for her mother's intellect, contributed to Ginsburg's feminism. She attended Cornell University, where she met Martin, universally known as Marty. After graduation, they married and attended Harvard Law School together. She earned excellent grades and was named to the *Harvard Law Review*. She also had her first child, Jane, while she was in Cambridge. When Marty, a year ahead of her in law school, landed a job with a New York law firm, Ginsburg transferred to Columbia University for her third and final year of law school. She had the distinction of becoming an editor on a second law review. When she graduated, she tied for first place in grades in the Columbia class of 1959. But, like other women of her day, Ginsburg had trouble finding a job in the law. She turned to teaching and eventually became the first tenured woman professor at Rutgers University. In 1972 she helped found the American Civil Liberties Union Women's Rights Project and gained national prominence for her litigation against sex discrimination. Wearing her mother's earrings and pins for her appearances before the Supreme Court, she argued six cases, winning five of them and helping to develop legal standards for sex discrimination challenges.

Some liberals in Washington, D.C., opposed Ginsburg as a possible successor to Justice White because of her moderate rulings over thirteen years on the District of Columbia Circuit appeals court and her criticism of the constitutional underpinnings of *Roe v. Wade*, which made abortion legal across the country. It was somewhat surprising resistance, given Ginsburg's established record of supporting women's rights. But hard-core liberals favored other candidates, including Judge Patricia Wald, who was also on the District of Columbia Circuit and whose votes were more consistently on the left.

Ginsburg had disparaged the reasoning of *Roe* as going too far in "the change it ordered" under the right to privacy, and she had insisted that the sweep of the ruling effectively mobilized antiabortion advocates and ultimately hurt women's choices.[13] Her husband sought to reassure administration power brokers that her positions did not threaten liberals. Even as the White House was focused on other possible nominees, Marty Ginsburg persuaded law professors and other friends connected to the Clinton administration to write to the president and his counsel, Bernard Nussbaum, to emphasize that Ginsburg supported abortion rights. Letters poured in, and although they did not inspire the White House to settle on Ginsburg at that point, they provided crucial reassurance when her time came.[14]

Senator Moynihan had suggested Ginsburg's name to Clinton in May 1993. According to Moynihan's account in his personal correspondence, the president had responded, "The women are against her." Moynihan said he countered, "That is your problem, Mr. President. You have too many friends. You cannot govern without enemies."[15]

Only after Clinton's awkward lunch with Stephen Breyer did the president arrange to meet with Ginsburg. There was potential for more awkwardness with her. No one would have disputed her intellect and seriousness, but the woman who wore her hair pulled back tightly in a short ponytail had a soft voice and had trouble looking people in the eye. She was also known for being so serious that as a youngster her daughter, Jane, made a booklet called *Mommy Laughs* that recounted the rare episodes when her mother revealed her sense of humor.

As severe or as shy as she seemed, Ginsburg was passionate about the law and could turn on the charm. She did so with Clinton. In the meeting with the president, her warmth and sense of a larger mission surfaced. Hearing about her litigation on behalf of women's equality, Clinton understood why Moynihan and others had described her as "the Thurgood Marshall of women's rights." In another plus for diversity, Ginsburg could also become the first Jewish justice in nearly a quarter century. The last Jew, Abe Fortas, had resigned under pressure in 1969 after a financial scandal.

When President Clinton made Ginsburg's nomination public on June 14, 1993, the day after their meeting, he emphasized that she would become only the second woman on the Court. In her remarks in the Rose Garden ceremony, Ginsburg paid tribute to her late mother: "I pray that I may be all that she would have been had she lived in an age when women could aspire and achieve and daughters are cherished as much as sons." Tears rolled down Clinton's cheeks as Ginsburg spoke.

The Senate confirmed Ginsburg with a 96–3 vote.

Hispanic leaders had wanted one of their own, but there had been no significant public pressure on the White House to select a minority candidate. The atmosphere was different the following year, when Justice Harry Blackmun made his resignation intentions public, and the drumbeat for a Hispanic nominee grew louder.

Blackmun had been hinting for months that he might step down. The justice best known for authoring *Roe v. Wade*, the 1973 ruling that made abortion legal across the country, was the last liberal of his generation on the Court. Through much of 1993 and into early 1994 Blackmun had been telling friends he was weary and frustrated. He increasingly disagreed with the conservative majority's views. One of the strongest public signals of Blackmun's impending exit had come in February 1994, when the eighty-five-year-old justice denounced capital punishment. In a dissenting opinion when the Court majority rejected an appeal from a Texas death row prisoner, Blackmun said he would no longer "tinker with the machinery of death."[16] He said he would refuse ever again to endorse capital punishment, which suggested that he was taking stock and considering his legacy. Two months later, he made it official in a letter to President Bill Clinton that said he would retire at the term's end.

José Cabranes, as it turned out, got a call that April as the news was breaking that Blackmun was going to retire. He heard first from Harold Koh, a Yale law professor who was a former Blackmun clerk with ties to the Clinton White House. Koh admired Cabranes, a former university general counsel, and was close to Cabranes's wife, Kate Stith-Cabranes, a professor at Yale. Koh believed that Cabranes could have the inside track as Blackmun's successor, and he urged Cabranes to connect with people who might help him get the attention of the Clinton administration.[17]

Cabranes had preceded Sotomayor to the federal bench by more than a decade. In 1979, when President Carter named him to the district court, he became the first Puerto Rican federal judge in the mainland United States, a designation he wore proudly. He rarely passed up an opportunity to talk of his parents' epic journey from the island to the mainland to give their children the opportunities of American life.

Koh was not the only person who thought of Cabranes as a successor to Blackmun. Legal analysts and veteran journalists tossed around the idea that President Clinton might want to make a big statement with the appointment of a Hispanic justice. At the time, Hispanics made up more than 10 percent of the population yet constituted about 3 percent of the nation's federal judges. But in the weeks that followed, divisions among Hispanic groups and behind-the-scenes liberal opposition undercut Cabranes's chances.

Sotomayor, still in her thirties, had not made any short list on this round. But she was working her way up in Hispanic networks, speaking at conferences and getting to know legal and political leaders. Through her connections, she was hearing of how liberals and Mexican Americans, the dominant Hispanic group, regarded Cabranes.

Irrespective of politics and ideology, Cabranes had a compelling personal story and record of accomplishment. Born in Mayagüez in December 1940, he had come to the mainland with his parents when he was five. They were middle class: his father, Manuel, had run social welfare programs in Puerto Rico, overseen a home for troubled youths in Mayagüez, and served as the chief probation officer for the federal district court in Puerto Rico. His mother, Carmen, taught elementary school.

When the family moved to New York, in 1946, Manuel took a job as executive director of the Melrose House, the South Bronx institution that sheltered and serviced Jewish immigrants and eventually Puerto Ricans. When the family moved from the Bronx to Flushing, Queens, in the early 1950s, Cabranes joined the mix of ambitious newcomers, attending public schools before going to Columbia College and Yale Law School. He practiced law in a New York City firm, taught at Rutgers University, and served as head of the Washington office of the Commonwealth of Puerto Rico before he became Yale's general counsel.

Now fifty-three, tall, broad-shouldered, still ambitious as well as savvy, Cabranes knew his Supreme Court prospects were not promising. He had come to this point before, only to be disappointed. When Justice White retired, Cabranes had been talked about in the press as a possible successor. But he was never really in the mix.

The possibility of the "first Hispanic" was much more in the air this time. At the Supreme Court, a private exchange between Justice Scalia and Justice Ginsburg proved that.

On April 19, two weeks after Blackmun told President Clinton he would be stepping down, Havana-born Silvia Ibanez happened to be at the lectern in the justices' white marble and crimson velvet courtroom to argue her case. Ibanez grew up in the United States, and prior to her legal career she had been an accountant. So she advertised herself as having a C.P.A. as well as a J.D. in order to attract business as a lawyer. Those dual credentials were the subject of litigation before the Supreme Court. The Florida Board of Accountancy banned advertising of an accounting credential if a person was not a practicing accountant. Ibanez insisted that she had a First Amendment free-speech right to advertise her professional qualifications, and she was arguing her own case.[18]

In the early 1990s it was unusual to see a woman at the lectern arguing a case, and it was even rarer to see a black or Hispanic woman. As Ibanez responded persuasively to the justices' questions, Scalia sent a note down the row to his friend Ginsburg: "Tell your president, she's his Hispanic."[19]

With one whimsical remark, Scalia—a conservative known for his irreverence—captured the reality of nomination politics.[20] He understood that Reagan and the senators who had supported his High Court nomination had relished the opportunity to support the first Italian American justice, and he recalled that in the weeks leading up to his September 1986 confirmation, Senator Robert C. Byrd, a West Virginia Democrat, had contacted him to see if he would attend a Columbus Day celebration in his state. Scalia immediately said yes, knowing that his presence at that favorite holiday of Italians would be a boost to Byrd. During Scalia's confirmation hearing, so many senators brought up Italian connections that Senator Howell Heflin, a Democrat from Alabama, told the nominee, "I believe that almost every Senator that has an Italian American connection has come forward to welcome you . . . I would be remiss if I did not mention the fact that my great-great-grandfather married a widow who was married first to an Italian American." Getting Heflin's joke, Scalia shot back, "Senator, I have been to Alabama several times, too."[21]

Justice Blackmun, who was now giving President Clinton an opportunity to fill a vacancy, had won his seat on the Court in 1970 as the result of a more traditional association, his long-standing friendship with Chief Justice Warren Burger. President Richard Nixon tapped Blackmun to fill the seat then being vacated by Abe Fortas, who resigned in the wake of a financial controversy. Blackmun was Nixon's third choice, after the Senate had rejected his first two nominees—U.S. appeals court judge Clement F. Haynsworth, Jr., of South Carolina and U.S. appeals court judge G. Harrold Carswell of Florida. Nixon turned to Blackmun, then a U.S. appeals court judge in Minnesota, on the advice of Burger, who had been a friend of Blackmun's since they grew up together in that state.[22]

Some Hispanic advocates thought that Blackmun's retirement would clear the way for Cabranes, a fifteen-year veteran of a U.S. district court and arguably the most prominent Latino on the bench.

Cabranes understood that his ethnicity might help him, but he did not think that it was all he had to offer. Merit and diversity were not mutually exclusive, he often reminded audiences. During a testimonial for two Hispanic judges on the Connecticut Superior

Court in 1992, Cabranes had scoffed at supporters of Clarence Thomas who said that race had nothing to do with President Bush's choice. "Our leaders, on all sides, failed to teach the American people that judicial appointments, even at the highest levels, are eminently political appointments," Cabranes said. "That there is nothing sinister about the word politics. And most important of all, that the politics of inclusion is not necessarily inconsistent with the politics of merit."[23]

Several judges were being mentioned to succeed Blackmun. Senator Kennedy was still pushing for Boston-based Judge Breyer, who had come close to being named in 1993, and supporters of U.S. appeals court judge Richard Arnold, based in Little Rock, thought he might be the favorite of the Arkansas-born Clinton. Arnold was sitting on the Eighth Circuit, the same court from which Blackmun had been elevated. "In some circles, at least," Emory law professor Polly Price later wrote, "there was an expectation that Blackmun's replacement would come from the same geographic region."[24]

Arnold was friendly with Clinton and had known White House counsel Bernard Nussbaum at Harvard Law School, where Arnold graduated first in the class of 1960. Arnold had become a U.S. district court judge in 1978, an appointee of President Jimmy Carter. The following year, Carter elevated him to the Eighth Circuit. President Clinton had briefly considered Arnold in 1993 for the position that went to Ginsburg, but he had been dissuaded by aides who thought an Arnold appointment might smack of cronyism at a time when the new president was bringing in other friends from Arkansas for top jobs.

Unlike Arnold and Breyer, Cabranes was still a district court judge. A year earlier he had lost a chance for elevation to a Connecticut-based opening on the Second Circuit, despite the backing of the two U.S. senators from that state. President Clinton instead chose Yale law dean Guido Calabresi, a more reliable liberal and an old friend of the Clintons from their Yale Law School days.

Liberals were suspicious of Cabranes, who had a moderate record as a trial judge and had been mentioned in news accounts as a possible Supreme Court choice for Republican president George H. W. Bush.[25] Mexican American leaders also opposed the Puerto Rican judge because they wanted the first Hispanic on the High Court to be of their heritage. "In those days, there was a lot of rivalry between Mexican Americans and Puerto Ricans," recalled Adelfa Callejo, a prominent Dallas lawyer and Democratic fund-raiser who was among the Mexican American Legal Defense and Educational Fund (MALDEF) leaders resisting a Cabranes nomination. "There was always the feeling that Puerto Ricans did not have the struggles that Mexican Americans had. The fact that he was a conservative had something to do with it, too."[26] Sotomayor, who was friendly with Callejo and her husband, Bill, a member of the Puerto Rican Legal Defense and Education Fund board, had begun to broaden her contacts beyond the East Coast. She heard the criticism from Callejo and others about Cabranes. She was grateful to her mentor for all he had done to help her get her start, but she was also becoming more aware—and wary—of his conservative inclinations.

Journalists seized on the conflicts among Hispanics, noting that, as a threshold matter, Clinton knew the appointment of the first Hispanic justice would secure him a place in history and, more immediately, improve his appeal among Hispanic voters, particularly Mexican Americans in California and Cubans in Florida. Cabranes "has been endorsed by some Hispanic organizations but is far from a favorite of other Hispanic groups, who view the Puerto Rican–born Cabranes as too conservative and would prefer a Hispanic of Mexican-American descent," The Washington Post's Ruth Marcus wrote.[27] Neil Lewis of The New York Times observed that White House officials were "considering straightforward political factors, as in, 'How might this affect the President's reelection?'" Lewis pointed out that the powerful Mexican American Legal Defense and Educational Fund had withheld support of Cabranes.[28]

The split among Hispanic groups could be traced to long-standing cultural differences, not just between Mexican Americans and Puerto Ricans but between, for example, prosperous Cubans and needy Dominicans.[29] In the early 1990s Cabranes was one of

the nation's most successful Hispanic lawyers, yet that stature did
not mean he would be backed by people of such diverse and rival
heritages.

While Hispanic organizations sought to maintain their individual ethnic identities, collectively they felt the need to pressure the
White House to name a Hispanic, even if they could not agree on
the nominee. "We can't afford to come out of this thing all frag-
mented," Esteban Torres, a Democratic member of the U.S. House
of Representatives from La Puente, California, told the *Los Angeles
Times*. "That sends a negative signal. There's a window of opportunity open to us now."[30]

Hispanic groups tried to close ranks. Antonia Hernández, president of the Mexican American Legal Defense and Educational Fund,
wrote to Clinton offering a lukewarm endorsement for Cabranes.
She said that the group usually did not take a position on a candidate before nomination, but they promised to support him if he
was selected. "He is bright, he is talented, and he of course has fifteen years of federal judicial experience," she wrote. Then, revealing
MALDEF's true sentiment, Hernández urged the president to consider other Latinos, including state judges Cruz Reynoso in Los Angeles and John Carro in New York.[31]

Neither man was a viable contender. Carro had not cleared the
political hurdles for a district court judgeship in the early 1990s, and
Reynoso, a former California Supreme Court justice, had been ousted
by voters on a judicial retention ballot in 1986. Hernández did not
mention Sotomayor, who was a generation behind those men.

Hernández's letter was an attempt at unity, but it magnified
the ambivalence about Cabranes. At the same time, liberal advocacy groups such as the Alliance for Justice were quietly opposing
him. An internal report for the group referred to "troubling patterns"
in rulings by Cabranes, particularly in employment discrimination
cases, and said that he appeared to lack "basic sensitivity to the poor
and disenfranchised." Such assessments circulated privately but set
a tone among key players connected with the White House and crucial Democratic senators.

There were other whispers about Cabranes. Some White House officials said they believed that he had quietly passed the word that he opposed abortion rights when it was possible he might have been nominated by President George H. W. Bush. Cabranes said there was no basis for such a belief. Clinton White House counsel Nussbaum, who had gotten to know Cabranes at Columbia when they were undergraduates, said later that he had heard the antiabortion tale but did not believe it was grounded in truth. Yet Nussbaum said he knew about the split among Hispanics. "If the groups were united," he said, "it would have helped."[32] The sense among the most liberal members of Clinton's administration was that Cabranes had hurt his chances with his conservative leanings. Unlike Ginsburg a year earlier, Cabranes had no one inside the administration expressly pushing for him. Ginsburg eventually also had an opportunity to make her case to the president. Cabranes was never called to the White House for an interview.

In May 1994 Clinton was still enchanted with the idea of nominating a larger-than-life, statesmanlike figure, just as he had been in 1993 when he tried to lure Mario Cuomo to the bench. "My first choice was Senator George Mitchell," who had announced his impending retirement from the Senate, Clinton wrote later. "He was a good [Senate] majority leader, he had been loyal and extremely helpful to me, and it was far from certain that we could hold on to his seat in the November election." Mitchell had been a federal judge before becoming a senator, and Clinton thought Mitchell "would be a big personality on the Court, someone who could move votes and whose voice would be heard, even in dissent."[33]

President Clinton's effort to persuade Mitchell to take the job ended the same way the overtures to Cuomo had played out a year earlier. Mitchell pulled himself out of contention. He said he wanted to devote his attention to work on legislation for comprehensive health-care insurance.

Clinton looked at Interior Secretary Bruce Babbitt, a former Arizona governor and attorney general who had been considered in 1993. But as the search went down to the wire, Babbitt was eliminated because of opposition from such Senate partisans as Republican Orrin Hatch of Utah, a leading member of the Senate Judiciary Committee, and because there was no obvious successor to run the Interior Department. Babbitt shrugged off the administration's snub and issued a brief statement when the nomination sweepstakes finally ended: "As enticing as the great indoors is, the great outdoors is where I want to spend my time."[34]

Clinton returned to the possibility of Judge Arnold, who had earned a stellar reputation on the bench but whose health presented a dilemma. Arnold had long suffered from chronic lymphocytic leukemia, and Clinton, after speaking to Arnold's physicians, believed there was no guarantee he would be able to serve at least fifteen years on the High Court. Clinton later wrote, "My Republican predecessors had filled the federal courts with young conservatives who would be around a long time, and I didn't want to risk giving them another position" by naming someone whose prognosis was not clear.[35] Arnold died in 2004, at the age of sixty-eight, from cancer of the lymph glands. If he had been appointed to the Court, he would have served ten years.

White House aides continued to tell reporters that Cabranes was under consideration.[36] This probably appeased the Hispanic National Bar Association without alienating such groups as MALDEF, because leaders of the latter knew that their opposition to Cabranes was being heard by the right people inside the administration. A top lawyer to Clinton recalled the president saying, "I'm not going to appoint someone the groups don't even want!"

As Senator Mitchell, Secretary Babbitt, and Judge Arnold fell out of consideration, Judge Breyer's chances improved. Lloyd Cutler, who succeeded Nussbaum as White House counsel in the spring of 1994, was an old friend of Senator Kennedy's and pushed for Breyer, too. Republican senators who had known Breyer when he worked as a Judiciary Committee staffer were putting in a good word. President Clinton began to appreciate the advantage in a nominee with bipartisan support, especially at a time when he was trying to pass major health-care legislation and was increasingly ensnarled in scandals related to the Whitewater land development project in Arkansas.

The president was running out of political capital, and Breyer became the politically expedient choice. Making history no longer mattered. Clinton realized that he would not gain many political points with the Breyer nomination, but he certainly would not lose many either.

Then, partly because of pressure from Hispanics who supported him, Cabranes was tapped for elevation to the New York–based U.S. Court of Appeals for the Second Circuit. Connecticut U.S. senators Christopher Dodd and Joseph Lieberman, longtime Cabranes backers, engineered a compromise with New York senator Moynihan to help Cabranes and to protect their respective pieces of Second Circuit turf.[37] Clinton announced that he was submitting Cabranes's name for the Second Circuit two weeks after he nominated Breyer for the Supreme Court.[38] The Senate approved Cabranes unanimously on August 9, 1994, less than two weeks after the Senate confirmed Breyer by a vote of 87–9.

Some Hispanic leaders were not mollified. Wilfredo Caraballo of the Hispanic National Bar Association wrote later, "We believed the promise that the face of justice was finally going to include ours . . . There exists a moral imperative that all who are among the judged have the right to expect that they may be represented in the faces of those who judge."[39]

Hispanics also disagreed with one another on strategy. Raul Yzaguirre, chair of the National Council of La Raza, which, like the Mexican American Legal Defense and Educational Fund, resisted Judge Cabranes, said, "They said we all have to be centered behind Cabranes and nobody else, and we didn't think that was a winning strategy."[40] Some in the Hispanic community reacted negatively to such sentiment. Howard Jordán, managing editor of *Critica*, a journal of Puerto Rican policy and politics, declared at the time, "The real blame goes to President Clinton, but I think the situation was exacerbated by the inability of the Hispanic community to come together with one voice."[41]

In the end, Clinton's Supreme Court choices did not appear to cost him Hispanic voters. Two years after the Breyer appointment, Clinton won reelection, with 72 percent of the Hispanic vote, over

Republican senator Bob Dole, who drew only 21 percent. When Clinton first ran for president, in 1992, he attracted 61 percent of the Hispanic vote as he claimed victory against George H. W. Bush, who then drew 25 percent of the Hispanic vote.[42]

Cabranes realized that even if the reelected Clinton got another chance to fill a vacancy on the Supreme Court, he would not be the nominee. Cabranes had faced that reality when Breyer was selected and he read in *The New York Times* that Clinton had considered choosing a Hispanic but was so "cool" to Cabranes that he "turned to his advisers and asked in exasperation if they could find him a Hispanic candidate other than Judge Cabranes."[43]

◆

Through the late 1990s Hispanics continued to be the fastest-growing minority group in the United States, and the White House redoubled its efforts to find Latinos to appoint to the lower federal courts. Sonia Sotomayor was one of them. In June 1997 President Clinton nominated her for a seat on the U.S. Court of Appeals for the Second Circuit, where Cabranes had landed three years earlier.

She almost did not make it. The stakes were higher for her—and for Republicans—because she was being considered for a position just below the Supreme Court. During her first judicial nomination, in 1991–92, Sotomayor had confronted a GOP administration that naturally was not as interested in a nominee sponsored by leading Democrat Moynihan. Five years later, key Republicans understood that if she were confirmed to the appeals court, she would be in line for the High Court.

This time around, she was as poised for battle as the Democratic White House and the Republican-controlled Senate. Her political instincts were sharp, her list of contacts long. She also had a team of loyal boosters, led by Xavier Romeu, a Puerto Rican native who had worked for her as a law clerk in her early years as a district court judge. Sotomayor and Romeu had become friends and had stayed in close contact as she continued to serve as a trial court judge and Romeu moved on to other positions, including executive director of the Puerto Rico Federal Affairs Administration.

Romeu, who was also vice president of the Puerto Rican Bar Association, became the kind of shrewd and tireless backer that Marty Ginsburg was for his wife, Ruth, and that Senator Kennedy and his aides had been for Breyer. Romeu served as Sotomayor's troubleshooter, working with her supporters and criticizing her opponents. Even though she had a fat Rolodex with a network of connections, Sotomayor was still a judge, and she still had to act like one. Romeu could press her case in a way that she could not.

Romeu secured an endorsement from Puerto Rico governor Pedro Rosselló and persuaded him to commit, as Sotomayor later said, "all of his office's resources to my confirmation."[44] Within a few weeks of her nomination, Romeu visited the White House to talk to top Latino aides in the administration. He kept in close touch with the lawyers handling nominations. He helped organize constituents to write letters to senators. He obtained testimonials from several Latino legal groups, which urged a speedy Senate Judiciary Committee hearing for Sotomayor. He prepared fact sheets listing her strengths and quickly circulated information to counter any criticism emerging in the Senate or from such outside opponents as conservative talk-show host Rush Limbaugh, who was branding Sotomayor a liberal activist.[45]

When the Senate Judiciary Committee held its hearing in September 1997, the session was rockier than what Sotomayor had experienced when she was being considered for the district court in 1992. Republican senators focused on her criticism of federal sentencing rules that many judges thought too rigid and harsh. She said that despite her personal feelings, she "imposed what the law required."[46]

GOP senators also brought up a 1992 *New York Times* story in which she had been asked whether she had sat on her hands when Justice Clarence Thomas addressed a conference she attended. She said in response to the reporter's question, "I'll take the Fifth."[47]

"Did you see fit to stand and applaud?" Alabama senator Jeff Sessions asked Sotomayor.

"He was my Supreme Court Justice of my circuit," she answered, backing away from the suggestion in the *New York Times* report. "I stood up."[48]

The Senate Judiciary Committee recommended her to the full Senate in March 1998, but the nomination stalled in the Republican-controlled chamber. There were rumors that Justice John Paul Stevens, then seventy-eight, might retire. Republican senators, including majority leader Trent Lott, worried that Sotomayor would be in line for the Stevens position if she were confirmed to the appeals court.

So even though she had yet to make it onto the Hispanic National Bar Association's list of possible Supreme Court candidates, she was very much on the Republicans' radar screen. GOP partisans, who had been astutely playing judicial selection politics since the Reagan years, understood that Sotomayor could be an unstoppable Supreme Court candidate. They thought that if this rare Latina jurist were confirmed, Republicans would not be able to stop the president from making history by appointing her to the Supreme Court. Mississippi senator Lott understood and refused to allow a floor vote.

Talk radio host Limbaugh stoked Republican concerns about where she could go from there by saying she was on a "rocket ship" to the Supreme Court. *The Wall Street Journal* also editorialized against her, citing a similar view that Clinton was laying the groundwork for her eventual elevation to the High Court. "We'd like to think the Republicans may be having second thoughts about Judge Sotomayor and are deliberately delaying her confirmation until seeing whether Justice Stevens announces his retirement when the current Court term ends this month," the editorial in early June 1998 said.[49]

The Wall Street Journal referred to several Sotomayor trial court decisions that it considered antibusiness. In one, Sotomayor had ruled that a law school graduate with learning disabilities was entitled to accommodation under the Americans with Disabilities Act while taking the New York State bar exam. The *Journal* wrote in its editorial, "By now New Yorkers are accustomed to this sort of antic judicial thinking. But why impose it on the whole country?" Romeu dissected that *Wall Street Journal* editorial and circulated a fact sheet responding to the criticism, writing that the would-be lawyer "suffers from a neurological impairment that prevents her from automatically recognizing words, thereby requiring her to read and reread sentences in order to decode their meaning." He pointed out that Sotomayor's decision had been affirmed by the U.S. Court of Appeals for the Second Circuit.[50]

There was no split among Hispanics, as there had been four years earlier over a Cabranes nomination. A diverse coalition of Hispanic groups backed Sotomayor.

Yet in the end it would not be action by the Clinton White House, Democratic senators, or even Latino advocates that propelled Sotomayor's nomination forward. It would be Republican senator Alfonse D'Amato who engineered the crucial Senate vote. This occurred a little more than a month before the 1998 November election, when D'Amato faced Democratic challenger U.S. representative Charles E. Schumer of New York.

D'Amato was trailing among Hispanic voters in the state. Sotomayor's supporters convinced him that if he went to Senate majority leader Lott and secured a floor vote for her, Hispanics would be more inclined to vote for him over Schumer. So D'Amato pressured Lott to schedule the vote. On October 2, 1998, the Senate approved Sotomayor's elevation to the Second Circuit appeals court by a vote of 67–29. All the votes against her were cast by Republicans.

A few weeks later, at her investiture at the Manhattan courthouse, it was clear that Sotomayor had kept up with her networking even after she put on the black robe of a trial court judge. She thanked a multitude of women's groups and Hispanic organizations. "Hispanic leaders from across party, partisan, and island status lines not only endorsed my nomination and confirmation but also exerted their influence publicly and privately to make this confirmation happen," she said.[51]

She referred to D'Amato's crucial role and the many people who talked him into intervening, including U.S. representatives José Serrano and Nydia Velázquez and various local Bronx officials. "State Senator Efrain Gonzalez of the 31st District in the Bronx, a man of his word and action, even withheld his endorsement of Senator D'Amato until the senator got me a Senate vote," she said. (D'Amato lost to Schumer, failing to garner support from several important constituencies, including women, Jews, and Hispanics, but he harbored no hard feelings toward Sotomayor, and in 2009 he urged his former colleagues to support her Supreme Court confirmation.)

Sotomayor's vast personal networks also were on display at the appeals court swearing-in. Cousins from Puerto Rico made the trip to New York, as did a Fendi lawyer from Italy whom Sotomayor had known when she represented the luxury-goods maker at Pavia & Harcourt. High school friends attended. Her dentist was there, and Sotomayor observed—as if it were as natural as could be—that she had gotten to know her dentist's husband and become godmother to one of their children. She praised her mother and, when she referred to her father, said that he died at forty-two in part from the heart complications that had kept him out of the army during the war.

In one of the most personal moments of the investiture, before hundreds of supporters, Sotomayor addressed her then fiancé, Peter White, a New York construction contractor: "Peter, you have made me a whole person, filling not just the voids of emptiness that existed before you, but making me a better, a more loving and a more generous person . . . Many of my closest friends forget just how emotionally withdrawn I was before I met you."

But she and White did not marry. The relationship ended early in her tenure on the Second Circuit.[52]

Another man who had been a constant in her adult life, José Cabranes, addressed the crowd. "This is a wonderful day in New York . . . ," he said. "I have been accorded the honor of speaking to you on this happy occasion because, in a professional sense, I was 'present at the creation.'"

Much had changed since Cabranes and Sotomayor first met in 1976. She had connected with such other powerful people as Senator Moynihan and had earned the loyalty of men and women in the trenches such as Xavier Romeu. She understood the political milieu of judicial nominations and knew that many forces needed to align for any one individual to reach her goal.

"There's no question that between 1992 and 1994 Cabranes was the most talked about, most prominently talked about Hispanic candidate," recalled Carlos Ortiz, the Hispanic National Bar Association official who worked for Hispanic appointments to the bench. "[Sotomayor] was an avid reader of all this. She learned to make the right connections. There is no question about that. She knew who to be in contact with, who to tell about her interests. I don't want to say she was campaigning for the court of appeals, but she let people know."[53]

SIX

The Right Hispanic

Washington lawyer Miguel Estrada bristled at what he was hearing from the three attorneys who had come down from New York to his office one spring day in 2002 to talk about his nomination to an important federal appeals court. Officials from a Puerto Rican advocacy group, they had already made their criticism known, one going so far as to say in a letter to senators that Estrada might lack the compassion and open-mindedness to be a good judge. And now they were suggesting that any Hispanic nominated to the upper echelons of the federal judiciary should have strong ties to the community— and be proud of those connections. The Honduran-born Estrada, who had graduated from Harvard Law School, earned a prestigious clerkship at the Supreme Court, and was now specializing in appellate advocacy, believed that candidates for elite judgeships should stand on their legal credentials and their character. He thought an emphasis on his heritage conjured up the worst kind of "identity politics" and the presumption that his views would be determined by his ethnic heritage.

The differences between Estrada and his visitors would hurt his chances for appointment as judge. Other factors were in play as well, including Estrada's strong conservatism. As President George W. Bush tried to position Estrada for possible appointment as the first Hispanic Supreme Court justice, he became a pawn in the nasty partisan competition over the federal judiciary. What developed would link the fates of Miguel Estrada and Sonia Sotomayor, situated so differently in the eyes of organized Hispanic advocates. Their experiences would reveal what effects prominent Hispanic groups were having in the nation's capital and what happens when a nominee is opposed or, alternatively, championed.

◆

About a year after Estrada had first been nominated to the U.S. Court of Appeals for the District of Columbia Circuit, he found himself looking across his desk at the three men from the Puerto Rican Legal Defense and Education Fund.[1] Spread out before him were newspaper articles about his nomination. Estrada had made special note of the criticism, some of it from the lawyers who now sat in his Washington, D.C., office.

The three visitors, Carlos Ortiz, Juan Figueroa, and Benito Romano, were Latinos who had made it to the top of the legal profession, just as Estrada had.[2] For Estrada and Ortiz, particularly, the meeting marked a significant moment in their respective efforts related to the judiciary. Estrada, forty, had been nominated by Bush to be a judge on the powerful Washington, D.C., appeals court, which was regarded as a springboard to the Supreme Court. Ortiz, forty-seven, held a job in the top ranks of an international food distributor and was chairman of the board of PRLDEF and a past president of the Hispanic National Bar Association. Ortiz had been working for a decade to persuade administrations in Washington to appoint a Hispanic Supreme Court justice. He had taken it personally when Judge José Cabranes was spurned in 1994 for the top court and had cultivated relations with other Hispanics—including Sotomayor—who might be in a position to be nominated for the next vacancy. Sotomayor had been on PRLDEF's board before becoming a judge.

Estrada and Ortiz were each highly respected and had wide circles of admirers in the law. Both men exuded polish and professionalism in their demeanor, down to their starched white shirts and pressed dark suits. And at this moment, each man resented what the other was saying. Their competing views related to Hispanic connections and credentials would represent two sides of a debate over

who might be in the best position to be nominated as the first
Hispanic for the Supreme Court.

Estrada was subjected to far more scrutiny than the typical nominee for the D.C. Circuit because his supporters—and opponents—
recognized that President George W. Bush could be positioning him
for the High Court. His nomination led to a record seven filibusters in
the Senate and exposed ethnic stereotyping and infighting among
organizations that had not been seen since the conflict over Judge
José Cabranes during the Clinton administration. *Slate* columnist
Dahlia Lithwick wrote, "As the debate grows uglier, it's now becoming
a contest among Mexicans, Cubans, and Hondurans about who—to
paraphrase *Snow White*—is the most Hispanic of them all."[3]

Estrada's nomination also reflected the lingering bad feelings
among Democrats over the Clarence Thomas confirmation. Democrats recalled how Thomas had been appointed to the D.C. Circuit
not long before his 1991 elevation to the Supreme Court—made
possible in part because Southern Democrats who might have opposed him were worried about a racial backlash. Critics of Estrada
did not want him to be similarly positioned for elevation from the
D.C. Circuit. Because of the nation's growing Hispanic population,
the possibility of a first Hispanic justice was even more in the political atmosphere than it had been during the Clinton administration
a decade earlier.

Estrada's father, a lawyer, and his mother, an accountant, divorced when he was young, and he eventually moved to the United
States to be with his mother, who worked as a bank examiner in
New York. He was seventeen when he arrived, knowing little English, but he caught up quickly and graduated with honors from
Columbia College and Harvard Law School. After his clerkship
for Justice Anthony Kennedy at the Supreme Court, Estrada became a federal prosecutor in Manhattan and then worked in the
U.S. Office of the Solicitor General, which represents the federal
government before the Supreme Court. In public service and now at
the private law firm Gibson, Dunn & Crutcher, Estrada had racked
up fifteen oral arguments before the Supreme Court.

This was a special achievement, for Estrada had a stutter that he had to overcome every time he stepped up to the lectern to argue before the justices, and he sometimes struggled to get out the first word of a sentence. The embodiment of intelligence and determination, he also was a conservative, drawing early opposition not only from Latino groups but also from liberal advocates who had begun to mobilize against him even before President Bush formally nominated him. If he made it to the Supreme Court, they speculated, he would undercut progressive gains on abortion rights, affirmative action, and death penalty appeals.

Another dynamic shaped the debate. Estrada, smart and smart-alecky, was known for saying exactly what he thought, sometimes to the point of offense. In many other parts of the professional world, a contrary or combative personality might not matter. But during a high-stakes judicial nomination, amid the egos of the Senate, a nominee bore the burden of showing deference and respect. Estrada's regard—or lack of it—for some Democratic leaders would exacerbate his difficulties during the confirmation process.

Carlos Ortiz was born in the Bronx and grew up in Harlem. He attended the City University of New York, became an accountant, and then went to Brooklyn Law School. He became general counsel at a food manufacturer and rose in the leadership of Puerto Rican and Hispanic legal groups that wanted more Hispanic representation on the nation's courts. Ortiz had made the appointment of the "first Hispanic" justice a personal mission. He insisted that it did not matter whether the first was a Democratic or Republican appointee, although most of the activists pressing for the appointment were in the liberal rather than the conservative camp.

Since the George H. W. Bush administration in the early 1990s, Ortiz and fellow Hispanic advocates had been meeting with presidents and their top aides to promote this cause. It had been at a 2001 session with President George W. Bush's White House counsel Alberto Gonzales that Ortiz first heard Miguel Estrada's name as a possible Supreme Court candidate. Ortiz had visited Gonzales soon after Bush assumed the White House to press again for a Hispanic justice. Gonzales mentioned that Estrada could soon be on deck for such an appointment.

Now, in the April 2002 meeting in Estrada's law firm office, the nominee and his critics from the Puerto Rican Legal Defense and Education Fund, including president Juan Figueroa, thought they might find common ground. The Puerto Rican leaders feared that Estrada was too conservative and out of touch with the Hispanic community. Yet there was no reason, at this point, to think the nominee would be in serious trouble or blocked in the Senate. Estrada had accepted their request for a meeting partly because he knew the third man in the group, Benito Romano. Estrada and Romano had both served as prosecutors in the U.S. attorney's office in Manhattan. Romano, who had led the office's anticorruption unit and then temporarily held the top U.S. attorney post, was now on PRLDEF's executive committee. Estrada would later say he was "delighted" to set up the meeting: "I think of myself as a fair-minded person, who is very concerned that there is anybody out there who may think that I am biased or that I have any character trait that would make me less of a person."[4]

Estrada went into the session irritated, however, because PRLDEF had laid out its cards with a disparaging letter to Senate Judiciary Committee chairman Patrick Leahy, a Democrat from Vermont, before the group's leaders had talked to him. Written just about a month after President Bush had nominated Estrada, the letter raised concerns about "the nominee's ultra-conservative views." Without citing specifics, the June 11, 2001, letter, signed by Figueroa, said, "If the views attributed to Mr. Estrada are accurate, they would place his views well outside the mainstream of American political and legal thought." The group said it was also disturbed that Estrada "appears to have had no involvement or participation whatsoever in the Hispanic community" and asserted that he "may not have the compassion, open-mindedness, sensitivity, courtesy, patience and freedom from bias . . . to be an effective jurist on any court."[5]

The meeting in his office, which Estrada said lasted more than three hours, did not allay those concerns.

Things grew tense when the visitors expressed a series of views that, according to Estrada, boiled down to: "'You, Mr. Estrada, were nominated solely because you are Hispanic; that makes it fair game for us to look into whether you are really Hispanic. We, having been involved in Hispanic Bar activities for lo these many years, are in a position to learn that you are not sufficiently Hispanic.' To which my response was—and I felt that very strongly—to point out that the comments were offensive, and deeply so, and boneheaded."[6]

Boneheaded? Ortiz drew back. He had been warned that Estrada could be dismissive and insensitive to the concerns of the Hispanic community. Now he and the others felt they were seeing those qualities firsthand. "Based largely on our personal observations," the Puerto Rican advocates would later write in a public assessment, "we now firmly believe that Mr. Estrada lacks the maturity and temperament that a candidate for high judicial office should possess."[7]

Estrada was offended. He believed he was being held to a different standard simply because he was Honduran. In his mind, he was as qualified as any high-performing lawyer, regardless of race or ethnicity. He felt he was being squeezed into a mold of what a Latino nominee should be and tested according to criteria he believed were irrelevant to judicial office.

But there was no escaping the bitter history between the two political parties over lifetime appointments to the bench. To Democrats, Estrada represented an assault on liberalism. Since Ronald Reagan's presidency in the 1980s, Republicans had used the courts to promote their agenda of conservatism and smaller government. They stacked the bench with jurists who thought that such social problems as overcrowded prisons, environmental disasters, and lingering school segregation should be the province of elected legislators, not appointed judges. Perhaps most significantly, they wanted to curtail the right to abortion embodied in the 1973 *Roe v. Wade* decision that protected women who sought to end a pregnancy.

As Barack Obama, then a Democratic senator from Illinois, wrote, "Gaining control of the courts generally and the Supreme Court in particular had become the holy grail for a generation of conservative activists—and not just, they insisted, because they viewed the courts as the last bastion of pro-abortion, pro-affirmative-action, pro-homosexual, pro-criminal, pro-regulation, anti-religious liberal elitism."[8]

When he was running for president against Vice President Al Gore, George W. Bush had said he wanted to appoint justices in the mold of Justices Antonin Scalia and Clarence Thomas. Bush had also strongly suggested that he wanted to name the first Hispanic justice, which meant getting someone positioned, possibly on an important lower court such as the D.C. Circuit, for the moment when a vacancy on the Supreme Court occurred.

Bush won the election in 2000 with an assist from the Supreme Court in the dispute over the decisive Florida election results. The Supreme Court's ruling in *Bush v. Gore* cut off recounts of Florida's ballots. Despite the saga that stretched from the November 7 election day until the December 12 ruling, Bush arrived in office with a plan for the federal bench, particularly the U.S. appeals courts, and quickly put forward an impressive slate of nominees that included Estrada.

The D.C. Circuit, to which he was nominated, was aptly dubbed the nation's second-highest bench. It handled challenges to federal regulations and passed judgment on policies covering such matters as the environment, campaign finance, and workplace safety. The stakes for any nominee to that court were high, especially because so many of its judges moved on to the Supreme Court. In 2001, three of the nine sitting justices were from that bench: Antonin Scalia, Clarence Thomas, and Ruth Bader Ginsburg.

◆

Bush's selection of Estrada was part of his own grander plan for the federal courts, first unveiled in an East Room ceremony on May 9, 2001. With more White House flourish and invited media attention than ever before for a set of appeals court candidates, President Bush introduced Estrada and ten other nominees: eight men and three women; eight whites, two blacks, one Latino. Estrada stood smiling, his hands clasped in front of him. The carefully orchestrated unveiling included the nominees' families and other supporters, as well as Attorney General John Ashcroft and Senate Judiciary Committee leaders Orrin Hatch, a Republican from Utah, and Patrick Leahy, the Democrat from Vermont. News reporters were handed three-ring binders with the nominees' biographies and supporting testimonials.

Among conservative luminaries nominated along with Estrada were former Reagan and first Bush administration lawyer John Roberts, also nominated to the D.C. Circuit; University of Utah law professor Michael McConnell, for the Denver-based Tenth Circuit; and Ohio solicitor general Jeffrey Sutton, for the Cincinnati-based Sixth Circuit. Like Estrada, they all were former Supreme Court law clerks and leading conservative thinkers, screened and recommended by members of the Federalist Society, a group that had helped scour the nation for conservatives for the courts since the early 1980s. Estrada and Roberts also had been part of George Bush's legal team during the disputed Florida election battle in December 2000.

Roberts had the deepest history in GOP administrations, having helped screen judicial candidates during the Reagan and George H. W. Bush years, including when Senator Moynihan was trying to win Sotomayor a U.S. district court seat. The first President Bush had tried to place Roberts, a native of Buffalo who grew up in Indiana, the son of a steel-plant executive and a homemaker, on the D.C. Circuit a decade earlier. At the time, Hispanic activists were pushing for more representation on prominent courts. A White House "talking points" memo in Roberts's file with the first Bush administration addressed why a Hispanic had not been chosen in early 1992. The memo defended the Roberts decision by calling him "a superstar" candidate and asserting that "the President does not need to nominate a Hispanic to this seat to demonstrate commitment to reaching out to Hispanics."[9]

Senate Democrats blocked Roberts's nomination back then. They believed that the Reagan protégé who rose quickly in the first Bush administration was a conservative ideologue. Some Democratic committee staffers took an "anyone but Roberts" attitude at the time, and Senate Judiciary Committee chairman Joseph Biden refused to schedule a hearing on his nomination. When President Bush lost to Bill Clinton in November 1992, Roberts went into private practice and began adding commercial clients and pro bono work to his résumé. From his base at the firm of Hogan & Hartson, Roberts became a preeminent Supreme Court lawyer.

President George W. Bush's interest in Estrada, also a leading Supreme Court lawyer, stemmed in part from the administration's attention to an increasingly powerful constituency. Hispanics had become 12.5 percent of the U.S. population, some 35.3 million of the total 281.4 million residents, according to the 2000 census. Mexicans represented 7.3 percent of the total U.S. population, Puerto Ricans 1.2 percent, and Cubans 0.4 percent. Overall, the Hispanic population had increased by 57.9 percent since 1990, up from 22.4 million.[10]

Such numbers fueled the expectation that whoever won the presidency in 2000 would want to have a Hispanic poised for appointment to the High Court. Both Texas governor Bush and Vice President Al Gore had suggested as much. At this point, the forty-six-year-old Sotomayor, a two-year veteran of an appeals court, was being mentioned in news stories about possible Supreme Court changes if Democrat Gore won the presidency.

Shortly after Bush defeated Gore and took office, it appeared that the most likely Hispanic candidate would be White House counsel Alberto Gonzales, a Mexican American who grew up in Texas and graduated from Harvard Law School. As governor, Bush had appointed Gonzales to the Texas Supreme Court and brought him to Washington as White House counsel in 2001. But it quickly became evident that many conservatives in the nation's capital did not trust Gonzales, who took a moderate approach to such Republican agenda items as abortion rights and affirmative action.

Estrada emerged as a Supreme Court contender in the view of

many Republicans and the news reporters following Bush's deliberations. When Bush nominated Estrada to the federal appeals court
in Washington, D.C., the president highlighted his Honduran roots,
noting that he was the first Hispanic ever offered a spot on the D.C.
Circuit. To counter Estrada's reputation as a conservative, the White
House recruited high-profile Democrats to support him, including
Walter Dellinger and Seth Waxman, former top officials in the
Clinton solicitor general's office. Administration officials also obtained a letter of endorsement from Ronald Klain, a Harvard Law
School classmate of Estrada's and a political operative whose Demo-
cratic credentials were unquestioned. Klain had been chief of staff
and counsel to Vice President Gore and was a close adviser to him
during the 2000 election, including as chief counsel overseeing the
Florida recounts.

When Bush officials enlisted him to help with Estrada in 2001,
Klain was in private practice in the Washington office of O'Melveny
& Myers. But as he endorsed Estrada, Klain reinforced the reality
that nomination politics was as much about the past as the present.
He noted that earlier Democratic nominees, including Elena Kagan
during the Clinton administration, had run into roadblocks and
been denied seats on the D.C. Circuit.[11] "I think it is unfortunate
that this vacancy exists at all due to the Senate's failure to confirm"
prior nominees, Klain wrote. He then said he believed Estrada
would be an independent thinker, not a reflexive conservative.[12]

Klain's fellow Democrats were not convinced. The Estrada opposition had come out early and was working in plain sight. In an
opinion piece published in *The New York Times* just six weeks after
President Bush announced his first batch of nominees, Senator
Charles Schumer of New York wrote, "The not-so-dirty little secret
of the Senate is that we do consider ideology, but privately . . . If the
President uses ideology in deciding whom to nominate to the bench,
the Senate, as part of its responsibility to advise and consent, should
do the same in deciding whom to confirm. Pretending that ideology
doesn't matter—or, even worse, doesn't exist—is exactly the opposite of what the Senate should do."[13]

The liberal Alliance for Justice had contacted Democratic senators, including Senate Judiciary Committee chairman Leahy, with concerns about Estrada's conservatism, specifically on civil rights issues. The group also began working with Senators Schumer and Dick Durbin, Democrats who represented key Hispanic constituencies in New York City and Chicago, respectively, to block the Estrada nomination. Alliance for Justice staff met regularly with Senate aides to strategize about how to raise suspicions regarding Estrada in the press and among moderate senators. As one Democratic staffer on the Senate Judiciary Committee told columnist Jack Newfield for a piece in the liberal *Nation* magazine, "Estrada is 40, and if he makes it to the circuit, then he will be Bush's first Supreme Court nominee. He could be on the Supreme Court for thirty years and do a lot of damage. We have to stop him now."[14]

Meanwhile, Puerto Rican, Mexican American, and other liberal-leaning Hispanic groups were trying to persuade Chairman Leahy to move slowly on Estrada's nomination.[15] The Puerto Rican Legal Defense and Education Fund, whose lawyers had visited Estrada in the spring of 2002, was one of the first to issue a full report on the nominee. "Of greatest concern to the Latino community is Mr. Estrada's clear lack of any connection whatsoever to the issues, needs, and concerns of the organized Hispanic community," the Puerto Rican organization asserted in the September 2002 report. "It is indeed ironic that someone promoted as a Hispanic has neither shown any demonstrated interest in, nor has had any involvement with, any Hispanic organizations or activities throughout his entire life in the United States."[16] The Mexican American Legal Defense and Educational Fund and the California La Raza Lawyers Association submitted a letter and report to the Judiciary Committee, concluding that they could not be sure Estrada would be fair to Hispanics trying to vindicate their rights in the courts.[17]

Estrada never tried to portray himself as a standard-bearer for Latinos, as White House officials such as Alberto Gonzales and Republican senators such as Senator Orrin Hatch had done on his behalf. Nor did he try to make himself out to be poor or disadvantaged. "I have never known what it is to be poor, and I am very thankful to my parents for that," he said.[18]

But in the atmosphere surrounding the nomination, his background was an issue. His opponents did not believe he shared or could understand the lives of many Hispanics. "Being Hispanic for us means much more than having a surname," U.S. representative Robert Menendez, a Democrat from New Jersey, told *The Washington Post* as he criticized Estrada for being disconnected from Hispanics.[19] Around this time, Sotomayor was complaining in speeches that minority candidates for the federal bench often stalled and that no Hispanic had ever been appointed to the D.C. Circuit. But her concern related to Democratic nominees. When she addressed the judicial bickering as Estrada's nomination was pending, she did not mention him.

Estrada's hearing before the Senate Judiciary Committee, just like the meeting with the Puerto Rican advocates, failed to boost his chances of confirmation. On September 26, 2002, the day after he celebrated his forty-first birthday, Estrada sat alone at a long table draped with a green cloth. Behind him were his mother, his sister, and his wife. In this venue, Estrada was not belligerent or especially defiant, but he did not answer senators' questions to their satisfaction. He also tripped up regarding his screening of young attorneys who sought clerkships with Justice Kennedy, his former boss at the Supreme Court. The issue was whether Estrada had tried to eliminate liberal applicants, a notion he initially resisted and then conceded he may have done.

Even though he was not as combative as he had been in other settings, his day of testimony was tense and stressful. At several points during the session, his wife, Laury, wiped her eyes. Dressed in a dark suit, white shirt, and red striped tie, Estrada said he was "exceptionally proud of every piece of legal work" he had undertaken.

Senator Schumer, who was chairing the Judiciary Committee hearing, reminded everyone about an earlier racially charged nomination and warned that he and others had not forgotten what happened. "Clarence Thomas came before this distinguished committee and basically said he had no views on many important constitutional issues of the day . . . But the minute Justice Thomas got to the Court, he was doctrinaire," Schumer asserted. "Whether you agreed with him or not, he obviously had deeply held views that he shielded from the committee. It wasn't a confirmation conversion. It was a confirmation subversion. And there is still a lot of simmering blood up here about that."

Some White House officials had thought that in the early 2000s Estrada's ethnicity would neutralize criticism about his conservatism the way Thomas's race deflected such issues in 1991. But they were wrong. The aftershocks of the Thomas confirmation hurt Estrada.

Schumer insisted that he was not questioning Estrada's legal abilities, but rather his ideology and whether he would be fair. Peering over brown-rimmed reading glasses at Estrada, Schumer referred to Estrada critics, including Arizona State University law professor Paul Bender, who had been Estrada's supervisor in the U.S. Office of the Solicitor General. Bender, who did not testify before the committee, had claimed in news reports cited by senators that Estrada lacked judgment and was "too much of an ideologue to be an appeals court judge."[20]

Schumer asserted that because of such criticism, the solicitor general's office should release memos Estrada wrote about cases when he served as an assistant from 1992 to 1997. "Everyone I have spoken with believes such memoranda will be useful in assessing how you approach the law," Schumer said, noting that the SG's office determines the government's position on important constitutional questions.

But in fact not everyone thought the memos should be turned over. Seven former U.S. solicitors general, including Democrats Seth Waxman, Walter Dellinger, and Drew Days, had written to Senate Judiciary Committee chairman Leahy to stress the need for confidentiality in the solicitor general's office correspondence.[21]

Estrada told Schumer he did not want to press the Bush administration to release the memos; he did not want his personal interests to eclipse regard for the institutional interests of the SG's office.

Under separate questioning by a number of senators, including California Democrat Dianne Feinstein, Estrada refused to give his view of past cases or to say how he would have voted. He stressed that he was committed to the process of judging, not necessarily the end result.

The most awkward moments came when senators asked him about a story in *The Nation* that said that Estrada had screened out liberals who were seeking clerkships with Justice Kennedy.[22] Estrada denied the reports that he told candidates they were too liberal for a job in the chambers of Kennedy, a conservative who often swung toward the liberal side in key cases such as the death penalty and punishments for juveniles. Estrada said that if he did say such a thing, it would have been only as a joke.

But then, after a lunch break from the committee hearing, Estrada told senators he needed to elaborate on his comments. He said there could have been circumstances under which he believed an applicant had an extreme view that would do a disservice to Kennedy. If the candidate would not follow the justice's wishes because of the candidate's strongly held views, Estrada posited to senators, he would not believe the candidate had the proper ideology for Kennedy.

"I think we have some credibility problems," Schumer said, accusing Estrada of changing his story.

That charge prompted Senator Hatch, the ranking Republican on the committee, to interject, "This is really offensive . . . This is a question of fairness." Hatch said that Estrada should not have to be confronted with anonymous sources. As he complained about how Estrada was being treated, the senator said, "The extreme left-wing Washington groups go after judicial nominees like kids after a piñata. They beat it and beat it until they hope something comes out that they can then chew and distort . . . Detractors have suggested that because he has been successful and has had the privilege of a fine education, he is somehow less than a full-blooded Hispanic."[23]

Estrada met with a weary look Republicans' assertions that he was the Latino embodiment of the American dream. Few Latinos came to his defense. Not many even knew the hearings were under way. The Pew Hispanic Center and other groups that regularly tap into ethnic sentiment did not poll on Estrada's nomination to the appeals court. Democrats realized that they could criticize him without fear of fallout. That included Senator Feinstein, from the heavily Mexican American state of California. Feinstein, more moderate than Schumer, might have been inclined toward Estrada because she had supported other controversial Bush nominees. But she was suspicious about his answers regarding the screening of law clerks for Justice Kennedy, and she complained that Estrada had stonewalled the committee.

As often happened in judicial nomination fights, Feinstein conjured the bitter memories of other Democratic candidates who Republican senators had stalled, including Mexican American Enrique Moreno, a Harvard-educated El Paso lawyer who had been nominated by President Clinton for a U.S. appeals court in Texas and waited years for a vote that never came. She mentioned Moreno even as she protested, "I want to clearly state this is not an issue of retaliation, as some have suggested. It is true that the Republican Senate did block a number of very qualified Hispanic nominees—female nominees, and so on—under President Clinton."[24]

Committee chairman Leahy raised Sonia Sotomayor's name and recalled the tactics used when she was being considered for the Second Circuit in 1998. "She was supported by every Hispanic organization," Leahy declared, underscoring what mattered to Democrats. "She had first been appointed to the federal bench by the first President Bush," he continued. "This should have been very easy, but every time we wanted to bring her up for a vote on the floor, there was an anonymous hold on the Republican side. Nobody wanted to step forward."[25] Sotomayor got her vote only because GOP senator D'Amato interceded.

Some news reporters emphasized Estrada's personality in their accounts of his nomination. "Mr. Estrada turned out to be a difficult, even prickly interview subject when he made courtesy calls on some Hispanic groups and when he appeared before the Senate Judiciary Committee," Neil Lewis reported in *The New York Times*. "His friends say he is principled and cannot avoid speaking straightforwardly, which means he is unwilling to provide benign, even courteous, responses when a line of questioning strikes him as foolish."[26] And much struck Estrada as foolish. His brutal honesty and wit drew some people to him but put off others.

Estrada might not have helped himself at some points, but Senate Republicans shepherding his nomination stumbled more. Part of their problem was bad timing. Three weeks after Bush put Estrada's name up, Republicans lost their majority in the Senate when Vermont's Jim Jeffords dropped his Republican affiliation and switched to Independent.

The GOP leadership remained in turmoil during key moments of the Estrada nomination even after Republicans won back the Senate majority in 2002.

Republican senator Trent Lott of Mississippi was forced to give up his leadership post because of racially insensitive remarks made during a celebration for long-serving senator Strom Thurmond. At a birthday party for the South Carolina Republican, who was turning one hundred in December 2002, Lott declared that if Thurmond had been elected president in 1948, the country would not have "all these problems over all these years." Thurmond had been a segregationist candidate. Amid public outcry Lott apologized, saying his "poor choice of words conveyed-to some the impression that I embrace the discarded policies of the past."

Fellow Republicans ousted Lott and chose William Frist of Tennessee to be Senate majority leader. Less skilled at hardball nomination politics, Frist was unable to advance Estrada's nomination, and Senator Lott took the extraordinary step of telling a reporter he disapproved of Frist's handling of the situation.[27]

Frist, a surgeon who had graduated from Princeton two years before Sotomayor and trained at Harvard Medical School, vowed to get Estrada confirmed. "I want people to see that we don't fold, period, when we're right on principle," he said. "I know that half of my own caucus thinks we've prolonged this too long. But before this is over it will show that patience pays off, just like it does in medicine—persistence, when you know deep inside that you are right on an issue."[28]

But Democrats were more skillful, and they repeatedly blocked a straight up-or-down vote on Estrada's nomination in February 2003. For days, they engaged in a filibuster, standing at their individual wooden desks in the well of the Senate. They criticized Estrada and also filled time by talking about everything from the ongoing war with Iraq to personal tales from their childhoods. Robert Byrd of West Virginia recalled how in 1934 he used chewing gum and candy to court a girlfriend who eventually became his wife.[29]

The filibuster could have been stopped only by a "supermajority," the votes of 60 of the 100 senators. At the time, the Senate consisted of 51 Republicans, 48 Democrats, and 1 Independent. Neither side had an incentive to compromise. Meanwhile, some Hispanic groups, such as the Mexican American Legal Defense and Educational Fund, kept up the pressure against Estrada. "Estrada has neither demonstrated that he understands the needs of Latino Americans nor expressed interest in the Latino community," Antonia Hernández wrote in a commentary piece for the *Los Angeles Times*. "Simply being a Latino does not make one qualified to be a judge."[30]

Hernández and others drowned out Estrada's support from such Republicans as Linda Chavez, a Mexican American who had been a top aide in the Reagan and first Bush administrations. Chavez complained that liberal groups that traditionally sought racial and ethnic considerations "in everything from college admissions to judicial appointments now want the right to define just who qualifies for inclusion in their racial and ethnic categories."[31]

◆

In the spring of 2003, two men who had stood on risers at the White House with Estrada when President Bush unveiled his initial slate of judicial nominees, and who had controversial records of their own,

Sonia Sotomayor strides into the East Room of the White House with President Barack Obama and Vice President Joe Biden on May 26, 2009, for the president's announcement of her nomination to the Supreme Court. (Official White House Photo by Pete Souza)

Emphasizing her point, Sotomayor speaks to President Obama on the day of her nomination to succeed the retiring justice David Souter; Vice President Biden looks on. (Official White House Photo by Pete Souza)

In late June 2009, during preparation for Sotomayor's July confirmation hearings, White House staff celebrated her birthday with her. Sotomayor laughs with Deputy White House Counsel Cassandra Butts (left). Behind Sotomayor is Cynthia Hogan (far right), counsel to Vice President Biden. Butts and Hogan took the lead on much of the preparation. (Official White House Photo by Johnny Simon)

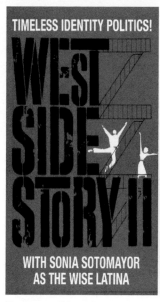

TIMELESS IDENTITY POLITICS!

WHEN YOU'RE A WHITE YOU'RE A WHITE ALL THE WAY FROM YOUR FIRST CLASS BIRTHRIGHT TO YOUR COUNTRY CLUB DAYS!

SENATE REPUBLICANS

SENATOR LEAHY

MATSON
THE NEW YORK OBSERVER
caglecartoons.com

WEST SIDE STORY II

WITH SONIA SOTOMAYOR AS THE WISE LATINA

Sotomayor's nomination set up ethnic and racial tensions that were captured by political cartoonists. Senate Judiciary Committee Republicans were featured in this spoof on *West Side Story*'s "Jet Song," by the cartoonist R. J. Matson in *The New York Observer*. (Courtesy of Cagle Cartoons)

SOTOMAYOR IS RACIST

VOTE GOP

YOU'RE IN OUR WAY....

RUSH

NEWT

Nate Beeler's cartoon in the *Washington Examiner* conjures up criticism by Rush Limbaugh and Newt Gingrich against Sotomayor, particularly for her "wise Latina" remark, suggesting their commentary may have been unwelcomed by other Republicans looking ahead to elections. (Courtesy of Cagle Cartoons)

Jimmy Margulies, a cartoonist for *The Record* in New Jersey, plays off Sotomayor's record of breaking through glass ceilings. (Courtesy of Cagle Cartoons)

This Taylor Jones caricature of Sotomayor appeared in *El Nuevo Día* in Puerto Rico. Sotomayor was confirmed by the Senate on August 6, 2009, by a 68–31 vote. Most Republicans voted against her.
(Courtesy of Cagle Cartoons)

At a White House reception on August 12, 2009, after So-
tomayor's Senate confirmation, President Obama and First
Lady Michelle Obama congratulate the new justice. (Official
White House Photo by Pete Souza)

Supreme Court justices welcome Sotomayor during her September 8, 2009,
investiture events. President Obama speaks with Justices Sotomayor, Antonin
Scalia, and Ruth Bader Ginsburg. (Steve Petteway, Collection of the Supreme Court of the
United States)

After an investiture ceremony at the Supreme Court on September 8, 2009, Chief Justice John Roberts escorts Sotomayor, the nation's 111th justice, across the west plaza toward the assembled news media. (Steve Petteway, Collection of the Supreme Court of the United States)

Sotomayor joins her family after the ceremony on the Supreme Court's plaza: (from left to right) Omar Lopez (stepfather), Celina Sotomayor (mother), Tracey Sotomayor (sister-in-law), and Juan Sotomayor (brother). (Steve Petteway, Collection of the Supreme Court of the United States)

After Obama and Biden won a second term, Vice President Biden asked Justice Sotomayor to swear him in on January 20, 2013, his official inauguration taking place one day before the ceremonial one. But Sotomayor had a book signing in Manhattan that afternoon, so she asked him to move the event from the traditional noon to 8:00 a.m. As she rushed out after the ceremony, he thanked her for the honor, saying he hoped he hadn't caused her to miss her train. (Steve Petteway, Collection of the Supreme Court of the United States)

The presidential inauguration was held at the U.S. Capitol on January 21, 2013. Justice Sotomayor greets Biden just before that ceremony. Standing on the platform waiting for the ceremony to begin are Chief Justice Roberts and Associate Justices Anthony Kennedy, Clarence Thomas, Ruth Bader Ginsburg, Stephen Breyer, and Antonin Scalia. (Steve Petteway, Collection of the Supreme Court of the United States)

The current Supreme Court, together in their robes in 2010 (Steve Petteway, Collection of the Supreme Court of the United States)

Justice Sotomayor gets ready to press the button for the countdown ball for the celebration of the New Year on January 1, 2014, in Times Square. (Getty Images)

were confirmed. Jeffrey Sutton, the former Ohio solicitor general, was approved by the Senate in a vote of 52–41 for the U.S. Court of Appeals for the Sixth Circuit. John Roberts, the former deputy U.S. solicitor general under the first President Bush, was confirmed by a voice vote to the D.C. Circuit.

A few months later, Estrada pulled out. He had been filibustered seven times. "I believe that the time has come to return my full attention to the practice of law and to regain the ability to make long-term plans for my family," he wrote to President Bush. Bush had been personally urging Estrada to stick it out, but the ordeal was taking a toll on Estrada and his wife. They believed that people were going through their garbage looking for information, watching them, and spying on them. They had been trying to start a family, and Laury miscarried.[32]

From the start, Estrada had quarreled with the White House on how officials should portray him. They highlighted his ethnicity, but that ended up exacerbating his difficult situation. Rather than rally behind him, Hispanics who kept up with developments in his nomination generally opposed it. Veteran Mexican American commentator Carlos Conde wrote, "It was about pitting Latinos against Latinos with one side claiming that Estrada was not sufficiently Latino to merit the post and the others arguing that his detractors were clueless about the genesis of being Latino." Conde, who was an aide in the Richard Nixon White House and worked on the campaigns of President George H. W. Bush, questioned whether Estrada was nominated for a federal judgeship because of his talent or because he was the conservative type of Latino Republicans were seeking.[33]

◆

If Estrada had ended up on the D.C. Circuit, he might have been in a position to be considered for the Supreme Court openings that occurred in 2005, when D.C. Circuit judge Roberts was elevated and when Third Circuit appeals court judge Samuel Alito was nominated. The first vacancy occurred when Justice Sandra Day O'Connor announced her retirement on July 1, 2005. O'Connor, then seventy-five, said that she wanted to spend more time with her husband, John, who was suffering from Alzheimer's disease. President Bush chose Roberts, who, after he graduated from Harvard Law School, had earned a clerkship with Associate Justice William Rehnquist and then rocketed through the Reagan and first Bush administrations.

In early September 2005 Roberts was heading toward his Senate Judiciary Committee hearings for the associate justice spot vacated by O'Connor when Chief Justice Rehnquist died from complications related to thyroid cancer. President Bush immediately decided to nominate Roberts, who had won initial rave reviews from senators and the media, for the open chief justice spot.

To fill the O'Connor vacancy, Bush selected White House counsel Harriet Miers, a longtime friend from Texas. Miers, a graduate of Southern Methodist University's law school who had had virtually no constitutional law experience, was criticized by Bush's own Republican allies, who thought she could not be counted on as a conservative. Robert Bork, a former appeals court judge and conservative lightning rod who had been rejected by the Senate for a Supreme Court appointment in 1987, called the Miers nomination "a disaster on every level."[34] He argued that she was not qualified and would set back the conservative cause. Miers pulled out, and President Bush nominated Samuel Alito, a low-profile Trenton, New Jersey, native and Yale Law School graduate who had worked in the U.S. Office of the Solicitor General, served as a U.S. attorney, and in 1990 been appointed to the Philadelphia-based U.S. Court of Appeals for the Third Circuit. Liberals, including Senator Barack Obama, opposed Roberts and Alito but could not muster enough Democratic support to block their confirmations.

The Senate confirmed Roberts by a vote of 78–22 on September 29, 2005, and Alito by a vote of 58–42 on January 31, 2006, mainly along party lines.

◆

Estrada continued his appellate advocacy at the private firm of Gibson, Dunn, gaining more clients and increasing his arguments before the High Court. On one occasion the justices decided to appoint him specially to argue a case for them—certainly a seal of approval.[35]

Yet on Capitol Hill his 2003 rejection for the D.C. Circuit continued to stir passions among Democrats and Republicans who invoked his name to make their respective points about the rough-and-tumble politics of race and ethnicity that persisted in judicial nominations.

Democrats pointed to the fact that Estrada had no record as a judge and few legal writings to assess. They said he evaded their questions, and they complained that he was impertinent. Republicans would not let go either. They believed he was a victim of racial politics, pure and simple.

In 2009 at least one Republican senator told Sonia Sotomayor that Estrada, not she, deserved to be up for Supreme Court appointment.

"No Republican would have chosen you, Judge," Lindsey Graham of South Carolina told her during a Senate Judiciary Committee hearing. "That is just the way it is. We would have picked Miguel Estrada. We would all have voted for him."[36]

The Estrada ordeal remained an open wound the next year, nearly a decade after he had been nominated by President Bush, when Elena Kagan appeared before the Senate Judiciary Committee as a Supreme Court nominee.[37]

Kagan and Estrada had been study partners during their student days at Harvard Law School, and, despite his politics, he heartily endorsed her 2010 nomination by Democratic President Obama.

"I think it's one of the great tragedies for the country that he was never able to sit on an appellate court," Senator Graham told Kagan, who in turn testified of her friend, "He is qualified to sit as an appellate judge. He's qualified to sit as a Supreme Court justice."

When Oklahoma Republican senator Tom Coburn asked Kagan if, were she a sitting senator, she would have voted for Estrada, she said yes. But then, as Coburn was thanking her for the answer, Kagan slipped in, "I hope I would have, anyway. You know, who knows what it feels like to be one of you guys and to be subject to all the things that you guys are subject to."

It was a nod to the truth that politics, whether in the Senate, at the White House, or among advocacy groups, always won out.

SEVEN

The Wise Latina

Like most Americans of a certain age, Sonia Sotomayor remembers where she was on September 11, 2001, when al-Qaeda terrorists attacked the United States. She had a physician's appointment in midtown Manhattan, and like many New Yorkers, she made her way to safety through streets clogged with people and filled with smoke and ash. As she staggered to her home in Greenwich Village, she passed people with their car doors open, their radios relaying the latest news. She heard a report—false, it turned out—that a courthouse had been hit, and she worried that she had lost old colleagues.

Six weeks after 9/11, as the nation was still engulfed in the chaos and deaths of nearly three thousand people from the al-Qaeda hijackings, Sotomayor flew to California as previously scheduled. She had been invited to deliver the opening speech for a two-day symposium at the University of California, Berkeley, entitled "Raising the Bar: Latino and Latina Presence in the Judiciary and the Struggle for Representation."

As one of the most prominent Latinas in the country at the time, U.S. appeals court judge Sotomayor was a natural choice for Latino organizers of the event, which would address such topics as "The Politics of Appointment" and "The Need to Increase the Role We Play as Lawyers, Judges, and Professors." The conference also commemorated the fortieth anniversary of the first Latino appointment to the federal bench. In 1961 President John F. Kennedy had named Mexican American Reynaldo Guerra Garza, a University of

Texas Law School graduate and Brownsville attorney, to be a U.S. district court judge in the Southern District of Texas. President Jimmy Carter elevated Garza to the U.S. Court of Appeals for the Fifth Circuit in 1979. A little over two decades later, in 2001, the number of Latinos on the federal bench was still disproportionately low compared with their population. At the same time, as civil rights and defense organizations pointed out, Latinos, like African Americans, were caught up in the criminal justice system in disproportionately high numbers.

Sotomayor's speech at the conference on October 26 drew scant news attention in a nation still consumed by the devastation at the hands of al-Qaeda. But eight years later, her comments at Berkeley—one phrase relating to a "wise Latina," in particular—would dominate commentary on her nomination to the Supreme Court.

Sotomayor gave the "wise Latina" speech without fanfare on a Friday afternoon in a standard state university auditorium, but critics charged that what she said was anything but ordinary. Her assertion: "I would hope that a wise Latina woman with the richness of her experiences would more often than not reach a better conclusion than a white male who hasn't lived that life."[1] Some detractors later called her "racist," and former House speaker Newt Gingrich, a Georgia Republican, posited, "Imagine a judicial nominee said, 'My experience as a white man makes me better than a Latina woman.' Wouldn't they have to withdraw?"[2]

The "wise Latina" remark would take on a life of its own and elicit competing responses typifying the enduring reactions to Sotomayor. Ultimately, the remark would become a rallying cry for Hispanics. Sotomayor's comments at this unguarded moment in Berkeley would also foreshadow chords she would strike after she became the most public justice ever. With candor and an everywoman style, she would separate herself from the usual elite world of the judiciary, emphasizing her disadvantaged background, her lingering feelings of being "different," and a life of seized opportunities.

Sotomayor's speech at Berkeley, given as the new president George W. Bush was nominating more conservative judges, offered a liberal counterpoint to the view that personal life experiences do not inform judicial decisions. In his election campaign, Bush had held up as a model Justice Antonin Scalia, who insisted that judges should keep themselves out of the equation and look only to the original meaning of a constitutional provision when it was adopted, whether in the eighteenth-century text or at the time of amendment. Sotomayor had endorsed the idea that the Constitution's meaning evolves and judges' decisions are affected by many factors, including their backgrounds and ideologies.[3]

Yet Sotomayor, who in 2001 was three years into her tenure on the U.S. Court of Appeals for the Second Circuit, was a pragmatist, and on that October afternoon in Berkeley she had not set out to give a weighty speech about jurisprudence. With her customary style, she was interweaving her aspirations about judging with childhood references: nights playing Bingo with her grandmother Mercedes, meals of pigs' feet and beans. These childhood experiences permeated her adult life, no matter how far she moved from life in the Bronx.

When she stood before any audience, Sotomayor was acutely aware of where she was in her own journey as a Latina, and she knew that her up-from-nothing story inspired others and reinforced her own success.

Sotomayor also would have understood the poignancy of this moment for Latinos across the country. In the early 2000s their numbers were swelling, but their educational and employment opportunities were not keeping pace. The 1990s had brought a series of statewide ballot initiatives aimed at curtailing affirmative action and immigration.

Ethnic tensions were evident at the places where many Latinos were able to find work: poultry plants, carpet mills, and construction sites. The steady economic gains of Latinos were threatened by the efforts to stop educational affirmative action in such states as Texas, California, and Florida.[4]

Affirmative action had made the difference in Sotomayor's life, and she wanted it to survive for others. A time would come when she could actually influence its survival, as a justice, but for now, as an appeals court judge out on the stump, she was addressing such dilemmas in only the most cautious terms.

She had been invited to the Berkeley conference by student organizers and Rachel Moran, a Latina law professor who had attended Yale Law School with Sotomayor in the 1970s. Moran, whose mother had come from Mexico, was born in Missouri, grew up in Arizona, and graduated from Stanford University before going to Yale, where she was two years behind Sotomayor. Like the judge, Moran was a rising star in the law. She would become dean of the University of California Los Angeles School of Law in 2010. Moran's accomplishments as a law professor even in the fall of 2001 prompted Sotomayor to quip, "I warn Latinos in this room: Latinas are making a lot of progress in the old-boy network."[5]

Sotomayor built on planks laid in other speeches as she spoke, using her fairly standard device of "Who am I?" She launched into the familiar refrain professing her identity as a Nuyorican. "For those of you on the West Coast who do not know what that term means: I am a born and bred New Yorker of Puerto Rican–born parents who came to the States during World War II." Speaking in a voice that retained its throaty accent, Sotomayor related the glossy version of her parents' success and happiness on the mainland, rather than offering the blunt honesty that would come later when she revealed that her father was an alcoholic and her mother cold and distant.

Because she was in California, speaking to an audience that included many Mexican Americans, Sotomayor acknowledged the differences among Hispanics in heritage and culture. She joked that she did not know about tacos until she was in college, where she had a Mexican American roommate.

She segued from "how wonderful and magical it is to have a Latina soul" to tensions among Hispanics and the recurring controversy over affirmative action. She did not mention California's Proposition 209. But her audience certainly would have been aware that five years earlier, state voters had adopted the referendum that

banned California state schools and public entities from considering race in the acceptance of applications or hiring of faculty and
staff. It was a potent response to decades-old affirmative action that
critics said wrongly discriminated against whites. Even as Sotomayor was speaking in October 2001, white students who had been
rejected for admissions at the University of Michigan's undergraduate and law school programs were challenging policies that gave minorities a boost. Sotomayor knew how it felt to be tested on this
issue: in 1978, a law firm partner had asked her whether she had
gotten into Yale because of affirmative action.

"We are a nation that takes pride in our ethnic diversity, recognizing its importance in shaping our society . . . ," Sotomayor told
the Berkeley audience, "yet we simultaneously insist that we can
and must function and live in a race- and color-blind way. That
tension . . . is being hotly debated today in national discussions
about affirmative action." She left her reference to affirmative action
at that. She was trying to encourage, not challenge, this audience.
There would be other occasions to accentuate what she achieved
through affirmative action and to make sure that it did not go down
without a fight.

She turned her attention to the federal judiciary and noted that
no Hispanics had ever made it to the U.S. Court of Appeals for
the District of Columbia Circuit and a handful of other powerful
appeals courts. Miguel Estrada had been nominated to a vacancy on
the D.C. Circuit at the time, but Sotomayor made no reference to
the Republican nominee. She referred instead to the stalled nominations of women and minorities to appeals courts during the
Democratic administration of President Bill Clinton.

Sotomayor usually avoided the overtly political. But this time
she said, "I need not remind you that Justice Clarence Thomas represents a part but not the whole of African American thought on
many subjects," referring to the skepticism many African Americans
directed toward the conservative Thomas.

Students and professors hearing Sotomayor speak at Berkeley
would say later that she was inspiring the Hispanics in her audience.

Professor Moran, who extended the invitation, said that Sotomayor's remarks about the value of a wise Latina "didn't raise any eyebrows" at the time, that Sotomayor was encouraging students to elevate their aspirations: "She made people feel that she was really there for them."[6] That was part of Sotomayor's natural pattern in such public settings. She developed a kinship with an audience. She welcomed questions, and if a student who took the microphone sometimes fumbled or faltered through nervousness, it was not unlike Sotomayor to move closer to where the student stood and offer words of encouragement.

Certainly in Berkeley, she was suggesting to students that her story of success could be theirs, too. But she went further to make a qualitative comparison that Latinas might make better decisions and to assert that one's background necessarily made a difference in making those decisions. "People of color," Sotomayor emphasized, "will make a difference in the process of judging." She also called "the aspiration to impartiality" in judicial decision making "just that—it's an aspiration because it denies the fact that we are by our experiences making different choices than others."

Sotomayor contrasted her views with those of a former colleague, U.S. district court judge Miriam Cedarbaum, a 1986 appointee of President Reagan who had said that judges should transcend their personal sympathies and prejudices for greater fairness and legal integrity. "I wonder whether achieving that goal is possible in all or even in most cases," Sotomayor said. "And I wonder whether by ignoring our differences as women or men of color we do a disservice both to the law and society."

When Sotomayor began to unspool the observation that would become most controversial during her 2009 Supreme Court nomination, she did it with remarkable casualness. She said she was not sure whether it was Supreme Court justice Sandra Day O'Connor or someone else who originally observed that a wise old man and a wise old woman would reach the same conclusions in the law. (The adage can be traced to Minnesota Supreme Court justice Mary

Jeanne Coyne.)[7] Whoever first uttered those words about wise judges, Sotomayor said, she disagreed with them because she hoped that a wise Latina "would more often than not reach a better conclusion than a white male."

A *better* conclusion? That was a startling assertion, as even Sotomayor's Democratic White House vetters would later concede.

Sotomayor had been voicing versions of this "wise Latina woman" sentiment for years. One of her earliest public references on the topic came in 1994, when she was not yet even on the federal appeals court. Speaking at a convention hotel in Puerto Rico for the 40th National Conference of Law Reviews, she said that she hoped a "wise woman"—not specifically a wise Latina woman—would reach a better conclusion than a man.[8]

But by the time of the Berkeley speech, Sotomayor had become more forceful in her claim that judges are influenced by their personal experiences and her assertion of the value of her own background. "Personal experiences affect the facts that judges choose to see," she said, as she implied that she was speaking from her own experience and what she had observed in her colleagues. Yet, she acknowledged, "I simply do not know exactly what that difference will be in my judging. But I accept there will be some based on my gender and my Latina heritage."

Intriguingly, she closed on a defensive note, one that suggested that for all her talk of opportunity and success, she was always struggling with the fear that her Puerto Rican identity and experience merited less respect in the world of the white male judiciary: "Each day on the bench I learn something new about the judicial process and about being a professional Latina woman in a world that sometimes looks at me with suspicion."

She felt that suspicion deeply, often from lawyers who practiced before her. Sotomayor had generally good relations with her fellow judges on the Manhattan-based Second Circuit, but reviews from lawyers were mixed, as seen in the commentary of the *Almanac of the Federal Judiciary*, a respected volume on all U.S. judges. Compiled by Aspen Publishers, it listed a judge's academic and professional

background, honors, and noteworthy rulings, along with lawyer assessments based on interviews, and was a common resource for practicing attorneys, law professors, and news reporters. Over the years,
the assessments of Sotomayor's temperament grew increasingly critical. In 2001, the year she spoke at Berkeley, the following lawyer
comments were representative: "She can be tough. She's not rude in
any way but she's exacting." "I've never had a problem with her, but I
know that some lawyers don't care for her temperament." "She's very
accomplished and clearly very smart, and in truth, I think they're
intimidated." By 2009, the year she was nominated, the tone was
harsher. "She seems angry." "She is overly aggressive—not very judicial." "She does not have a very good temperament." "She is nasty
to lawyers."[9]

Such mixed reviews would continue through the years. In 2009
a committee of the American Bar Association, which had been
screening Supreme Court nominees for decades, analyzed Sotomayor's writings and interviewed lawyers who practiced before her.
The report said that some found her "aggressive" during oral arguments and expressed concern that the "wise Latina" comment reflected bias. The ABA committee chalked the first issue up to her
being "an assertive and direct questioner," and when it came to the
second claim, its panel found no bias in her work.[10]

It also would become evident that Sotomayor, more than other
judges and justices, would be communicating to multiple audiences.
In 2001 she was speaking at a conference about Latinos, largely attended by Latinos. In that setting, her remark about the value of a
"wise Latina" attracted no attention. Only when a broader audience
read her words were her motives questioned.

A few years after the Berkeley appearance Sotomayor observed
in a speech to Cornell University students that the differences minorities face do not "magically disappear" after an Ivy League education or professional success. "We people of color have problems
that we struggle with throughout our careers, throughout our lives."
She said that it sometimes seemed as if she lived a charmed life,
with her Manhattan apartment and opportunities that brought her

into the company of Aretha Franklin, Bernadette Peters, and Robert De Niro. Yet, she told the students, "despite everything I've accomplished, I'm always looking behind my shoulder, wondering if I measure up."[11]

If the Berkeley speech is viewed in the broader context of her other speeches to student groups, perhaps what one sees most is Sotomayor's ongoing drive to define herself in a world where she breaks the mold. Asked about that effort in the context of the Berkeley speech, she said, years after becoming a justice, "It's very hard for people who haven't lived my life to know what it's like to have your experiences looked down upon, to be viewed as inferior, to be viewed as not smart enough. You need to affirm that you have value."

◆

She would, however, have to eat her words about the "wise Latina" during her 2009 Senate confirmation hearings. It was painful for Sotomayor but necessary in the view of her White House supporters. "I want to state up front and unequivocally and without doubt," she said early in the hearings, "I do not believe any ethnic, racial, or gender group has an advantage in sound judging."[12]

Senator Lindsey Graham, a South Carolina Republican and an important member of the Senate Judiciary Committee, put Democrats on notice within days of President Obama's nomination that he would be seeking an apology for her sentiment that a Latina would reach a better conclusion than a man. For him, she delivered, testifying, "I regret that I have offended some people. I believe that my life demonstrates that that was not my intent to leave the impression that some have taken from my words."

That appeased Graham, but not other Republicans. Senator Jeff Sessions, a former federal prosecutor from Alabama, said that the "wise Latina" comment revealed a distaste for the "American ideal" that all judges should be able to "put aside their personal biases and prejudices."[13]

Sotomayor rejected that characterization and continued to minimize her original sentiment. "My rhetorical device failed," she said.

"It failed because it left an impression that I believe something that I don't . . . It left an impression that has offended people and has left an impression that I didn't intend."

She said she was speaking only of how a person's varied experiences would naturally affect her view: "Life experiences have to influence you. We're not robots who listen to evidence and don't have feelings. We have to recognize those feelings and put them aside. That's what my speech was saying."

Most Senate Republicans were not satisfied. Outside the Beltway, however, the "wise Latina" phrase would take off in 2009. Cartoonists seized it, and not at Sotomayor's expense. *Roll Call's* R. J. Matson combined it with Sotomayor's childhood passion for Nancy Drew detective stories to depict *The Case of the Wise Old Latina*, with Nancy Drew pursuing the "Hardly Boys." On the mock book cover, the Sotomayor figure searches with a flashlight for the nervous-looking caricatures of Newt Gingrich and Rush Limbaugh. In a cartoon by Mike Luckovich of *The Atlanta Journal-Constitution*, Sotomayor sits before senators and above her are the words "Keep talking. The more you say, the better I look." In the bubble above one of the senators: "That's one 'Wise Latina.'"

For the Supreme Court nominee, the "wise Latina" assertion turned out to be more of a plus than a minus and foreshadowed Sotomayor's popularity in upcoming years. Rossana Rosado, publisher of *El Diario* in New York and of Puerto Rican descent, wrote in the *Los Angeles Times*: "Women in my professional and personal circles are busy ordering T-shirts and buttons with the phrase. We want to be wise Latinas."[14]

EIGHT

Race and the *Ricci* Case

By 2008, Sonia Sotomayor and José Cabranes had served together on the U.S. Court of Appeals for the Second Circuit for a decade. Their relationship had changed as their fourteen-year age difference became less significant. The young woman who once looked up to Cabranes was now his equal. As she worked from a courthouse in Manhattan and he in New Haven, they remained friends, but ideological differences created tension between them. She had not always taken his advice when she was young, and she was less inclined to be guided by him now. That may have been inevitable. What drew Cabranes to Sotomayor in the first place was that she was certain of herself and pushed hard for what she wanted. And Cabranes was simply more conservative than his protégée, especially when it came to the validity of government actions to right the wrongs of discrimination.

On a February weekend in 2008 Cabranes was at home in New Haven, reading the newspaper, when an article about a new judicial decision caught his attention. He saw that a three-judge panel of the Second Circuit had rejected a discrimination claim brought by a group of white firefighters. The men had sued New Haven city officials who had discarded the results of promotion tests because no African Americans and only two Hispanics had qualified for the rank of lieutenant or captain. The city contended that the test format was flawed and could expose officials to lawsuits by minority firefighters who would argue that they had been disproportionately and unlawfully kept from promotion. The city had long been trying to counteract past discrimination and had hired an outside consulting firm to help design tests that would not, through subtle and inadvertent bias, hurt the chances of minority candidates. That strategy had apparently not worked.

The firefighters' lawyer, Karen Torre, had told the *New Haven Register* newspaper that she was appalled that the firefighters had received only a cursory, unsigned order rather than a reasoned legal opinion "on . . . the most significant race case to come before the Circuit Court in 20 years."[1]

Sotomayor was a member of the three-judge panel that had issued the brief order in *Ricci v. DeStefano*, denying the firefighters' appeal. The other judges were Rosemary Pooler and Robert Sack. Both had joined the Second Circuit as appointees of President Bill Clinton in June 1998, five months before Sotomayor had been confirmed.

The *Ricci* case themes of racial bias and resentment had long threaded their way through Sotomayor's life. She had benefited from, and continued to support, policies that boosted the chances of minority applicants in education and on the job. And she knew firsthand the controversy over whether such policies led to the hiring of people unqualified for the post. Developments in the case also revealed a different side of her as a judge. Throughout her career Sotomayor had been sure to tread carefully and generally avoided controversy. But in this case she exposed herself to charges of activism or, at least, a cavalier disregard for the firefighters who were alleging discrimination.

The case had been dispatched with a brief order issued on a Friday. It might have escaped public attention. But lawyer Torre had alerted the *New Haven Register* and expressed sufficient outrage to catapult the story onto the front page, catching the interest of one important reader, Cabranes, who could blow the whistle even louder and eventually attract national attention to the case.

Cabranes took provocative steps of his own as he began working behind the scenes to try to have the case heard again by the full Second Circuit. But Torre and her clients, seventeen whites and one

Hispanic, did not know that this veteran judge on the Second Circuit was helping their cause and about to set off a brawl. So after the panel's February 15 order, Torre began work on a petition to the Supreme Court. In her office just steps away from the federal courthouse on Church Street in New Haven, Torre crafted arguments to try to win a Supreme Court review of the firefighters' claim that city officials had discriminated against them.[2] She filed the petition in early May. Only in June would divisions on the Second Circuit break out into the open.

When they did, the *Ricci* case would not only highlight the conflicts between two jurists and friends, both of Puerto Rican heritage, but also would exemplify Sotomayor's other allegiances on the Second Circuit. Rosemary Pooler, the senior judge on the *Ricci* panel, had become a dear friend. They were among the first women ever to sit on the New York–based federal appeals court. Two other Second Circuit judges who would later go out of their way to support the three-judge panel's decision had deep ties with Sotomayor, too.

◆

As the Second Circuit wrestled with the *Ricci* case internally, Democrats Hillary Clinton and Barack Obama, the strongest female and African American contenders ever to vie for the U.S. presidency, were in a tight battle for the party's nomination. If either Clinton or Obama ended up taking the White House, any subsequent Supreme Court vacancy would likely generate a renewed interest in diversity. President George W. Bush's two appointees were white men (John Roberts and Samuel Alito), and the High Court was at this point made up of eight men and one woman. All were white except for Clarence Thomas. There had never been a Hispanic appointee, and on any list of possible candidates could be the fifty-three-year-old Sotomayor—a fact not lost on people inside and outside the Second Circuit.

The judges knew the *Ricci* case could take on greater prominence because it dealt with issues of race and diversity, and because Sotomayor was in the middle of it. As it progressed up toward the

Supreme Court, commentators focused on Sotomayor's role and the disagreement between the two prominent Puerto Rican jurists. Cabranes would reject any suggestion that he was trying to call specific attention to Sotomayor and hurt her chances at a time that she might be under Supreme Court consideration. This was the spring of 2008, he would observe, and who knew what would transpire with the presidential election or future Court vacancies.[3]

Then age sixty-seven, Cabranes was no longer a rival to Sotomayor in the Supreme Court sweepstakes. He was probably too old to be considered for elevation after the election. Age might have contributed to their dueling views on government-imposed racial remedies, too. Cabranes rose to prominence in the legal profession before affirmative action was common, and he was often the lone Latino in places of power and prestige. For Sotomayor, fourteen years made a huge difference, allowing her to ascend with a class of, as she would say, "affirmative action babies."

Since her days at Princeton, Sotomayor had lived with the dilemmas and resentment raised by the *Ricci* case. She had climbed the ladder of the law not just because she was smart and worked hard but because people in positions of power (including Manhattan district attorney Robert Morgenthau and U.S. senator Daniel Patrick Moynihan) sought to hire and promote blacks and Hispanics. Sotomayor understood that she was sometimes chosen over white candidates because of her ethnicity, but she objected to contentions that she was not as qualified or as competent because of the boosts she received. She believed she was chosen because she had vaulted herself over academic and professional hurdles that most people, regardless of their color or ethnicity, could not.

Many Americans disagreed with her on the larger issues. They viewed the antibias initiatives begun in the 1960s as discrimination against whites rather than as important ways to help qualified minorities. The white firefighters in New Haven said that the city's decision to toss the test results perpetuated the very practice of racial discrimination it was seeking to eradicate.

For decades, cities like New Haven had struggled with the legacy of race discrimination in municipal fire and police departments. The question was to what extent municipalities could act to ensure new diversity. For the judges who reviewed New Haven's actions, the answers came down to the racial disparity of the test results and the city's real reasons for throwing them out.

The dilemma involved two parts of Title VII of the 1964 Civil Rights Act. One section, aimed at intentional discrimination, forbade employers from hiring or promoting someone based on race or sex, which is known in the law as "disparate treatment." Another section banned employers from using a test or other practice that caused a "disparate impact" on the basis of race or sex unless the practice was related to the job. These dual mandates put the city of New Haven in a difficult position. The white firefighters sued under the first part, saying they were being denied score-based promotions because of race. Black firefighters had threatened to sue under the second part of Title VII, based on the disproportionately poor scores and their diminished chance for promotions.

Allowing Title VII challenges to the discriminatory *effects* in hiring, as opposed to those aimed at discriminatory *intention*, flowed from the federal understanding that employer practices may appear neutral but actually arise from hidden bias. Under past Supreme Court cases, a key question in the analysis was whether a screening test was actually necessary for legitimate, nondiscriminatory business reasons. If not, such a test might derive from structural racism and an implicit desire to keep minorities out of management positions.

A Title VII claim based on a statistical imbalance did not require a showing of discriminatory intent for a plaintiff to prevail. The lower threshold for such lawsuits troubled conservative judges who believed that America had moved beyond its racist past and should focus on remedying only specific instances of bias.[4] Opposition to such group remedies had been simmering for several years on the High Court. In 2007, Chief Justice John Roberts had revealed little patience for public school assignment plans that considered students' race to ensure district-wide diversity: "The way to stop

discrimination on the basis of race," he wrote, "is to stop discriminating on the basis of race."[5]

But such a color-blind approach was not so easily carried out in
municipal fire stations, including in New Haven, where even in the
2000s blacks and Hispanics were rare in the fire department's
command positions although they comprised about 60 percent of
the population. There was considerable debate over how well pen-
and-paper tests even measured leadership in firefighting. Perhaps,
some suggested, simulations that tested applicants' judgment under
pressure were better. Eventually it would fall to Supreme Court justice Ruth Bader Ginsburg, not Sotomayor or the other Second Circuit judges who had considered the case, to declare, "Relying heavily
on written tests to select fire officers is a questionable practice, to
say the least."[6]

When the tests were given in New Haven, 118 applicants took
the written and oral exams in hopes of being promoted to captain or
lieutenant. Of the 41 firefighters applying for captain, 25 were white,
8 were black, and 8 were Hispanic. In the end, no blacks and 2
Hispanics scored high enough to be eligible for promotion. Of the
77 firefighters who sought promotion to the rank of lieutenant, 43
were white, 19 were black, and 15 were Hispanic. For this rank, no
blacks or Hispanics scored high enough to be considered.[7] The city's
lawyer told the board that the scope of the statistical disparity could
lead to a claim of racial discrimination. A representative from the
black firefighters association argued against certification, as did a
vocal African American minister who was an important vote-getter
for Mayor John DeStefano. The New Haven Civil Service Board
deadlocked on certification, which prevented the results from being
used to determine promotions.

Frank Ricci, who is white, took the lead in suing DeStefano
and other New Haven officials over that 2004 decision against certification. Ricci said he had studied up to thirteen hours a day to
prepare for the lieutenant test. Because he was dyslexic, he had paid
an acquaintance more than a thousand dollars to read the books
onto tapes. He said he studied harder than he ever had. "Reading,

making flash cards, highlighting and reading again all while listening to prepared tapes," he recalled of his study habits. "I went before numerous panels to prepare for the oral assessment. I was a virtual absentee father and husband for months because of it." Another firefighter, Benjamin Vargas, the only Hispanic in the group of challengers, said he gave up a part-time job while he prepared for the exams and that his wife took a leave of absence from her job to care for their three children while he studied.[8]

At their first stop in federal court, the firefighters' claims failed. U.S. district court judge Janet Bond Arterton ruled that the city acted properly by discarding the test results. Judge Arterton said that officials justifiably worried that an insufficient number of minorities would be promoted if the test results were certified, exposing the city to a disparate-impact lawsuit. She rejected the white firefighters' arguments that the city required more proof that it faced a possible lawsuit based on flaws in the exams. Arterton, a 1995 appointee of President Bill Clinton's, concluded that officials need not pinpoint deficiencies or offer a better test if they decide against certification.[9]

◆

By the time the firefighters appealed Arterton's ruling, Sotomayor had been a member of the Second Circuit for nearly a decade. Much had changed in her life. When she was sworn in to the New York–based federal appeals court, she was engaged and looking forward to marrying New York construction contractor Peter White, whom she had been seriously dating for four years. Before an investiture audience of a thousand people at the federal courthouse on Pearl Street in Manhattan, Sotomayor had spoken tenderly about how White had kept her spirits up as the appeals court nomination dragged on for months. But their romance ended soon after she took her spot on the appeals court in late 1998. "Not every relationship ends with such mutual respect and dignity as Kevin and I somehow salvaged from our youthful mistakes," she would later write, referring to her 1983 divorce from Kevin Noonan. "I would discover what it is to go down in flames romantically, disappointment that shakes your foundations."[10] After her relationship with White ended, Sotomayor settled alone into her Greenwich Village condo and found comfort in her vast networks of friends.

One of those friends was Rosemary Pooler, who would preside when the three judges heard the *Ricci* case.

Sixteen years older than Sotomayor, Pooler was a veteran of Syracuse city and New York state politics. She had served on the Syracuse common council, held a state consumer-protection post, and run unsuccessfully for Congress in the late 1980s. She had strong political instincts and a protective fondness for Sotomayor, whom she called "Toots." The two women often dined out after sitting together on court panels. When Sotomayor made the four-hour trip up to Syracuse to see her brother, Juan, and his family, she made a point of visiting Pooler, who lived there, too.

The third judge on the Ricci court, Robert Sack, had been in private practice, specializing in press law, before his 1998 appointment. He had first come into the orbit of the Clintons in 1974 when he worked with Hillary on the U.S. House of Representatives special impeachment inquiry related to President Richard Nixon and the Watergate scandal. On the day of the *Ricci* oral arguments, in December 2007, Sack was out ill. He caught up with the written briefs and a tape of the hearing.

For the oral arguments in the Manhattan courtroom, the firefighters wore their dress uniforms. Karen Torre added to the drama by lugging in stacks of textbooks the firefighters had used to study for the promotional exams.

As soon as Judge Pooler opened the session, Sotomayor launched into her trademark hard-hitting approach. Since her days at Yale, she had heard criticism that she was overbearing. But the former student debater offered no apologies. This was simply the way she was. During oral argument she often talked over her fellow judges and interrupted lawyers as they tried to answer her barrage of questions.

In *Ricci v. DeStefano*, she did not wait for lawyers to answer her initial questions before she fired off additional queries. And, as was her practice, she referred to herself as she asked a question: *"My* problem with your . . . cause of action is . . . ," she said as she aimed one line of inquiry at Torre. When Sotomayor felt she had not gotten an answer, she would say, "You beg my question."[11]

Yet her queries cut to the core issues in the case. "Can a state ever look at its practices to ensure there's no adverse impact?" she asked Torre, who insisted that any review based on race was forbidden and that, by doing so, the city had treated men seeking promotions as "garbage collectors" whose jobs did not require special skills.

"This is a command position of a first responder agency," Torre said. "The books you see piled on my desk are fire-science books. These men face life-threatening circumstances every time they go out . . . This is a high-level command position in a post-9/11 era no less. They are tested for their knowledge of fire behavior, combustion principles, building collapse, truss roofs, building construction, confined space rescue, dirty bomb response, anthrax, metallurgy . . ."

Sotomayor bristled. "We're not suggesting that unqualified people be hired. The city's not suggesting that. All right?" Moving past her impatience with what she believed was exaggerated rhetoric on Torre's part, Sotomayor said, "But if your test is always going to put a certain group at the bottom of the pass rate so they're never, ever going to be promoted, and there is a fair test that could be devised that measures knowledge in a more substantive way, then why shouldn't the city have an opportunity to try and look and see if it can develop that?"

Torre said that the city had, in fact, developed a fair test, verified by the outside consulting company. Sotomayor was not sympathetic. "It assumes the answer is . . . the test is valid because we say it's valid."

When Richard Roberts, the lawyer for New Haven's city officials, took his turn at the podium, Sotomayor was equally confrontational: "You haven't told *me* . . . ," she said. She also homed in on a key issue—the validity of the test—telling Roberts, "If you're going

to say it's unfair, point to specifics, of ways it wasn't, and make sure
that there really are alternatives."

Pooler said later that Sotomayor's style of questioning never
bothered her. "When I sat with her, I always found it worthwhile to
hear her questions. I always thought that she made such a valuable
contribution. She is what she is."[12]

◆

In the weeks that followed the *Ricci* hearing, Sotomayor, Pooler,
and Sack could not agree on how to resolve the thorny case. Sotomayor agreed with district court judge Arterton that the varying
pass rates among racial and ethnic groups posed a problem. She
also thought the city had a good argument that it was following
what the law required. Judge Sack was more ambivalent about Arterton's approach and resisted signing on to an opinion affirming her
rationale.

A substantive compromise eluded them, and it would not have
fallen to Sotomayor to broker a deal. This was an area of the law she
knew well, certainly. And she had strong views on racial and ethnic
policy. But she had generally kept them quiet. And in terms of persuasive force, some judicial colleagues said later that although Sotomayor was clear in making her own opinions known, she was not apt
to influence colleagues whose legal views differed from hers.

The Second Circuit judges would not disclose all that went on
behind the scenes. Speaking generally, Pooler described Sotomayor
as a judge who steeped herself in the facts and the law of a case.
She said she could sometimes hold tight to her position, wondering
of colleagues, "Why can't you see it?" Yet in these years as an appeals
court judge, Sotomayor was cautious and not known for heated dis-
sents or splitting off from her colleagues.

At the time of the *Ricci* case, Sotomayor had already written
hundreds of opinions, most falling into the run-of-the-mill center of
federal court rulings: solidly written and hewing to precedent. She
leaned to the left but not reflexively so. The Supreme Court reversed
few of her opinions. In general assessments of her work, the Ameri-

can Bar Association and the Congressional Research Service would characterize her opinions as well reasoned and well organized.[13] The American Bar Association screening committee in 2009 said that some of its members criticized her opinions as "less than imaginative, lacking in flourishes, and lengthy," adding, "these criticisms are about writing style, not substance."[14]

Sotomayor had shown similar competence as a U.S. district court judge. During the seven years she spent overseeing trials in Manhattan, her most high-profile action came in a labor dispute in the nation's long-running Major League Baseball strike of 1994 and 1995. Sotomayor ruled in favor of the players by granting a National Labor Relations Board request for an injunction temporarily restoring the terms of an expired collective bargaining agreement. In her order ending the 232-day strike, she required team owners to reinstate lapsed provisions of their earlier contract, including salary arbitration and competitive bidding. The order gave the two sides an incentive to return to negotiations, which eventually produced a deal.[15] Baseball fans across the United States and in Canada cheered her. *The Globe and Mail* newspaper wrote that Sotomayor "moved into the early lead for an MVP award" and the New York *Daily News* said, "The judge who ordered baseball to clean up its act knows her game."[16]

Sotomayor's opinions typically included a long recitation of the facts, a listing of all arguments, and a lengthy explanation of the applicable law. But that was not going to happen in the firefighters' dispute. After several weeks and insufficient unity to issue an opinion on the law, Judges Pooler and Sotomayor thought the best course was a brief summary order affirming the lower court judge but not establishing any Second Circuit precedent for future cases. Judge Sack eventually went along. It was a big case, but the only way they could resolve it was by acting as if it was small and sidestepping a precedent-setting opinion.

All told, it might have been a missed opportunity for Sotomayor, who understood practices that had long kept blacks and Hispanics at lower ranks. She could have elucidated the societal justifications for policies intended to help minorities. She used to speak candidly about how she had fared on tests that she felt were biased.

In a 1994 appearance at a legal conference in New York, Sotomayor said of her admissions to Princeton University and Yale Law School: "If we had gone through the traditional numbers route of those institutions, it would have been highly questionable whether I would have been accepted." Sotomayor, a relatively new trial judge at the time, explained to women at a Practicing Law Institute session, "With my academic achievement in high school, I was accepted rather readily at Princeton and equally as fast at Yale. But my test scores were not comparable to that of my classmates." Offering her theory on the statistical gap with her classmates, she said, "There are cultural biases built into testing. And that was one of the motivations for the concept of affirmative action, to try to balance out those effects."[17]

But she would not speak about such issues when deciding the *Ricci* case. Maybe it was fruitless when the three judges could not agree on a legal justification for the New Haven officials' action. And why go out on a limb? That was not her way on the law. And she knew the political pitfalls of appearing to be an activist on the bench. Three years earlier, in an appearance at Duke University, she had backtracked after blurting out, "The court of appeals is where policy is made." She caught herself and said, "I know this is on tape and I should never say that, because we don't make law, I know. Okay. I know. I'm not promoting it, I'm not advocating it."[18]

In the *Ricci* case, a simple affirmation of the district court order would suffice—and avoid the political hazards of a new opinion. The relevant part of the panel's February 15, 2008, decision said:

> We affirm, substantially for the reasons stated in the thorough, thoughtful, and well-reasoned opinion of the court below. In this case, the Civil Service Board found itself in the unfortunate position of having no good alternatives. We are not unsympathetic of the plaintiffs' expression of frus-

tration. Mr. Ricci, for example, who is dyslexic, made intensive efforts that appear to have resulted in his scoring highly on one of the exams, only to have it invalidated. But it simply does not follow that he has a viable Title VII claim. To the contrary, because the Board, in refusing to validate the exams, was simply trying to fulfill its obligations under Title VII when confronted with test results that had a disproportionate racial impact, its actions were protected.[19]

Judge Cabranes was surprised at the abrupt handling of the case. After he read the newspaper account, he fired off a memo to the three judges telling them he had seen the front-page story in the *New Haven Register,* reporting on *Ricci v. DeStefano.* He had logged on to the court website and read the summary order, which struck him as fairly opaque. He speculated that readers could even think that the suit challenged discrimination against those suffering from dyslexia. Cabranes asked Pooler, Sack, and Sotomayor to reconsider their terse order and issue a fuller opinion explaining the case.

Pooler responded that they would not change the order. Cabranes countered by saying he would ask the Second Circuit clerk to place a hold on the issuance of the mandate in the case. That was the prerogative of any individual judge.[20] He subsequently checked the nearly two-thousand-page record in the case and proposed that the full circuit hear the firefighters' appeal of the district judge's ruling.

The full Second Circuit put the possibility of a rehearing to a vote, and Cabranes lost 7–6. The split was made public in mid-June 2008, when a series of opinions were filed. Sotomayor, Pooler, and Sack opposed reopening the case, and they were joined by Judges Guido Calabresi, Chester Straub, Robert Katzmann, and Barrington Parker. With Cabranes were Chief Judge Dennis Jacobs and Judges Reena Raggi, Richard Wesley, Peter Hall, and Debra Ann Livingston. It was a bitter ideological split. All the judges who voted for rehearing—with the exception of Cabranes—were appointed by Republican presidents. All the judges who opposed a rehearing were selected by Democratic presidents. Parker, although appointed by President George W. Bush to the Second Circuit, had originally been a choice of President Bill Clinton for a trial court position.

In seeking a new hearing, Cabranes pointed a finger at the Sotomayor panel for failing to consider circuit court precedent and Supreme Court rules for race-based decision making. He said it was "arguable that the deck was stacked" against the high-scoring white applicants. "Whether such action amounts to an impermissible racial quota was not addressed in the district court's opinion or in the decisions issued by the panel," he wrote. "What is not arguable, however, is the fact that this Court has failed to grapple with the questions of exceptional importance raised in this appeal. If the *Ricci* plaintiffs are to obtain such an opinion from a reviewing court, they must now look to the Supreme Court. Their claims are worthy of that review."

Judges Calabresi and Katzmann denounced Cabranes's view in separate opinions. Katzmann, a Moynihan protégé whom Sotomayor had known since her days on the district court, insisted the majority was right to follow a tradition of deference, "a tradition which holds whether or not the judges of the court agree with the panel's disposition of the matter before it." Chief Judge Jacobs, who had aligned with Cabranes, countered, "To rely on tradition to deny rehearing . . . starts to look very much like abuse of judicial discretion."[21]

The vote and resulting opinions caught Torre, the firefighters' lawyer who had already submitted a petition to the Supreme Court, off guard. She immediately sought advice from lawyers sympathetic to the firefighters' cause, including those in the conservative Federalist Society network. She then revised her appeal to take advantage of Cabranes's favorable view of her position. Torre also began working with Gregory Coleman, a former law clerk to Justice Clarence Thomas, who had served a stint as Texas solicitor general and then in private practice litigated against government racial policies. In the spring of 2008 Coleman was already preparing arguments for the Supreme Court, challenging a key part of the Voting Rights Act of 1965. Section 5, as it was called, required certain states with a history of racial bias, mainly in the South, to seek federal approval for any change in electoral policies.[22]

The Supreme Court granted the firefighters' revised petition, and by the time the justices heard oral arguments on April 22, 2009, Barack Obama had been elected president and had been in office for three months.

It had also become evident by now that the conservative Supreme Court majority was interested in using the *Ricci* case to curtail bias lawsuits tied to statistical disparities. In a series of earlier actions, Chief Justice Roberts and Justice Alito, the successor to Sandra Day O'Connor, had signaled their suspicion of policies intended to benefit minorities as a group. Critics beyond the Court pointed to Obama's presidential victory as a sign that America had closed its ugly chapter on race discrimination and it was time to abandon the remedies that had been needed in the past.

The Obama administration tried to chart a narrow course in its legal response to *Ricci v. DeStefano*. Administration lawyers contended that New Haven had acted lawfully in discarding the test results. But the administration also argued that the case should be returned to the lower courts because neither district court judge Arterton nor the Sotomayor appeals panel had "adequately considered" whether the city's justification for the action—fear of lawsuits— had been a pretext for the intentional race discrimination the white firefighters claimed.[23] Critics of New Haven's actions, including Justice Alito, would later emphasize that not even the Obama administration endorsed the Second Circuit resolution devised by Judges Sotomayor, Pooler, and Sack.

When the case was heard at the Supreme Court, lawyer Gregory Coleman was up first. He had taken over the firefighters' advocacy from Torre. "Racial classifications are inherently pernicious," Coleman began, "and, if not checked, lead as they did in New Haven to regrettable and socially destructive racial politics."[24] Justice

David Souter, at the time just days from revealing the retirement that would open the door to Sotomayor, asked whether New Haven was in a "damned if you do, damned if you don't situation." Souter was suggesting that New Haven faced two fraught and complicated paths regarding the test results: one that would allow it to avoid potential litigation from a "disparate-impact" claim by minority fire-fighters and another that would head off a discriminatory intent lawsuit from the white firefighters. Coleman disagreed with Souter's assertion and said that the city, instead of acting in good faith, had simply decided that the exam came "to the wrong racial result" and concluded that "there must be something wrong with the test."

When Deputy U.S. Solicitor General Edwin Kneedler, repre-senting the Obama administration, stepped to the lectern, Chief Justice Roberts questioned whether the administration was being hypocritical: "Can you assure me that the government's position would be the same if . . . black applicants scored highest on this test in disproportionate numbers, and the city said we don't like that result . . . The government of [the] United States would adopt the same position?" Kneedler said the government would have taken the same position if whites had been hurt by the test in the way Roberts described. But Kneedler also wanted to make it clear that the ad-ministration was not fully backing the Second Circuit. He stressed that neither the district court nor the appellate panel had adequately considered whether New Haven's claimed purpose of avoiding a lawsuit from minority firefighters was valid.

Christopher Meade, who argued on behalf of New Haven, de-fended the Second Circuit's handling of the case. He told the jus-tices that employers who wanted to follow Title VII's goal of rooting out barriers to opportunity were required to scrutinize practices that hurt blacks and Hispanics. He said New Haven acted appropriately when it threw out the test results because the disparate scores would have allowed black challengers to "substantiate an inference of discrimination." Meade said that employers should be able to take action when they become aware of such flaws in a test.[25]

The ruling in the case came on the last day of the Court's

2008–09 term, and it appeared hard fought. A narrow majority rejected the city's position and sided with the white firefighters. In the 5–4 opinion of June 29, 2009, Justice Kennedy wrote that an employer must have "a strong basis in evidence" that, had it not taken the action, it would have been liable under Title VII. Kennedy, who had become the crucial vote in the middle on race-related cases after the departure of Justice O'Connor, was joined by Roberts, Scalia, Thomas, and Alito.

Kennedy wrote that New Haven had *no* evidence—let alone the required "strong basis in evidence"—that the tests were flawed because they were not job-related. The majority said that the fear of litigation failed to justify New Haven's actions, and in the end, the city had intentionally discriminated against the men.[26]

Justice Alito, an Italian American whose modest roots in Trenton were not unlike those of the firefighters in New Haven, wrote a sympathetic concurring opinion. Joined by Justices Scalia and Thomas, Alito reviewed the longtime connections between Mayor DeStefano and a prominent African American minister as he insisted that a jury could have found that the city's real reason for scrapping the test results was not fear of litigation, but to please an influential political constituency.

As Justice Ginsburg took the lead for the dissenting liberals, she opened her opinion by recalling the history of discrimination in fire departments. She noted that in 1972, when Congress extended Title VII of the Civil Rights Act of 1964 to cover public employment, fire departments across the country pervasively discriminated against minorities. "The extension of Title VII to cover jobs in firefighting effected no overnight change," she wrote. "It took decades of persistent effort, advanced by Title VII litigation, to open firefighting posts to members of racial minorities . . . Firefighting is a profession in which the legacy of racial discrimination casts an especially long shadow."

Ginsburg said that the majority's approach in *Ricci* would undercut voluntary efforts by local governments to comply with Title VII. When the law became effective in 1965, she wrote, employers

responded by eliminating practices that explicitly barred racial minorities from the workplace. "But removing overtly race-based job
classifications did not usher in genuinely equal opportunity," she said.
"More subtle—and sometimes unconscious—forms of discrimination replaced undisguised restrictions." That is why the Supreme
Court had interpreted Title VII to allow remedies tied to statistical
imbalances to counter such less obvious discrimination.

Judge Sotomayor's critics, including some Republican senators,
would use the *Ricci* case during her Supreme Court nomination
hearings to question whether she was a fair judge. They would not so
much target the kinds of issues the nine justices thrashed out but
rather the minimal decision her panel issued. She would defend
her part in the dispute by saying that she decided it on "the basis of
the very thorough 78-page decision by the district court and on the
basis of established precedent." As far as Sotomayor was concerned,
the city faced possible lawsuits over a test "that everybody agreed
had a very wide difference between the pass-rate of a variety of different groups."[27] She believed the city had taken the necessary steps,
with hearings and witnesses, to assess the situation. She said the
only question before her Second Circuit panel was: Did the city do
what it was required to do?

To her, the answer was yes. But she passed up all opportunities
as the case was resolved, and then at her hearings, to explain why
disparate statistical results in a Civil Service text could expose hidden bias. A vigorous defense of the Title VII approach might have
illuminated the dilemma at the New Haven Fire Department. Sotomayor wanted to minimize her role in the case, repeatedly telling
senators that the district court judge's opinion was seventy-eight
pages long and substantively comprehensive. As for what happened
after her panel summarily endorsed that opinion and the full Second Circuit weighed whether to rehear the case, she stressed the
company she was in: "Judge Cabranes had one view of the case. The
panel had another. The majority of the vote—it wasn't just my
vote—the majority of the court, not just my vote, denied the [Ca-
branes] petition" for a hearing by the full court.[28]

White House lawyers were watching as the *Ricci* case played out. They said later that they were not so concerned that the Roberts Court had reversed the Sotomayor panel. That was predictable, given the five-justice majority's views of racial policies. "The reversal was less important to us than the question of whether she had done an adequate job on the Second Circuit in writing the opinion," said White House counsel Gregory Craig. Did she take it seriously, they wanted to know, or simply engage in a politically expedient move? "Did she phone it in?" asked Craig.[29]

It would be just one of the questions White House lawyers would raise and balance along with everything else when the time came to decide who would get the first Supreme Court nomination of President Obama's tenure.

Firefighter Ricci would have his own moment in the national spotlight when he testified in 2009 at her confirmation hearing. Wearing a crisp blue dress uniform as he appeared before the senators, he said the disputed tests were critical to public safety: "When your house is on fire or your life is in jeopardy, there are no do-overs."

In the end, Ricci lamented that "the more attention our case got, the more some people tried to distort it."[30]

NINE

The President's Choice

A few weeks after Barack Obama's November 2008 presidential election, he huddled with legal advisers in his Chicago transition office to thrash out priorities. The Supreme Court came up almost immediately. Obama believed he would have at least two opportunities to make nominations. Justices David Souter and John Paul Stevens—two Republican appointees who had moved to the liberal camp over time—appeared likely to step down during the next four years.

Obama knew that his lawyers were gathering names of potential nominees for all levels of the federal bench, but the president-elect wanted to make sure three names were definitely on the Supreme Court list: Diane Wood, a judge on the U.S. Court of Appeals for the Seventh Circuit and an Obama teaching colleague from the University of Chicago; Cass Sunstein, a former professor at the University of Chicago who had just taken a position at Harvard Law School; and Elena Kagan, another former University of Chicago professor, who had become dean of the Harvard Law School. As Obama mused about other possibilities, he mentioned Sonia Sotomayor. "Clearly, she has to be in the mix," Obama said, according to Gregory Craig, who became the White House counsel.[1] Obama understood the potential historic and political benefits of naming the first Hispanic justice to the Supreme Court.

As a former law professor at the University of Chicago who had written about the "high wire" thrill of teaching students the Constitution, Obama also understood the sheer magnitude of a Court appointment. In his 2006 book *The Audacity of Hope*, he extolled the individual liberties enshrined in the Constitution and said, "We would be hard pressed to find a conservative or liberal in America today, whether Republican or Democrat, academic or layman" who did not embrace the constitutional values espoused by the High Court.[2] Yet he knew that appointments to the bench were polarizing affairs, where the past was prelude. Obama observed that "each side has claimed incremental advances . . . and setbacks." In the latter category, he noted that conservatives lamented the leftward drift of David Souter, an appointee of President George H. W. Bush.[3]

◆

Two decades earlier, the reserved, bookish Souter had come to the White House's attention through his connections with Republican U.S. senator Warren Rudman and White House chief of staff John Sununu, natives of New Hampshire who had previously worked with him. Souter had been state attorney general and a state court justice. In early 1990 Bush named him to the Boston-based U.S. Court of Appeals for the First Circuit and then tapped him in August 1990 to succeed the retiring Supreme Court justice William Brennan. Sununu promised Republicans that the relatively obscure Souter would be a "home run for conservatives," but this prediction could not have been more wrong. Souter ended up being one of the liberal members of the Court during the late 1990s and the 2000s, which prompted a "no more Souters" mantra among conservatives.

And almost immediately after the 2008 election, Souter was ready to give the new Democratic president an opportunity for a Supreme Court appointment.

Souter loved the law but had disliked Washington, D.C., from the start. Soon after moving to the nation's capital in the autumn of 1990, the fifty-one-year-old bachelor known for his ascetic life made it clear that he did not want to mix with the town's elite. He turned down the many invitations for social occasions that came his way and preferred to eat a lunch of apple and yogurt alone at his desk. He longed for the years when he could read Thoreau and the other classics of literature that enthralled him, rather than face mounds of legal briefs piled on the desk in his chambers, where he liked to keep on few lights and work in semidarkness. When the Supreme Court term recessed each summer, Souter took off in his Volkswagen Jetta for his small family farmhouse in New Hampshire.

As he become a reliable vote for the liberal wing, in 1992 he was critical to the five-justice majority in *Planned Parenthood of South-eastern Pennsylvania v. Casey* that upheld a woman's right to abortion. He joined the left on other social policy issues, opposing the death penalty and supporting affirmative action. Souter, who succeeded the liberal Brennan and became his friend, also dissented in a succession of cases in which the conservative majority curtailed the federal government's authority to enforce civil rights laws against the states. In 2000, when the conservative majority decided the case of *Bush v. Gore*, cutting off the Florida election recounts and giving Texas governor George W. Bush the White House, Souter was devastated. He believed that the decision, reversing Florida state court action, undermined the integrity of the federal judiciary. He thought the Supreme Court should leave it to the Florida state judges to establish uniform standards for problematic ballots rather than halt the recounts and effectively declare Bush the winner over Vice President Al Gore. He felt betrayed by his conservative colleagues in the majority.

Souter told friends he might retire after the 2004 presidential election, no matter who won, but when George W. Bush defeated U.S. senator John Kerry and earned another four-year term, Souter decided to stay. By 2008 it was well known at the Supreme Court that Justice Souter was hanging on for a Democrat to win back the presidency.

In the November 8, 2008, election, Democratic senator Obama of Illinois beat Republican senator John McCain of Arizona to become the first African American to take the White House. Obama overwhelmingly won the black vote—96 percent—yet also won the largest share of white voters of any Democrat in a two-man race since 1976, as well as a wide margin of the Hispanic vote. Hispanics had voted for Obama over McCain by a ratio of more than two to one, 67 percent versus 31 percent, according to an analysis by the Pew Research Center's Hispanic Trends Project. All told, 9 percent of the 2008 electorate was Hispanic.[4]

Obama, the son of a white mother from Kansas and a black father who had grown up in Kenya, prided himself on transcending America's enduring racial divisions. He also understood and appreciated that he could make history in another important way—by putting a Hispanic on the Supreme Court.

When he met with legal advisers in Chicago after his victory, Obama was keenly aware, too, that the Court had only one woman. The nation's first female justice, Sandra Day O'Connor, had retired in January 2006 to care for her husband.[5] Justice Ruth Bader Ginsburg, who had been appointed by President Bill Clinton in 1993, was the sole woman left.

Ginsburg, the former women's rights advocate, made sure the nation knew she was there, even if alone. When President Obama addressed a joint session of Congress for the first time in February 2009, Ginsburg was recovering from pancreatic cancer and chemotherapy treatments, but she dragged herself to the evening event and sat with her brethren. She said she wanted to make sure that people watching the nationally televised address saw that the Supreme Court had at least one woman.[6] Around the same time, Ginsburg also said in the most emphatic terms that she thought the Court needed another woman—that the presence of a single female justice sent a discouraging message about women's roles in society. The "worst part," she remarked, is the image projected to students who visit the Court: "Young people are going to think, 'Can I really aspire to that kind of post?'"[7]

Anyone paying attention to the politics of judicial nominations knew that President Obama would be inclined toward a woman appointee for an opening on the Court and be drawn to the idea of naming the first Hispanic.

Sonia Sotomayor was paying attention.

With sharp political instincts, she was also her own best agent. That quality had been apparent since childhood. She occasionally protested that she was simply going with the flow of national events, but her ambition and drive set her apart. As Sotomayor wrote in her autobiography, once she set herself on the path of a legal career, "I saw no reason to stint on ambition."[8]

In early 2009, Sotomayor, at fifty-four, had not lost the urgency of youth. Soon after Obama took the White House, she invited Carlos Ortiz, the former president of the Hispanic National Bar Association, to her Greenwich Village condominium for breakfast. Ortiz had been at the forefront of Hispanic lawyers' efforts to win Supreme Court representation. She showed him around the apartment that she had redecorated, served hot cocoa and cookies, and then got down to business.[9] She wanted advice on how she could be ready for a Supreme Court opening.

"She happened to volunteer that line about how getting to the Supreme Court is like being struck by lightning, twice," recalled Ortiz. "She was trying to be humble. She said, 'If you have advice, I'm happy to hear what you would say.'" Ortiz said he urged her to think about connections she had, who she could tap in the administration, and any potential obstacles she might need to confront. He said she mentioned her diabetes. "She had been afflicted with this since [childhood] and has been really good about keeping it in check. I told her she shouldn't be as concerned about it." Like others, he had observed that she never hid the condition or let it slow her down. "She just pulls out her kit," Ortiz said, referring to the insulin shots she gave herself. "And boom!"[10]

For nearly twenty years Ortiz had been working with other Hispanic lawyers to try to persuade a president to name the first Hispanic Supreme Court justice. For years, they had been putting up names. Now, in 2009, Sotomayor, with her Ivy League credentials and seventeen-year tenure on the federal courts, looked like an unstoppable contender, at least to Hispanic groups.

◆

Beyond the Hispanic community, well-connected Sotomayor supporters were already speaking on her behalf to people who would
matter. Legal insiders knew that this was important. Groundwork
had to be laid. Other possible contenders on Obama's early list—
notably Wood and Kagan—had surrogates reaching out to administration officials and other opinion shapers in the nation's capital for
early support.

Two colleagues of Sotomayor's from the Second Circuit appeals
court, Judges Guido Calabresi and Barrington Parker, arranged a
visit with White House counsel Gregory Craig a few weeks after
Obama's inauguration. Calabresi had long known Sotomayor, a former student of his at Yale Law School, and Parker was an old pal
from the federal trial court in New York (they shared a Yankees
ticket package).[11] Calabresi said that their mission did not arise from
an effort to promote Sotomayor; they wanted to draw Craig's attention to a range of judicial issues important to them. Still, when the
topic of the Supreme Court came up, he wanted to set Craig straight
on an element of Sotomayor's reputation. "You're going to hear how
she's tough in court and she's aggressive," Craig recalled Calabresi
saying. "But she's a great judge, and she runs an exciting hearing. It's
nothing out of the ordinary."

The former Yale Law School dean, then a fifteen-year veteran
of the Second Circuit, said in a later interview that he wanted
to demonstrate, preemptively if possible, the sexism at the heart
of criticism that Sotomayor was too aggressive during oral arguments. Because of past complaints about her from lawyers, Calabresi said, he had been keeping track of her questions and those
of male judges. If anyone asked, he said, he "was able to give
chapter and verse on how this was entirely sexist." Calabresi found
her tough and demanding but not beyond the norm of what lawyers and other spectators should expect from the bench. "She
isn't rude," he said, "but she goes after you." He believed that Sotomayor was being criticized for behaving as he and other male
judges might.[12]

Summing up the conversation with the Second Circuit judges, Craig said, "They were anticipating what was going to come out of the lawyers from the Second Circuit who were pushed around a bit by her."[13] Even before Souter had announced his retirement, Sotomayor allies were trying to counter such comments as those found in the *Almanac of the Federal Judiciary*, which news reporters and legal analysts often used as a guide: "She abuses lawyers" and "She really lacks judicial temperament."[14] The groundwork laid by Calabresi to counter such statements, along with his willingness later to praise Sotomayor's intellect and abilities in interviews with reporters, would be crucial to her appointment. Judge Parker said that a few weeks after their meeting he received a call from associate counsel Susan Davies, who worked with Greg Craig, mentioning criticism about Sotomayor's intellectual caliber. "I told her, what you've got to remember is that she won the Pyne Prize and she was summa at Princeton."[15] In the early weeks of Obama's new administration, Davies and Cassandra Butts, a deputy to Craig, were troubleshooting potential nominees.

Justice Souter had quietly informed the Obama administration that he would be leaving at the end of the term in late June, and he had asked for advice on the timing of his public announcement. The White House suggested that he wait until June. There were other, more pressing legal dilemmas to address. During the presidential campaign Obama had vowed to close the U.S. naval prison on Guantánamo Bay, where more than two hundred detainees taken into custody from around the world were being held because of suspected links to terrorist activity after the September 11, 2001, attacks. Ending their indefinite detention seemed simple at first. On January 22, 2009, the new commander in chief issued an executive order to close the prison. But each prisoner's case required careful review before he could be released, prosecuted, or transferred to a foreign nation. Further complicating matters, foreign countries were reluctant to take back their nationals who had been linked even indirectly to terrorism.

President Obama also faced scores of vacancies on the lower

federal courts, and the administration was running into trouble with Senate Republicans over nominees. Obama's ideological opponents had laid groundwork early. Former Reagan administration attorney general Edwin Meese and other outspoken conservatives wrote a letter to Republican senators in January 2009, two days after the inauguration, predicting that Obama was planning to appoint judges who reflected "the most radical judicial activist philosophy of any president in American history." Meese, an architect of conservatives' thirty-year drive for control of the bench, and other like-minded conservatives kept the pressure on by going to see Senate minority leader Mitch McConnell and Senate Republican whip Jon Kyl. Their message: "President Obama's unprecedented call for judicial activism must be met with an unprecedented level of Senate scrutiny."[16]

That rhetoric did not reflect the reality of Obama's approach to nominations for the bench. He was seeking racial and gender diversity more than a set ideology. Nonetheless, many Senate Republicans were ready to believe the dire predictions of activism. In the president's first major nomination, he chose U.S. district court judge David Hamilton for a seat on the U.S. Court of Appeals for the Seventh Circuit, which covered Illinois, Wisconsin, and Indiana. The administration considered Hamilton a moderate choice and a peace offering to conservatives after years of judicial wars. The nephew of former U.S. House member Lee Hamilton, an Indiana Democrat, he had the support of the state's senior Republican senator, Richard Lugar. Despite his bipartisan bona fides, Judge Hamilton's nomination was stalled in the Senate for most of 2009. Republicans justified their action by citing a 2005 district court decision in which Hamilton barred the Indiana House of Representatives from holding an opening prayer session that mentioned Jesus Christ as the Messiah. Hamilton said such references were "sectarian in the Christian tradition" and violated the Constitution's separation of church and state.[17]

It became clear that if Hamilton—with his moderate record on the bench, connection to Washington, and support of an influential

Republican senator—had confirmation problems, it was likely that Obama's future nominees were going to run into trouble as well. And they did. The only way Obama was able to win Senate action on his nominees to the powerful D.C. Circuit, in fact, was through Senate Democrats' change in filibuster rules in 2013, allowing the nominees to get a straight up-or-down vote.

In the spring of 2009 Justice Souter was content to wait to make his retirement announcement, but his hand was forced during the last week of April. National Public Radio's Nina Totenberg and NBC TV's Pete Williams aired stories on April 30 reporting that the justice was expected to retire. The next day, Souter made it official.

"I just got off the telephone with Justice Souter," President Obama told reporters in the White House press briefing room that Friday, May 1. "And so I would like to say a few words about his decision to retire from the Supreme Court . . . Justice Souter . . . came to the bench with no particular ideology. He never sought to promote a political agenda. And he consistently defied labels and rejected absolutes, focusing instead on just one task—reaching a just result in the case that was before him."

Obama then described the qualities he would seek in Souter's replacement. He said he wanted someone with stellar academic and professional credentials. He also said those credentials needed to be grounded in real-life experience. Specifically, he said, the candidate needed to possess "that quality of empathy, of understanding and identifying with people's hopes and struggles as an essential ingredient for arriving at just decisions and outcomes."[18] Conservative critics of Obama seized on his aspiration for "empathy," declaring it an invitation to judicial activism—as if empathy could not coexist with impartiality—and later made it a subtext of their confirmation complaints.

After Souter's formal announcement, people who had been quietly making moves behind the scenes on behalf of possible nominees shifted into high gear. They wrote to President Obama. They lobbied top aides. They connected with news commentators and other opinion shapers. In an earlier era, there was value in a surprise nominee, but by the 2000s it seemed that the best strategy was an air of inevitability for a candidate in the media and the corridors of power.

The administration's lawyers had already started talking to potential nominees, even though they thought they would have more time before Souter's retirement was announced. White House counsel Craig, along with Davies and Butts, had begun to reach out to candidates, including Sotomayor, with questions, and they wanted these individuals to start filling out paperwork about their records and finances. Sotomayor said she first heard from Craig on April 27.[19] Four days later, when Justice Souter announced he would be retiring, the calls from the White House team increased.

Meanwhile, Obama's legal and political advisers pored over candidate files they had gathered independently. The political team was anchored by Rahm Emanuel, Obama's chief of staff, who had been a policy adviser to President Clinton and served in the U.S. House of Representatives, and David Axelrod, a longtime adviser to Obama. Vice President Joseph Biden, who had experience as a Senate Judiciary Committee chairman, also played a central role in the discussions. Biden brought in two top aides who had worked on the Senate Judiciary Committee and been with him for years: Ronald Klain, his chief of staff, whose Supreme Court nomination experience dated back to the Robert Bork nomination in 1987, and Cynthia Hogan, his chief legal counsel, who had worked for Biden since 1991.

Top lawyers and political advisers scrutinized Sotomayor as well as Judge Wood in Chicago and Elena Kagan, who that spring had been confirmed as U.S. solicitor general, overseeing the government's appeals to the Supreme Court. Other names were added to the short list, including Department of Homeland Security secretary Janet Napolitano and former Michigan governor Jennifer Granholm. Judge Merrick Garland of the U.S. Court of Appeals for the D.C. Circuit was considered, but then his name was set aside as the process went along. Administration insiders wanted a woman nominee, and they also thought that Garland, who had won strong bipartisan support when he was confirmed to the appeals court in 1997, could serve as a compromise choice later if another vacancy opened in an election year and if the Senate at the time was controlled by Republicans.

In the early weeks of the search, advisers said, Obama leaned toward Judge Wood, who had served on the Seventh Circuit since 1995. She had been a law clerk to Supreme Court justice Harry Blackmun and then worked as an attorney at Covington & Burling, where she focused on antitrust and commercial litigation. She also taught courses at the University of Chicago Law School and wrote law review articles. Wood was a deep thinker who could offer an intellectual counterpoint to the Supreme Court's conservatives. In an expansive 2004 address at New York University, she argued that "our eighteenth-century Constitution, while a bit cryptic at the edges, is nonetheless a real treasure. Approached the right way, there is every reason to be confident that the dynamic process that has sustained it will continue to do so through the years, decades, and even centuries to come."[20] Such a view clashed with that of the reigning cónservative luminary, Justice Antonin Scalia, who believed the Constitution and its amendments should be interpreted in the context of when they were written.

Kagan, a former Harvard Law School dean, had the scholarly academic credentials, too. She was also a power player, having served in the Clinton White House as an associate counsel and policy adviser. At Harvard, she earned a reputation for easing tensions among faculty and bringing in more conservatives. She had no record as a jurist, so observers were not sure whether she had the liberal vigor of Wood. As a new U.S. solicitor general in the spring of 2009, Kagan had yet to argue a case before the Court. Then age forty-nine, she was also the youngest of the three leading candidates.

Sotomayor lacked the scholarly reputation of Kagan and Wood, but she had graduated from two of the most intellectually rigorous schools in the country. Sotomayor had a long, relatively uncontroversial judicial record; the *Ricci* decision stood out. She had served seven years as a trial judge and eleven years as an appellate judge. She did not have the direct personal link to the president that Wood and Kagan had, but she had other connections that proved helpful—her Second Circuit judicial colleagues, Manhattan district attorney Robert Morgenthau, and advocacy groups that had long been pushing for the first Hispanic justice. The Hispanic Congressional Caucus, chaired by Democratic U.S. representative Nydia Velázquez, was persuading African Americans in Congress to throw their support behind Sotomayor. Velázquez, a Puerto Rican who grew up in the Bronx, lobbied for the promise that if a black candidate did not make Obama's short list, the Congressional Black Caucus would back Sotomayor.

For Obama, ethnicity cut both ways. He understood the value of diversity, but as the man who had not asserted his own racial identity in his campaign, he did not want to be seen as choosing someone simply because of her color and ethnic heritage. He wanted someone he could say had a superior intellect and judicial demeanor. Almost immediately, critics of Sotomayor were raising doubts.

Three days after Justice Souter's retirement announcement on May 1, Harvard law professor Laurence Tribe, for whom Obama was a research assistant at Harvard, wrote to the president, recommending Kagan and criticizing Sotomayor. A leading constitutional scholar with a national following, particularly in liberal circles, Tribe first urged the president to use the Souter vacancy as an "opportunity to lay the groundwork for a series of appointments that will gradually move the Court in a pragmatically progressive direction." Tribe, the author of several casebooks, then dissected the impact of individual justices, saying,

> Neither Steve Breyer nor Ruth Ginsburg has much of a purchase on Tony Kennedy's mind. David Souter did, and it will take a similarly precise intellect, wielded by someone with a similarly deep appreciation of history and a similarly broad command of legal doctrine, to prevent Kennedy from drifting in a direction that is both formalistic and right-leaning on matters of equal protection and personal liberty.

If you were to appoint someone like Sonia Sotomayor, whose personal history and demographic appeal you don't need me to underscore, I am concerned that the impact within the Court would be negative in these respects. Bluntly put, she's not nearly as smart as she seems to think she is, and her reputation for being something of a bully could well make her liberal impulses backfire and simply add to the firepower of the Roberts/Alito/Scalia/Thomas wing of the Court on issues like those involved in the voting rights case argued last week and the Title VII case of the New Haven firefighters argued earlier."[21]

Tribe was referring to two pending challenges to racial policies, *Northwest Austin Municipal Utility District No. 1 v. Holder*, testing a crucial section of the 1965 Voting Rights Act, and *Ricci v. DeStefano*.

Former Harvard Law School dean Kagan was a natural choice, Tribe insisted. He told Obama she offered "a combination of intellectual brilliance and political skill that would make her a ten-strike, if you'll forgive my reference to bowling." The letter continued to sing the praises of Kagan compared with other potential nominees, including Wood, in terms of intellectual persuasiveness on the Court. The private correspondence became public in 2010, when *National Review* conservative commentator Ed Whelan posted a leaked copy online. Tribe responded to questions at the time of that disclosure by saying his reservations were refuted by Sotomayor's performance during her first term. In 2014, after studying her nearly five-year tenure, Tribe elaborated, "Simply put, I was totally wrong in ever doubting how strong a Supreme Court justice Sonia Sotomayor would be, as I had done when contrasting her with Elena Kagan, whose nomination I favored at the time."[22]

Yet Tribe was not alone in raising concerns about Sotomayor in 2009. On that same May 4, Jeffrey Rosen, a George Washington University law professor and regular columnist for *The New Republic*, wrote a piece for the magazine's website entitled "The Case Against Sotomayor." The article included comments from people

Rosen identified as having "worked with her, nearly all of them former law clerks for other judges on the Second Circuit or former federal prosecutors in New York," most of whom were Democrats. According to Rosen, none of the individuals in this group "raved about [Sotomayor]," and "they expressed questions about her temperament, her judicial craftsmanship, and most of all, her ability to provide an intellectual counterweight to the conservative justices, as well as a clear liberal alternative."[23]

Rosen said the most consistent concern "was that Sotomayor, although an able lawyer, was 'not that smart and kind of a bully on the bench,' as one Second Circuit clerk for another judge put it. 'She has an inflated opinion of herself, and is domineering during oral arguments, but her questions aren't penetrating and don't get to the heart of the issue.'" Her legal opinions were equally uninspiring: "Although competent, [Sotomayor's opinions] are viewed by former prosecutors as not especially clean or tight, and sometimes miss the forest for the trees."

Rosen offered a caveat in his public column, saying, "It's possible that the former clerks and former prosecutors I talked to have an incomplete picture of her abilities." But Rosen closed by recommending that President Obama tread carefully: "Sotomayor's detractors aren't motivated by sour grapes or by ideological disagreement— they'd like the most intellectually powerful and politically effective liberal justice possible. And they think that Sotomayor, although personally and professionally impressive, may not meet that demanding standard."

The provocative essay in the influential liberal-leaning magazine drew widespread attention. The public, of course, did not know about the Tribe letter at that point, but inside the White House the tenor of the Rosen criticism reinforced the Harvard law professor's private note.

Publicly, Rosen was excoriated. His article triggered hundreds of comments on the *New Republic*'s website, many of them negative, calling Rosen sexist and racist. Liberal writers, on *Salon* and *The American Prospect*, reacted with similar commentary against Rosen.[24]

His complaints touched a nerve about gender and class differences. Writing on *Salon.com*, Rebecca Traister called Rosen's column "a primer on how we talk about ladies when they are up for big (and traditionally male) jobs like being on the Supreme Court." She said that Rosen offered some "perfectly valid concerns about Sotomayor . . . including that former prosecutors have complaints about the tightness and quality of her opinions and that she may not present a 'clear liberal alternative' to the conservatives on the court. But when good questions about qualifications or politics are mashed together with low-budget aspersions about how brash, bossy and talkative a powerful woman is, it's hard to take them seriously."[25]

Rosen said later that he was not presuming to offer a "definitive" judgment but rather to encourage full consideration of Sotomayor's temperament. White House lawyers were making their own assessments. They were reading through her opinions and speeches, looking particularly at the circumstances of her assertion that a "wise Latina" might be a better judge and at her actions in the *Ricci v. DeStefano* case. They also considered her health, wondering whether her diabetes could limit her ability to serve as an effective justice or lead to a premature retirement.

Obama officials knew the "wise Latina" comment was inflammatory, but they also knew Sotomayor had expressed that view many times without criticism, including in 1994, well before her 1998 confirmation to the court of appeals. If it raised no red flags with detractors then, why should it now? They believed they could say the sentiment was intended mainly to bolster the confidence of Hispanic lawyers. What they did not realize is how much this assertion of Latina wisdom would ultimately win allegiance beyond women and across heritages.

The New Haven firefighters' case was an equally delicate matter—the administration did not entirely support Sotomayor's action there—and the White House was expecting the Roberts Court to reverse the Second Circuit panel's decision by the time the term closed in late June. But in the end, administration lawyers came to

believe that the Supreme Court reversal would be viewed in the public eye as more of a reflection on the conservative Court than on Sotomayor as an individual judge. The rest of her record was routine and generally unremarkable.

Sotomayor demonstrated that she had been keeping her diabetes under control and had avoided the eye and nerve damage that can accompany the disease. Early in her career she had kept her condition quiet, but after a hypoglycemic episode at a party at her house, she became more open about her needs. With that openness came the practice of giving herself a premeal injection right at the dinner table, no matter who was with her.

The White House contacted Sotomayor's physician and did its own research. Administration aides told reporters that "independent experts" had concluded that she could be expected to serve for many years.

Sotomayor did not mind talking about her health, especially given how public she was with her insulin shots. But the administration's probing of other aspects of her personal life, particularly related to former fiancé Peter White, made her bristle. Years later, she would complain about the process. "You know, and I don't mean to be graphic, but one day after I'd been questioned endlessly, for weeks at a time, I was so frustrated by the minutiae of what I was being asked about and said to a friend, 'I think they already know the color of my underwear.'"

She believed that the fact that she was a woman, a single woman, played a role in the queries. "There were private questions I was offended by. I was convinced they were not asking those questions of the male applicants . . . I wondered if they ever asked those questions of the male candidates. But the society has a double standard."[26] Administration lawyers said that at the time, Sotomayor grew angry with their questions, but they defended the queries about past personal relationships, saying the stakes were too high not to pursue all angles and insisting that was the routine for male and female candidates. Supreme Court nominees are also subject to FBI background checks.

By the end of May, President Obama's team had narrowed the finalists down to Sotomayor, Wood, Kagan, and Napolitano. Individual interviews were scheduled with the president. Judge Wood met with Obama on May 19, after which he told aides she was "as good as ever." Much was riding on Sotomayor's May 21 interview, and she prepared extensively. She polled former law clerks for advice, asking them to think of questions she might be asked. She reviewed transcripts of past nominations to anticipate issues that might be on the president's mind. She wanted to leave nothing to chance.

When she arrived at the West Wing, Sotomayor chatted first with White House counsel Craig, who had also gone to Yale Law School but whom she had never met. Before turning to an early career as a corporate lawyer, Craig had been a federal public defender, and they talked about that kind of defense work—which at one point in Sotomayor's life might have seemed the likelier career path.

When it was time for her meeting in the Oval Office, Sotomayor said she felt at ease and ready to represent herself to the utmost. She highlighted her regard for precedent and said she thought the way she challenged litigants on the bench was an effective way to probe a case. She said she could recall only one other interview during which she felt she was able to so effectively represent herself and her legal strengths—and that was with Moynihan, nearly two decades earlier, when the senator was interviewing potential district court candidates.

A graduate of Columbia College and Harvard Law School himself, Obama was also impressed that she had the topflight credentials from Princeton and Yale, from Morgenthau's office, and from her tenure as an appeals court judge on the Second Circuit. But it was her personal intensity and her continued connections to her community that really struck him. The Bronx Latina had not forgotten her roots. Knowing such struggles well, Obama admired how she had traversed worlds defined by race and ethnicity.

He kept her in the Oval Office for an hour—a good sign, because Obama had a reputation for winding up conversations quickly if he felt they were not going anywhere. As they parted, Sotomayor told him that no matter what he decided, he had made her "the happiest person" simply by his consideration of her.[27]

"Wow, she was great," Obama told top aides. Some said later that if the interview had not gone so well, Obama might have chosen Diane Wood. Said Craig, "As far as I was concerned, watching him, it was between her and Diane Wood."

Michelle Obama favored Sotomayor. The First Lady had attended Princeton University as an undergraduate and—almost a decade after Sotomayor—found refuge in the Third World Center. A lawyer, Michelle Obama believed Sotomayor was fully up to the job of a Supreme Court justice.[28]

Vice President Biden interviewed Sotomayor by phone on Sunday, May 24. On Monday, Memorial Day, it all seemed settled. President Obama was ready to elevate Judge Sotomayor. But it took him several hours—nearly the whole day—to call her as he had planned.

Some Obama advisers started to worry that he was having second thoughts. But it was his way to want to reflect on such a momentous choice.

Meanwhile, Sotomayor was waiting. And waiting.

"I had been told all weekend that the president would be making up his mind . . . sometime on Monday, and I had been sitting in my office from eight o'clock that morning waiting for a phone call," Sotomayor said, adding that the phone calls she was getting were from family asking whether they should begin making their way to Washington as preliminarily arranged.[29]

Time kept passing. It got to be 7:00 p.m., and Sotomayor called the White House. As she later recounted, "'Well, you're getting my family to Washington. Have any of you given any thought about how I'm going to get there?' And they stopped and said, 'Oh, I guess we should figure that out, shouldn't we?' Literally, that was the response. What I was told was that the president had gotten distracted with some important other business that was going on at the time, and that he would call me at about 8:00 p.m."

She was advised to get ready for the trip to Washington. So Sotomayor raced home to her apartment in Greenwich Village, pulled
out a suitcase, and began packing.

At 8:10 p.m., her cell phone rang. It was the White House operator. Sotomayor held her cell phone in her right hand. She put her
left hand over her chest to calm her beating heart. "And the president
got on the phone and said to me, 'Judge, I would like to announce
you as my selection to be the next associate justice of the United
States Supreme Court.' And I said to him—I caught my breath and
started to cry and said, 'Thank you, Mr. President.'" The moment
produced a blur of emotions, and she said it took many days, weeks
even, to get a sense of herself back.

At 10:30 a.m. on May 26 she entered with President Obama the
grandeur of the White House's East Room—gold silk drapes with
swag valances, cut-glass chandeliers, and a full-length oil portrait of
George Washington. "After completing this exhaustive process,"
Obama said, "I have decided to nominate an inspiring woman who
I believe will make a great justice." The president highlighted her
compelling personal story: "She's faced down barriers, overcome the
odds, lived out the American dream that brought her parents here
so long ago," he said.[30]

After thanking all the friends and family who had come to
Washington to share her joy, Sotomayor offered a tribute to her
mother: "I stand on the shoulders of countless people, yet there is
one extraordinary person who is my life aspiration. That person is
my mother, Celina Sotomayor. My mother has devoted her life to
my brother and me. And as the president mentioned, she often
worked two jobs to help support us after Dad died. I have often
said that I am all I am because of her, and I am only half the
woman she is."[31]

She made a vow regarding the kind of justice she'd be: "I strive
never to forget the real-world consequences of my decisions on individuals, businesses, and government."

Sotomayor often spoke of the "suspicion" she continued to face
about her qualifications, and that was seen in some responses to

her nomination. Dana Milbank, a liberal-leaning *Washington Post* commentator, wrote, "Some thought Obama would nominate Judge Diane Wood or Solicitor General Elena Kagan—big brains who could serve as a counterweight to the court's conservative philosophers . . . In selecting Sotomayor, Obama opted for biography over brains."[32]

Yet the broader public response was enthusiastic, notably from all corners of the Hispanic community. And it was not simply the expected organized advocacy groups lifting their voices. It was people on the streets, from grocery stores and beauty shops to university campuses and law firms. Writing in *The Washington Post*, reporter Eli Saslow captured the unity: "Sometime soon, Hispanics in the United States will once again subdivide into conservatives and liberals, natives and recent immigrants, Cuban Americans, Puerto Ricans and Mexican Americans . . . But at least for a few hours . . . America's largest ethnic minority seemed largely united in appreciation of a historic benchmark." He wrote that the collective response of the country's 45 million Hispanics was: "Finally. One of us."[33]

Hispanic groups had not previously coalesced around a single Court candidate, yet the tracks they laid in the prior decades influenced politicians who capitalized on the appointment when the time came.

In the end, Sotomayor had been in the right place at the right time for the right president. She had the tickets and the people: Princeton, Yale, Morgenthau, Calabresi. Fortified by the dreams of her mother, her personal smarts, and intense determination, Sotomayor had defied predictions from her youth.

Later on the afternoon of May 26, 2009, as President Obama was walking around the West Wing, tossing a football as he sometimes did to relieve stress, he ran into Ron Klain, Vice President Biden's chief of staff, who had helped vet Sotomayor.

The relief and satisfaction of the choice was on the president's face. Said Obama, "I feel really good about this."[34]

TEN

Standing Out

Before Sonia Sotomayor's appointment, a total of 110 justices had been named to the United States Supreme Court since its 1789 creation. All but 4 of these justices were white men, reflecting the traditional power base of the nation. Beginning with African American Thurgood Marshall in 1967, the groundbreakers navigated the public expectations and internal rituals of a tradition-bound institution.

Veteran civil rights litigator Marshall and women's rights attorney Ruth Bader Ginsburg remained advocates, to an extent, based on their respective identities. Sandra Day O'Connor and Clarence Thomas resisted being defined by their sex and race.[1] The four varied, too, in what they revealed of their personal difficulties traversing the overwhelmingly white male world.

None would be as publicly candid as Sotomayor. The way she presented herself to audiences—intimately, relentlessly—set her apart from all other justices. Commentators would begin calling her "the people's justice." But her style and all the attention did not always suit the other Supreme Court justices and the legal elite in their orbit.

Sotomayor knew that she stood out. She accepted that— embraced it—as part of her individuality and what she had long called her "lifelong commitment to identifying myself as a Puerto Rican Hispanic."[2] In the summer of 2010, two months after she had shaken Supreme Court decorum by dancing salsa at her first end-of-term party, Sotomayor was in Denver, talking to students about the value of diversity and the challenge of being different. She recalled the culture clash she experienced at Princeton University in 1972.

"The point is that I was different," she said. "It took a lot of hard work to make a life there." When a young woman asked Sotomayor whether she ever felt completely comfortable, the justice paused for several seconds. "Do you ever—when you're that different?"[3]

Even now, as a Supreme Court justice, Sotomayor told the students, she asks herself, "Am I really here? Do I really belong?" She looked directly at individual students before her and said, "Even if I'm a little bit different, it's okay. I keep getting knocked down and I just keep getting up."

This was the essence of Sonia Sotomayor's identity. In her fifties, at the pinnacle of the legal profession, she still defined herself as unlike others. Sotomayor made it clear that as she traversed the privileged side of life within the Supreme Court's velvet ropes, the difficulties of her past remained embedded in her psyche. As she intimated in Denver, she always felt as if she were being tested and had to prove herself.

But she turned this sense of siege to her advantage, and she took her tale of striving and success on the road, where it resonated, again, to her advantage.

◆

When she first moved into the Supreme Court building across from the Capitol, she chose a suite on the third floor, where she could have larger quarters for herself and her staff. The other justices occupied the second floor, where tighter spaces dictated that some of a justice's law clerks had to work in offices a few doors down or on another floor. The third-floor configuration, which Justice Ginsburg had initially chosen when she joined the Court sixteen years earlier, offered Sotomayor easy interaction with her law clerks.[4] She drafted opinions on a computer, papers spread out around her on the desk. "I like being able to call out to my law clerks with an idea and . . . popping out of my desk and running in to them and saying how about this, and engaging them with the idea," she said.[5]

Sotomayor did not stint on furnishings. She requested a custom-made oversize wooden desk with inlaid leather that was the talk of the Court's support staff because of its extravagance. She decorated with patterned rugs and upholstered furniture in soft peach and gold hues. The woman who had been intimidated during her interview at Radcliffe by an office that exuded pretentiousness—the fancy couch, the Oriental rug—now sat in surroundings that, in a material way, resembled the luxury she had once feared. Yet some visitors felt it had the welcoming atmosphere of a living room rather than a judicial office.

Sotomayor's novelty as the first Hispanic justice was evident in her chambers, too. The renovated kitchen and break room, shared with her staff, was filled with photographs and souvenirs from events that celebrated her groundbreaking status. There were snapshots of her appearances on the PBS children's show *Sesame Street*. In one episode she settled a dispute between Goldilocks and a bear whose chair she had broken. In another, she explained the idea of "a career" to the Muppet fairy Abby Cadabby, nudging her away from becoming a princess and suggesting that she aspire to be a judge. The hallway leading to Sotomayor's suite of offices was also filled with photographs, including those documenting her September 2009 Major League Baseball moment. Clad in a blue-and-white-striped jersey, she threw out the first pitch for the New York Yankees.

The pace of Sotomayor's chambers was hectic: a constant flow of law clerks and aides, friends, former colleagues, and other people she collected along the way to the nation's highest Court. She seemed to swim best in a sea of good company, and she found many people to be good company. Between appointments, her aides reminded her to monitor her blood sugar level to control the diabetes. They also kept her gym schedule to ensure that she got her exercise. Her telephones—office landlines and the pair of smartphones she carried—rang constantly. She interrupted conversations for another justice, for her mother, for a friend just out of surgery. Between her meetings with visitors and talks with law clerks and other staff, she often did not begin working on the nuts and bolts of cases until late in the day. That meant she frequently toiled late into the evenings.

Her rock remained Theresa Bartenope, who achieved unmatched status in the Sotomayor circle. She had served as an administrative assistant since the 1980s at Pavia & Harcourt and accompanied Sotomayor up through all three steps up the judiciary. Sotomayor deemed Bartenope "the soul and life of my chambers" when she saluted her in 1998 at the appeals court investiture. Bartenope was Sotomayor's "second Mom," and nearly as good at keeping her on track. Since Bartenope's husband and family remained in New York, she took the train down to Washington every week.

As was her way through life, Sotomayor stayed in close contact with friends—from Princeton, Yale, and her early legal career. She performed weddings for her former law clerks, attended theater openings, and tried new restaurants. She picked up new companions as she built a life in Washington, even as she regularly talked about how she missed the eclectic atmosphere of New York City.

When people approached her, at official events or in the grocery store, she shook hands and posed for pictures, exuding a sense of warmth and intimacy.

She dated occasionally. When she visited Puerto Rico early in her Court tenure, Sotomayor told an audience that she did not expect to find real romance anytime soon. "I understand from my girlfriends that I've been put on a most-eligible-bachelorette list," she said. "But right now I pity the man who tries to find a minute in my schedule."[6]

Thinking she would be happier in a relationship, friends sometimes tried to fix her up with men. Sotomayor was unusually candid about having had trouble getting close to people. At one public appearance she revealed that she went through a period in her life when she would ask her nieces and nephews for hugs, just to try to get more comfortable with intimacy.[7]

Sotomayor fell into Washington without adopting its stuffy ways. She was following the first two women justices, O'Connor and

Ginsburg, by a generation, and she eschewed their traditionally fem-
inine style. Sotomayor had mixed feelings about public expectations
regarding fashion and her own sense of herself: "It would take me
most of my life to feel remotely put together, and it's still an effort."[8]
She showed up for a dinner party in a sweater and slacks. She wore
little makeup and let her hair fall free. She still rushed across a
room in a way that would make her appearance-conscious mother
cringe.

Yet such authenticity was part of her attraction. And she acknowledged what few other prominent figures revealed: she sometimes felt awkward and out of place. In her speeches, she talked
about fighting the fear of missteps and failure. "Like yourself. Like
who you are," she advised young people trying to make their way in
the world.

Sotomayor's looks, particularly her bright nail polish and flashy
jewelry, were scrutinized by the news media. Latoya Peterson, a
black feminist commentator, praised her for spurning the "safe or
acceptable" and for revealing that she is "not ashamed of who she
is or where she has come from." Peterson noted that during the confirmation hearings Sotomayor minimized the nail polish and hoop
earrings and that as soon as she was confirmed returned to her
usual choices. "Assimilation requires a very high price and her refusal to do so is an amazing stand for individual truth. There is
nothing inferior about wearing colored nail polish, or wearing an
off-the-rack suit to work, or rocking hoop earrings. Just as many of
us are asked to remove our ethnic and regional markers in exchange
for success (straightening hair, tightening diction, and avoiding items
that call attention to the wearer) Sotomayor's subtle—but persistent—
refusal to fall in line implies much more than a love of candy apple
red polish."[9]

◆

During Sotomayor's first couple of years as a justice, her voice was
heard mainly outside the Court in inspirational speeches personal
to her situation. Even before she began putting her life story into a

book, people lined up to see her, to touch her, to hear her talk about what she had overcome as a Bronx Latina. Her tale of setback and success moved audiences.

When she spoke at an event sponsored by the Juvenile Diabetes Research Foundation, she drew gasps and tears from children—and many adults—as she related how she learned, at age seven, that she had type 1 diabetes. She was drinking so much water she began wetting the bed at night. When a physician tried to tell her that having diabetes was not so bad, she said she thought to herself, "If it isn't so bad, why is my mommy crying?"[10]

She maintained tight bonds with her Hispanic community. On the May 25, 2009, evening that President Obama had called to offer her the nomination, he had asked her to promise him two things: "The first," she recalled, "was to remain the person I was and the second was to stay connected to my community. I said to him that those were two easy promises to make, because those two things I could not change."[11]

She shunned interview requests with such traditional news organizations as *The Washington Post* and posed for a sophisticated photograph—her hair sleekly combed out, her makeup elegant—for *Latina* magazine. Taken in 2009 by the international photographer Pláton, the picture shows her in black robe, one hand pressed over her heart, the other on her lap. Her nails are fire-engine red. Her expression is penetrating, heartfelt.

In the accompanying feature story, *Latina*'s former editor in chief Sandra Guzman described Sotomayor as "a doting hostess [who] puts together cheese platters, makes tasty salads and hooks up a mean churrasco with a tangy lemon marinade." Guzman recalled asking for advice during dinner with Sotomayor and other friends. "She listened closely as I relayed my marital problems. I still recall her words, which I carry in my heart to this day. She told me that we have been wrongfully taught the Cinderella fairy tale as a paradigm of what happy relationships are supposed to be. And when we fall short of that, we suffer for it. To find happiness in love, she said, we have to make up our own rules."[12]

Guzman also recounted an exchange between President Obama and Sotomayor after her confirmation: She "pulled her hair back behind her ears, exposing her red and black semi-hoop earrings, a beloved accessory among Latinas across America—from the South Bronx to Houston to East Los Angeles. Obama joked that he had been briefed on the size of the earrings . . . Without skipping a beat, Sotomayor replied: 'Mr. President, you have no idea what you've unleashed.'"[13]

◆

Justice Sotomayor exuded a hurricane force that sometimes shattered the orderly, down-to-the-minute decorum so distinct to the Supreme Court. The symmetry of the marble-columned building completed in 1935 and the reserve of the dark-wood trappings were reinforced by the formality of the Court's people. The culture of the black robe naturally muted personalities. But not Sotomayor's.

She was particularly conspicuous in the Court's most public activity, oral arguments, when the nine justices questioned lawyers for both sides of a case. These were carefully choreographed events lasting one hour, with each side allowed thirty minutes. Small white and red lights on the lectern signaled to lawyers when they had five minutes remaining, then when they were out of time. Continuing with an argument after the red light went on visibly annoyed Chief Justice Roberts and, during the tenure of his predecessor, Chief Justice William Rehnquist (1986–2005), drew stern admonishment.

From the bench, Sotomayor was persistent and demanding. Most of the justices interrupted lawyers' answers to some extent, but she had a way of breaking in just as a lawyer was getting to the heart of an answer to another justice's question. Or she would start to speak as another justice was in the middle of a question. It was not rare to hear Chief Justice Roberts tell her to wait because a more senior justice was already speaking.

Yet her questions were not pointless. She sought clarity on the details of a case. "Are you talking about current figures or past? Tell us the date of the figures," she said to one lawyer in an exchange regarding statistics of prisoner suicides. In that same 2010 dispute over crowded conditions in California prisons and the impact on inmates' mental health, Sotomayor's intensity and some of the responses it engendered from colleagues were on display. She asked the attorney representing California how officials were meeting health-care needs. She wanted details, adding, "Slow down from the rhetoric."[14]

As the lawyer tried to answer, she repeatedly interrupted, saying such things as "When are you going to avoid the needless deaths that were reported in this record? When are you going to avoid or get around people sitting in their feces for days in a dazed state? When are you going to get to a point where you're going to deliver care that is going to be adequate?" Justice Scalia, more sympathetic to the state's dilemma than to the prisoners' condition, interrupted and added in a somewhat mocking tone, "But don't be rhetorical!"

In these early years, Sotomayor drew more than her share of grimaces from justices in the public courtroom.

Sotomayor asserted that she usually had a plan in mind when she jumped into the questioning: "Something most people will learn about me, I get so intensely engaged in argument that it's never fake," she said in an early interview. "Every question I ask has a purpose, it has some importance to something that is troubling me or that I'm curious about."[15]

Some colleagues said they believed her dominant presence on the bench and in conference was an attempt to challenge the doubters, to prove that she was prepared for cases. Others, however, said they believed her manner undercut her ability to work toward consensus.[16]

Overall, what did the other justices really think of her? It was a question that arose often among lawyers, journalists, and other close followers of the Court. The query naturally came up because of how Sotomayor stood out. Yet in these tradition-bound environs, where most justices shared backgrounds of privilege, it was a question complicated by the dimensions of ethnicity and class. And there was no single answer.

It was clear through interviews with her colleagues that Sotomayor engendered appreciation for her life story and respect for her work ethic. The justices varied in their personal assessments, as is natural with any group: some found her warm, amiable; others found her abrupt and exasperating. At the human level, these differences with her were not small. In the larger scheme of the law, they were.

The nine were appointed for life, and they had an incentive to get along. Any qualms expressed by colleagues about Sotomayor were minuscule compared with clashes among the nine in the great span of history.

As Justice Sotomayor neared her five-year mark on the Court, she joked about her reputation for interruptions and said she was trying not to break in so much. It was a hard pattern to stop. Breaking in is what she did.

◆

Sotomayor began her life as a justice at a momentous time. Her early terms brought unprecedented disputes over President Obama's health-care initiative, immigration policy, affirmative action, voting rights, and same-sex marriage.

Her first term was an especially grueling one for all the justices. During most of the 2009–10 session she and her colleagues watched Justice Ginsburg fight off exhaustion as she accompanied her husband to numerous physicians for cancer treatment and other health problems. He died the last week of the term. It had also been a difficult session for the ninety-year-old John Paul Stevens, the third-longest-serving justice in history. He decided to retire after concluding that age was getting the best of him. In January 2010 he had faltered and stuttered repeatedly as he read from the bench portions of a lengthy dissenting opinion in a major campaign finance case.[17]

All the justices were feeling the strain of ideological divisions exposed in that case—*Citizens United v. Federal Election Commission*. The five-justice conservative majority, which was seizing control in many areas of the law, had rolled back decades of precedent to strike down limits on corporate and labor union spending in elections.[18] Just days after the decision, President Obama, in a rare and highly public rebuke, denounced the ruling in his nationally tele-

vised State of the Union speech before Congress. Six justices—
three who happened to be from the *Citizens United* majority and
three from the dissenting side—were in the front rows in the U.S.
House of Representatives as the president condemned the decision.
Justice Samuel Alito, who had voted with the majority against the
campaign finance regulation, mouthed the words "Not true" as
Obama predicted that the decision would "open the floodgates for
special interests—including foreign corporations—to spend without limit in our elections."[19] It was a twenty-second moment that
went viral and exemplified the tensions between the executive and
judicial branches at the time.[20]

During Sotomayor's first term, the same five-justice conservative bloc that had written *Citizens United*—Chief Justice Roberts,
Samuel Alito, Antonin Scalia, Anthony Kennedy, and Clarence
Thomas—joined in a ruling that enhanced the right to own fire-
arms. Again over protests from the four liberals, including Sotomayor, the Court said that gun owners could challenge state and
city regulations that restricted gun possession. The majority declared
that the Second Amendment right to bear arms was fundamental to
American liberty and thus protected against local restrictions as
well as federal regulation. Four Chicago homeowners had challenged
a city law that banned handguns, saying they needed the guns for
their personal safety in dangerous neighborhoods. The Court's decision striking down the ban flowed from its 2008 ruling in *District of
Columbia v. Heller*, which established the right to keep and bear
arms under federal law.

Sotomayor's dissenting vote in the new case of *McDonald v. City
of Chicago* added to the evidence in her first term that she would be
a reliable liberal vote. It also provoked critics who thought that her
statements during Senate confirmation hearings should have led
to an opposite conclusion. During that testimony in the summer of
2009 she had expressed support for the Supreme Court's ruling in
Heller. She testified that she understood "the individual right fully
that the Supreme Court recognized in *Heller* . . . I understand how
important the right to bear arms is to many, many Americans."[21]

In that new case from Chicago, as she signed on to a dissent protesting the majority's view that the right to keep and bear arms is fundamental to liberty, Justice Sotomayor felt no need to write a separate opinion to provide an explanation. In her earliest terms she rarely broke off—beyond criminal procedure matters—to offer a concurring statement about her position, even in cases in which she was more naturally in the spotlight, such as on affirmative action and immigration.

Some of her moves were subtle. She brought a nuanced sensitivity to immigrant rights in her first signed opinion. The case involved a shift supervisor at a manufacturing plant who was fired after telling the human resources department that the company was hiring illegal workers, or, as Sotomayor wrote, "undocumented immigrants."[22] She later said that she had called the workers in question "undocumented immigrants" because calling "them illegal aliens seemed . . . insulting."[23]

Sotomayor's first major immigration case tested an Arizona law that, among its provisions, required police to check the immigration status of people stopped for routine offenses and to detain those who did not have proper documentation. Civil rights groups said that the requirement, signed into law by Republican governor Jan Brewer in April 2010, could lead to racial profiling and prolonged detentions. Hispanic advocacy groups, including the Mexican American Legal Defense and Educational Fund, vigorously protested it. More than half of the nation's estimated 11.5 million illegal immigrants were from Mexico. Critics of the law said that even people in the United States legally could be targeted because of their skin color and national origin. When the dispute came before the justices, however, it was not a constitutional dispute over racial profiling, but rather a test of state authority to enforce federal immigration law. The Obama administration was challenging all facets of the Arizona law, known as SB 1070, arguing that Congress, not individual states, should control immigration policy.[24]

As the Supreme Court hearing opened, Sotomayor was first in, firing a series of questions at Washington lawyer Paul Clement, a former U.S. solicitor general under President George W. Bush who was representing Arizona officials in their defense of the law. Sotomayor expressed concern that people stopped might end up in jail for long periods while local officers tried to check their immigration status. "What I see as critical is the issue of how long and . . . when is the officer going to exercise discretion to release the person," she said.[25]

Sotomayor was equally skeptical with U.S. solicitor general Donald Verrilli, attacking the "show me your papers" provision as being in conflict with federal immigration policy. "You can see it's not selling very well," she told him. At another point she said, "General, I'm terribly confused by your answer. Okay?" She challenged the reliability of federal databases that police officers might use to determine whether someone stopped locally is in the United States legally.

In the end, Sotomayor joined an opinion that upheld the provision allowing police officers to check the legal status of people they stop for other violations of the law yet struck down the bulk of SB 1070's disputed provisions. She and her colleagues viewed the stop-and-check section as reinforcing, rather than usurping, federal policy. Writing for a five-justice bloc that included Sotomayor, Justice Kennedy narrowly interpreted the provision's reach. He warned authorities not to use the law to delay the release of people or to target minor offenders—for example, jaywalkers who cannot produce identification. The modest scope and tone of Kennedy's opinion probably helped draw Sotomayor and the two other liberals, Ginsburg and Breyer. Chief Justice Roberts also joined the Kennedy opinion.

A majority, with Sotomayor, further declared that federal law preempted other provisions, including those that made it a state crime to be unlawfully present in the United States or to seek work without proper documentation. The justices highlighted the federal government's role in immigration and largely rejected the effort by Arizona and other states to institute their own sweeping measures to stop people from illegally crossing the border. Civil rights advocates and President Obama focused on the part of the decision that did not go their way. "No American should ever live under a cloud of suspicion just because of what they look like," Obama said in a statement.

If she were addressing a social policy matter rather than an issue of law, Sotomayor might have expressed similar sentiment. She did, in fact, tell students in Denver about crossing the border once with a dark-skinned Mexican American friend who was asked to get out of the car. Sotomayor believed the action might have stemmed from racial profiling. But as a jurist, she did not feel it was her place to elaborate on such views in a case.[26]

Nearly a generation behind the Court's most famous groundbreakers, Sotomayor did not see herself as an advocate for a cause. She did not come up through the ranks of Hispanic groups as a visible activist for her people, as Ruth Bader Ginsburg had done with women's rights. Sotomayor was not the leader who helped start the Puerto Rican Legal Defense Fund, as Thurgood Marshall had with the NAACP Legal Defense Fund. Marshall and Ginsburg accentuated broader group rights in their public writings and speeches rather than their personal experiences.

In the justices' private conferences, Marshall often regaled his colleagues with experiences he gathered in service to a cause. He knew firsthand Klan violence, jury bias, and judges who had been bought off. He told of seeing "whites only" signs on restrooms and at drinking fountains as he traveled the South and of being warned to get out of town "cuz niggers ain't welcome in these parts after dark." That perspective prompted Justice O'Connor to write after Marshall retired, "His was the eye of a lawyer who saw the deepest wounds in the social fabric and used law to help heal them . . . His was the mouth of a man who knew the anguish of the silenced and gave them a voice."[27]

Asked about the role Marshall played with his colleagues, Sotomayor said, "I am not a storyteller. I am not a flamethrower. That's not who Sonia ever was. If you look at my life, it's not that I don't support those legal issues or principles. It's not that the passion isn't there. It's that it's always done in a lawyerly, judicial way. That's who Sonia is. And it's effective."

◆

Sotomayor's early opinions were narrowly crafted, as they had been on the Second Circuit. Most distinctive, in a substantive vein, was her support for the rights of defendants and her concern for criminal law procedures. Sometimes her liberal colleagues would be with her, but often she was alone. "What I view as driving my jurisprudence is process," she said, telling audiences she wanted to ensure that people were given a fair chance within the legal system.[28]

In her first term she was joined by fellow liberals when she wrote the lead dissent to a 2010 majority ruling that sided with police when suspects had not clearly invoked or waived their Miranda right to remain silent during interrogations. The case tested the circumstances of questions put to a murder suspect in Michigan, Van Chester Thompkins, who had stayed silent but did not affirmatively say he did not want to talk to police. Near the end of a three-hour interrogation, when asked if he prayed to God to forgive him for the shooting, he said, "Yes." The trial judge refused to suppress the evidence during the trial, and Thompkins was convicted of murder. The Supreme Court majority upheld use of the statement at trial.[29]

Sotomayor, writing the first major dissent of her Supreme Court tenure, charged the majority with retreating from precedent that stood for the proposition that prosecutors have the burden of showing that a suspect had waived his rights. "Today's decision turns *Miranda* upside down," she said. "Criminal suspects must now unambiguously invoke their right to remain silent—which, counterintuitively, requires them to speak. At the same time, suspects will be legally presumed to have waived their rights even if they have given no clear expression of their intent to do so."[30]

Sotomayor's views were influenced by her experience as a Puerto Rican in the Bronx and also as an assistant district attorney in Manhattan. She knew firsthand how much raw power prosecutors and the police possessed.

During her early terms Sotomayor distinguished herself with impassioned statements when her fellow justices refused to take up defendants' appeals. Individual justices rarely went public with their concerns over which cases the Court decided to hear among the nearly eight thousand filed annually. But Sotomayor did so several times.[31] In *Pitre v. Cain*, she protested when the Court refused to hear the appeal of a Louisiana prisoner who claimed he was punished for not taking his anti-HIV medication. Anthony Pitre said that prison officials reprimanded him by "subjecting him to hard labor in 100-degree heat." Sotomayor believed that a constitutional issue was at stake: Pitre might have been able to demonstrate that his punishment was cruel and unusual. "To be sure, Pitre's decision to refuse medication may have been foolish and likely caused a significant part of his pain," she wrote, with no other justices signing on. "But that decision does not give prison officials license to exacerbate Pitre's condition further as a means of punishing or coercing him."[32]

Two years later, in the case of *Calhoun v. United States*, which the majority similarly refused to take up, Sotomayor objected to a prosecutor's racially charged comment during trial. The prosecutor asked a witness, "You've got African Americans, you've got Hispanics, you've got a bag full of money. Does that tell you—a lightbulb doesn't go off in your head and say, This is a drug deal?" The defendant argued that this remark violated his constitutional rights. The Supreme Court refused to accept his case, perhaps because he had not made this argument during an initial appeal. Although Sotomayor agreed with the Court's refusal to consider the matter, she wanted to make sure people knew that the justices were not "signal[ing] our tolerance of a federal prosecutor's racially charged remark."[33]

She elaborated: "There is no doubt . . . that the prosecutor's question never should have been posed . . . Such argumentation is an affront to the Constitution's guarantee of equal protection of the laws. And by threatening to cultivate bias in the jury, it equally offends the defendant's right to an impartial jury." With only Justice Breyer signing her opinion, Sotomayor wrote, "It is deeply disappointing to see a representative of the United States resort to this base tactic more than a decade into the 21st century. Such conduct diminishes the dignity of our criminal justice system and undermines respect for the rule of law. We expect the Government to seek justice, not to fan the flames of fear and prejudice . . . I hope never to see a case like this again."

It was difficult to read her words and not recall what she said about the slurs in the movie *12 Angry Men*—that she had heard about "those people" often in her life. Such experiences could not help but affect—to some degree—her idea about the place of law in America and what happens when the government fans the flames, as she said, "of fear and prejudice."

In another dissent from the Court's refusal to take up a defendant's appeal, Sotomayor suggested that an elected judge in Alabama was playing politics when he ignored a jury's decision to spare the life of convicted murderer Mario Dion Woodward and imposed the death penalty. The Supreme Court rejected Woodward's petition, with only Sotomayor, joined by Breyer, dissenting. "In the last decade, Alabama has been the only State in which judges have imposed the death penalty in the face of contrary jury verdicts," Sotomayor wrote. Why? she asked. "The only answer that is supported by empirical evidence is one that, in my view, casts a cloud of illegitimacy over the criminal justice system: Alabama judges, who are elected in partisan proceedings, appear to have succumbed to electoral pressures."[34] She said one judge who had overridden jury verdicts and imposed the death penalty had touted his support for capital punishment during his campaign for the bench. Sotomayor underscored her point by attaching a list of ninety-five defendants who were sentenced to death by Alabama judges after juries had imposed life in prison.

A capital punishment case the justices agreed to take up, *Cullen v. Pinholster*, revealed Sotomayor's concern for a defendant's early troubled life and pitted her against an ideological opposite, Clarence Thomas. The legal question centered on the effectiveness of the trial lawyer who represented convicted murderer Scott Lynn Pinholster. A federal appeals court had overturned Pinholster's death sentence after he claimed that the lawyer should have presented evidence to the jury of his mental problems and childhood trauma as mitigating evidence against the death penalty.[35]

The Supreme Court, on a 5–4 vote, reinstated the sentence. In emotionally charged opinions, Justices Thomas and Sotomayor presented two visions of the relevance of the defendant's childhood, the sufficiency of state hearings on such evidence, and the federal oversight role. Thomas opened his opinion by describing how Pinholster had stabbed two victims to death and threatened to murder his accomplice if the accomplice went to the police. Thomas mentioned Pinholster's childhood trauma in limited fashion. He and others in the majority said a deeper investigation into Pinholster's background would not have made a difference in the jury's sentence.

In contrast, Sotomayor, writing for dissenters, avoided the details of the crime and focused on the defendant's troubled youth and how it could have significantly affected the outcome of the trial. Pinholster was "raised in chaos and poverty," she wrote, noting that a relative saw the children mix flour and water for something to eat. Pinholster's stepfather beat him regularly. The key question, Sotomayor said, was whether there was "a reasonable probability" that at least one juror would have struck a different balance if that background were known. "It is not a foregone conclusion, as the majority deems it, that a juror familiar with his troubled background and psychiatric issues would have reached the same conclusion regarding Pinholster's culpability," she wrote, adding that fair-minded judges could not conclude that at least one juror would have struck a different balance.

Responding sharply to her position, Justice Thomas called Sotomayor's analysis "quite puzzling" and argued that her conclusions rested "on a fundamental misunderstanding" of the statute at issue in the case.

◆

A year later, it was liberal justice Ginsburg who claimed that Sotomayor had a fundamental misunderstanding of precedent in a criminal case. The episode would become part of a pattern after a few years in which Sotomayor separated from her usual allies and went it alone—over harsh criticism that she was misguided. She alone dissented when, in January 2012, the Court ruled that trial judges need not subject suggestive eyewitness evidence to a special review unless the police officers involved engaged in misconduct. She was driven by doubts about the reliability of eyewitness identifications and by studies saying that they have been a source of convictions of innocent people.

Barion Perry was convicted of car theft after a woman said she saw him at the scene of the crime. The Supreme Court eight-justice majority said that it was enough that jurors were able to assess the reliability of the eyewitness evidence in the regular course of the trial. In a dissent, Sotomayor noted that Perry, the only African American at the scene, was talking with police when the witness identified him. "The Court's holding enshrines a murky distinction," she insisted, "between suggestive confrontations intentionally orchestrated by the police and, as here, those inadvertently caused by police actions—that will sow confusion."[36]

Sotomayor's characterization of the Court's departure from precedent and her reliance on social studies about misidentifications particularly riled Ginsburg, the senior justice on the left. Joined by the remaining seven colleagues, Ginsburg objected to Sotomayor's assertion that the majority had applied a "significant limitation on our long-standing rule" about scrutiny for eyewitness identifications involving the police. Ginsburg noted that Sotomayor offered no prior case in which the Court had required pretrial screening absent any police-arranged identifications. "Understandably so, for there are no such cases," Ginsburg observed. "Instead, [Justice Sotomayor] surveys our decisions, heedless of the police arrangement that underlies every one of them, and [invents] a 'long-standing rule' that never existed."[37]

Being alone on the case and incurring such a heated rebuttal did not deter Sotomayor. Once she came to her own understanding of the correct approach to a dispute, she rarely budged.

During that same January, Sotomayor offered a unique approach
to a dispute over modern tracking devices. As part of an investigation of Antoine Jones, a Washington, D.C., nightclub owner suspected of drug dealing, police had placed a GPS tracker on a car
owned by Jones's wife.[38] Based on some of the evidence gathered,
Jones was convicted of conspiring to distribute and possess cocaine.
The U.S. Court of Appeals for the D.C. Circuit overturned the
conviction, ruling that admission of evidence from the warrantless
use of the GPS device violated the Fourth Amendment, which prevents the government from engaging in "unreasonable searches and
seizures."

The Supreme Court agreed that the attachment of a tracking
device was a "search" by a 9–0 vote. But the justices splintered in
their rationale, with Sotomayor playing an intriguing role. Writing
for a five-justice majority that included Sotomayor, Justice Scalia
said that the affixing of the GPS to the vehicle violated the Fourth
Amendment based on eighteenth-century notions of trespass. Sotomayor, who had given Scalia the key fifth vote for that rationale,
then wrote separately to suggest that the Court may need to develop
a new notion of informational privacy that matches the times. In her
concurring statement, signed by no other justice, she emphasized
that preventing physical intrusion (the traditional focus of anti–
search and seizure protections) might not be enough to ensure privacy in the digital age. She pointed out that technological advances
allowed the government to monitor people without actually intrud-
ing on their person or property and asserted that it might be time for
the Court to reexamine the way it analyzed Fourth Amendment
protections in the area of electronic surveillance.

Some academic commentators, including George Washington
University law professor Jeffrey Rosen, an early skeptic, deemed her
approach prophetic, particularly after it emerged that the United
States government was broadly collecting telephone and other digital data on Americans.[39]

Yet Sotomayor was not a natural favorite of the legal elite. That
was where Elena Kagan came in. President Obama had chosen his

U.S. solicitor general for his second appointment to the Court, to succeed Justice John Paul Stevens. True to Lawrence Tribe's prediction when he urged Obama to appoint Kagan over Sotomayor in 2009, Kagan quickly became a strategic force on the bench. A former law clerk to Justice Thurgood Marshall, she was deft during oral arguments, adroitly inserting herself into the flow as Sotomayor routinely interrupted. Kagan's written opinions were taut. She wrote in sharp declarative sentences with rhetoric that was not overtly flashy but memorable nonetheless.

The tactics and style that the former Harvard Law School dean brought to the Court were not lost on more senior colleagues, particularly veteran justice Ginsburg, who considered Kagan a persuasive force who might blunt the majority's move to the right. Even Kagan's ideological opposite, Chief Justice Roberts, publicly lauded her oral argument style and fluid writing.[40]

Justices Sotomayor and Kagan maneuvered differently among colleagues. Justice Sotomayor often operated autonomously, staking out a position and standing firm. She would not hesitate to write lone concurring opinions, differentiating her views from those of the other liberals. Justice Kagan saw herself more as one of nine in a collective process and during her early tenure never broke off to pen a solo concurrence.

Sotomayor resisted comparisons with other justices, saying she considered them counterproductive. Speaking generally, she said that throughout her life she knew there would always be someone who would seem smarter, faster, and better. She said the comparisons she preferred were personal to her: "Am I learning? Am I getting better?"

Some senior justices, too, rejected the inevitable comparisons between the two Obama appointees, both Princeton graduates and New Yorkers, noting that outside legal analysts were not equally quick to compare Roberts and Alito, George W. Bush appointees who joined the Court within months of each other.

Perhaps an alternative comparison revolved around Sotomayor's stature on the Court and off it. At the marble enclave she was one of nine, among the most junior and not known for her persuasiveness. But beyond its walls, she was magic. She was the Hispanic who had reached the absolute top of the exclusive world of the judiciary.

There was no denying her ongoing rise as a national figure. During her first year on the Supreme Court she was number three on CNN's list of "The 10 Most Intriguing People of 2009," behind President Barack Obama and First Lady Michelle Obama.[41]

There was plainly a national appetite for her story. Two other groundbreaking justices had written autobiographies—Sandra Day O'Connor, after she had reached the twenty-year mark on the Supreme Court, and Clarence Thomas, after he had reached fifteen years. But right from the start, Sotomayor knew she should write hers.

Within a year of her confirmation she signed a $3 million deal with the Knopf Doubleday Publishing Group to tell her life story. When the publication was announced, editor in chief Sonny Mehta said of Sotomayor's life, "Hers is a triumph of the Latino experience in America."[42]

ELEVEN

Equality and Identity

In her early years on the Supreme Court, Sonia Sotomayor's opinions lacked rhetorical fire. They were marked by exhaustive recitations of the facts of a case and legal precedent. Yet her life story made her a robust voice on race, and when the Court faced a pivotal case on university affirmative action in 2013, her willingness to write a scorching opinion led the majority to alter its course. That crucial opinion, however, would never be revealed to the public. Shades of it would emerge a year later in a dissenting statement in a different affirmative action case and spark a public sensation.

The first Hispanic justice drew a distinction between her approach and the methods of Thurgood Marshall and Ruth Bader Ginsburg. During her Senate confirmation hearings in 2009 Sotomayor had emphasized that unlike those justices, who had taken up their respective causes as litigators, she had served on the board— not in a courtroom—for the Puerto Rican Legal Defense and Education Fund. She simply did not see herself as at the forefront of an ideological cause. When Senator Arlen Specter of Pennsylvania[1] referred to the provocative rhetoric of conservative justice Antonin Scalia and asked, "Do you think it possible that if confirmed, you will be a litigator in that [Supreme Court] conference room, take on the ideological battles which pop out from time to time?" Sotomayor said no. "I judge on the basis of the law and my reasoning," she said.

"Well, perhaps you'll be tempted to be a tough litigator in the Court," Specter responded. "Time will tell, if you're confirmed, if you have some of those provocative statements."[2]

It turned out that she did, and in the university affirmative action case those statements would make a difference.

Through an unusually long nine-month set of negotiations over a case brought by Abigail Fisher, a white student rejected for admission to the University of Texas at Austin, the justices went from an initial vote to reject the Texas policy and sharply curtail affirmative action to a decision that permitted the Texas approach and widespread national practice to continue, at least for the near future. The tense debate occurred behind the scenes, and when it was over, there was no public sign of what Sotomayor had wrought.[3]

◆

The case of *Fisher v. University of Texas at Austin* was one of the most closely followed of the Supreme Court's 2012–13 term. Both sides speculated that the conservative-dominated Roberts Court was ready to roll back precedent dating to 1978 that had allowed universities to enhance racial diversity on campuses by favoring black and Hispanic applicants. The Court had reached out to take up the controversy, over protests from the University of Texas that there was nothing at stake anymore because Fisher had graduated from another university.

Civil rights advocates and education officials feared that the Court was poised to make it more difficult for public universities to enroll sufficient numbers of minorities, which they believed was crucial to a fulfilling academic experience for all students. On the other side, interests backing Fisher thought they might finally persuade the justices to reverse a course they had taken thirty-five years earlier in the case of *Regents of the University of California v. Bakke.*

When the University of Texas case was heard on October 10, 2012, the Supreme Court had just opened a new term, the fourth for Justice Sotomayor. This fractious affirmative action case was coming less than a month before the November 2012 presidential election. Former Massachusetts governor Mitt Romney was challenging Barack Obama. Racial issues such as those before the Court— with affirmative action in the *Fisher* case and voting rights in a dispute from Shelby County, Alabama—were not entirely divorced from controversies in the national election. A looming question was whether minorities who were apt to vote for Obama might be dissuaded from going to the polls because of stiffer voter identification requirements, registration restrictions, and limits on early voting. Republican proponents said the restrictions were needed to prevent fraud. Democratic opponents countered that they particularly burdened minorities, the poor, and the elderly, who might not have multiple forms of identification handy.[4]

As it rumbled in national politics, the affirmative action dispute was posing a personal challenge for Sotomayor. She had won admission to Ivy League schools, been chosen for a federal trial court position, and ultimately made it to the Supreme Court partly because of her Latina identity. She knew she had gotten a boost that whites had not, but she believed she had proven that she deserved those breaks.

Sotomayor, a Princeton and Yale graduate, epitomized one side of the debate. Abigail Fisher, who had turned to her second-choice school, Louisiana State University, represented the other.

The higher education dilemma traced to the 1978 *Bakke* case, when the justices had ruled by a 5–4 vote that government had a compelling interest in pursuing diversity on campuses and allowed universities to weigh an applicant's race as one of several criteria. The Court forbade schools from using quotas.[5] A quarter of a century later, in 2003, the Supreme Court upheld *Bakke* in a case involving the University of Michigan Law School. In that dispute, also decided by a 5–4 vote, Justice Sandra Day O'Connor reinforced the compelling governmental interest in campus diversity and stressed that programs needed to be narrowly crafted and based on individualized consideration of applicants.

Noting that a university education is a prerequisite for leadership in most professions, the first woman justice declared in *Grutter v. Bollinger* that such paths to leadership must be "open to talented and qualified individuals of every race and ethnicity." In a separate case decided on the same day, *Gratz v. Bollinger*, the Court struck down a University of Michigan undergraduate policy that automatically added points for minority applicants, stressing that such affirmative action had to involve individualized consideration and be narrowly crafted.[6]

Justice O'Connor's opinion in *Grutter v. Bollinger* regarding the law school touted Michigan's efforts to create a "critical mass" of minority students—so that those students would not feel isolated—and distinguished the approach from the racial quotas barred by *Bakke*. In another key point that would reverberate in the University of Texas case, O'Connor said that Justice Lewis Powell's controlling opinion in *Bakke* stood for the proposition that as part of their educational mission, universities were free to make their own judgments related to the selection of students and those who "will contribute the most to the robust exchange of ideas."

O'Connor closed her 2003 opinion by suggesting that America's need for university affirmative action was not likely to fade for another twenty-five years.

Yet a few years after the University of Michigan case, the ideological makeup of the Court changed and threw into doubt the future of programs designed to boost the chances of racial minorities. In September 2005 John Roberts succeeded William Rehnquist as chief justice. Beginning with his tenure as a Reagan administration lawyer in the 1980s, Roberts had worked on policy to curtail government's use of racial remedies. He sought to narrow the scope of the 1965 Voting Rights Act, specifically by advising the president in 1982 to oppose legislation intended to strengthen the federal government's hand in local cases of intentional voter discrimination.

Now, as chief justice, Roberts appeared willing to take more of a leadership role on racial disputes than Rehnquist had taken. In a 2006 case involving the drawing of voting district boundaries to enhance the political power of blacks and Latinos, Roberts referred to "this sordid business divvying us up by race." He later voted against race classifications in education and employment, the latter in the New Haven, Connecticut, firefighters' dispute that Sotomayor handled as an appellate court judge.[7]

When Justice O'Connor retired, in January 2006, she was succeeded by Samuel Alito, who also was more antagonistic to racial remedies, as seen in the 2009 challenge by Frank Ricci and other firefighters against New Haven officials trying to counteract the fire department's history of racial discrimination. In a 2007 case, *Parents Involved v. Seattle School District No. 1*, Alito and Roberts were part of a five-justice majority that rejected integration plans intended to even out the percentages of whites and blacks in schools throughout a district as a way to counteract segregated housing patterns.

The four liberal justices who dissented in the *Parents Involved* student assignment dispute declared that the new Roberts Court had put at risk the legacy of the 1954 *Brown v. Board of Education* decision that led to the desegregation of the nation's public schools.[8] "What of the hope and promise of *Brown?*" Justice Breyer said on behalf of dissenters as he read an impassioned dissent from the bench.[9]

That 2007 case signaled at least a retrenchment on racial policies in education, which raised the stakes as Abigail Fisher's challenge to the University of Texas policy worked its way toward the justices.

In 2004, with the seal of approval of the Supreme Court's 2003 affirmative action ruling, the University of Texas had changed its admissions policy and began considering the race of applicants. It was taking advantage of the Court decision and responding to the fact that the student body at its flagship Austin campus had grown less diverse over the decade. Texas officials began supplementing their so-called top-ten program, under which high school graduates in roughly the top 10 percent of their class were automatically admitted. The supplemental program considered an applicant's race along with other factors, such as family hardship or disability, to try to create diversity at the campus. University officials said that using race as a factor helped ensure the diversity needed to enhance the educational experience for all students.

Within a few years, as the makeup of the Supreme Court tilted more toward the right, critics—most notably Edward Blum, a former Houston stockbroker who was helping to finance lawsuits against race-based programs—sensed an opening for an attack on the University of Texas plan.

A businessman, not a lawyer, Blum had been targeting race-based government policies since he lost a 1992 congressional election in a racially gerrymandered Texas district. He had become a matchmaker of sorts, finding sympathetic white plaintiffs and hiring lawyers to take their cases. Under the auspices of the Project on Fair Representation, of which he was the sole employee, he raised money from conservative foundations and like-minded right-wing donors. Three of his earlier cases made it to the Supreme Court.[10]

To find someone to sue the University of Texas over its admissions policy, Blum set up a website that asked rejected applicants to contact him and share their experiences. Several students responded, but none seemed right for the long haul of a court case and news media exposure. Then Blum got a call from an old friend, Richard Fisher, whose daughter Abigail had been turned down by the University of Texas at Austin.

Her father and older sister had graduated from the state's flagship university, and she had always dreamed of attending the Austin campus. But Abigail, who had a 3.59 grade point average on a 4.0 scale and was ranked 82 out of her suburban Houston high school class of 674, was rejected. She believed she had been denied a space even as racial minorities with lower scores had been admitted.[11]

Blum promised the Fisher family that all legal costs would be covered if Abigail sued. Blum then hired Washington, D.C., lawyer Bert Rein, a founding partner of a half-century-old Republican-dominated law firm with whom Blum had worked on earlier cases.

Abigail Fisher lost before a district court judge and then in the U.S. Court of Appeals for the Fifth Circuit, where a three-judge panel stressed that the Supreme Court's 2003 University of Michigan decision recognized that universities are engaged in a distinct enterprise. Referring to that decision in *Grutter v. Bollinger*, the panel wrote, "*Grutter* teaches that so long as a university considers race in a holistic and individualized manner, and not as part of a quota or fixed-point system, courts must afford a measure of deference to the university's good faith determination." The Fifth Circuit added that the Texas admissions policy might be "superior" to the

Michigan law school approach approved in 2003 because Texas did not keep a running tally of minorities during the admissions process, which might have smacked of a quota.

When the Supreme Court took up Fisher's appeal on October 10, 2012, and lawyer Rein stepped to the lectern, there was a capacity crowd. All three hundred spectator seats were filled, and reporters packed into the courtroom's alcoves. Lawyers who could not get seats listened in a special room equipped to pipe in the audio from the courtroom. The justices' bench, however, had an empty chair. The newest justice, Elena Kagan, had recused herself because she had been U.S. solicitor general when the Obama administration filed a brief supporting the University of Texas in the lower courts. That left the bench without one of its strongest liberal voices and boosted what already seemed like a conservative advantage when the justices agreed to take up Fisher's appeal.

Standing at the lectern in the white marble courtroom, Rein was so eager to make his argument that he jumped in before Roberts could call the case. "Mr. Chief Justice, and may it please the Court—" the tall, silver-haired Rein began from his place below the bench.

"Well, I get to say," Roberts lightly interrupted him, "that this is case number 11-345, Fisher against the University of Texas at Austin, and you get to say . . ."[12]

Rein nodded and then repeated the salutation of, "Mr. Chief Justice . . . may it please the Court . . ." Rein was arguing that the University of Texas had violated Fisher's equality rights under the Constitution. "The central issue here is whether the University of Texas at Austin can carry its burden" to justify the decision, he said. Fisher was watching from a seat near the back of the spectator section. The slight, shy young woman sat with her parents and with Edward Blum.

Before Rein had gotten very far in arguing that Fisher was a victim of racial bias, Sotomayor made clear that she did not think the case belonged at the Court. Fisher had already completed her four years at Louisiana State University.

"She's graduated," Sotomayor said. "So what's the injury?"

"The denial of her right to equal treatment is a constitutional injury in and of itself," Rein answered. He said it did not matter that Fisher had turned to another school. She had been injured by the program's favoring of some races over others.

As the oral arguments shifted into the merits of the case, Sotomayor vigorously defended the university's attempt to generate a "critical mass" of minority students to make them feel comfortable and improve the educational experience for all. She referred to a study at the University of Texas that she said had found that "minority students overwhelmingly, even with the numbers they have now, are feeling isolated."

Sotomayor became increasingly demanding of Rein, cutting him off several times before he had a chance to answer. "So what are you telling us is the standard of 'critical mass'?" she asked. "At what point does a district court or a university know that it doesn't have to do any more to equalize the desegregation that has happened in that particular state over decades . . . and it has to change its rules. What's that fixed number?" She was addressing the statistical evidence that a university might need to continue an admissions process that uses race for the benefit of diversity.

Rein protested, saying it was the university's—not Fisher's— "burden to establish the number." But Sotomayor cut him off again before he could continue, saying that university officials "took a study of students. They analyzed the composition of their classes, and they determined in their educational judgment that greater diversity" was needed.

Sotomayor pushed Rein to provide evidence that the University of Texas had failed to follow the law. "Tell me what about their use of race did not fit the narrow tailoring . . . that *Grutter* required? How is race used by them in a way that violated the terms of *Grutter*?"

A few minutes later she said to Rein, "So now we're going to tell the universities how to run and how to weigh qualifications, too?"

"It's not the job of the Court to tell them how to do it," he responded. "It's their job to examine the alternatives available to them and see if they couldn't achieve the same thing."

When Rein's red light came on, indicating that he was out of time, Chief Justice Roberts referred to the few minutes advocates usually save to make final arguments, saying, "We will afford you rebuttal time, since our questions have prevented you from reserving it."

Many of those questions were from Justice Sotomayor.

◆

Next up was Gregory Garre, a generation younger than Rein, with his own impressive Republican credentials. Garre, a U.S. solicitor general under George W. Bush, was now in private practice at Latham & Watkins, the law firm that had successfully defended the University of Michigan law school program in 2003. The University of Texas hoped the hiring of the prominent national firm would again preserve campus affirmative action.

During his time at the lectern Garre argued that the University of Texas had complied with the 2003 Michigan ruling because the Austin campus was "taking race into account as only one modest factor among many for individualized considerations."

When Ginsburg and Kennedy separately asked how long race would have to be considered to achieve the requisite diversity, Sotomayor jumped in. "Mr. Garre, I think that the issue that my colleagues are asking is, at what point and when do we stop deferring to the university's judgment that race is still necessary? That's the bottom line of this case. And you're saying, and I think rightly because of our cases, that you can't set a quota . . . So if we're not going to set a quota, what do you think is the standard we apply to make a . . . judgment?"

Garre responded, "You would look to whether or not the university reached an environment in which members of underrepresented minorities, African Americans and Hispanics, do not feel like spokespersons for their race . . . an environment where cross-racial understanding is promoted, an environment where the . . . educational benefits of diversity are realized."

Chief Justice Roberts and the other conservative justices suggested that such an open-ended standard was unworkable and that the university's reluctance to fill in the contours of "critical mass" made it difficult to assess its constitutionality. Justice Kennedy, voicing skepticism throughout the argument for the university's position, focused on "this hurt or this injury" arising from screening by race.

Since he joined the Court in 1988, Kennedy had never voted to uphold an affirmative action program and had dissented in *Grutter v. Bollinger*, asserting that the majority's review of the University of Michigan Law School program was "nothing short of perfunctory." He insisted that "the Court's refusal to apply meaningful strict scrutiny will lead to serious consequences," notably that faculties and administrators will have little incentive to devise "new and fairer ways to ensure individual consideration."

In this new case, it appeared that Kennedy was ready to vote to strike down the University of Texas program and again try to curb the discretion of campus administrators. A big question was how sweeping the Court's opinion might be and how it would affect policies nationwide.

Blum was feeling optimistic that affirmative action was going down. After the arguments, he treated Abigail Fisher, her parents, Rein, and an entourage of thirty other people, including donors, to a meal at Morton's Steakhouse in downtown Washington.

Two days later, the justices took a preliminary vote in a private meeting, known as the "conference," as was the usual practice after a round of oral arguments. These justices-only conferences occurred in a small oak-paneled room off the chambers of the chief justice. At a rectangular table below an intricate glass chandelier they cast their votes in order of seniority. Then the most senior justice in the majority would decide who was to write the opinion for the Court. The most senior member of the losing side would decide who spoke for dissenters.

In the University of Texas case, it initially looked like a 5–3 lineup. The five conservatives, including Justice Kennedy, wanted to rule against the Texas policy and limit the ability of other universities to use the kinds of admissions programs upheld in *Grutter v. Bollinger*. The three liberals were ready to dissent.

Yet that division would not hold. The case would go down to the wire, unresolved until the final week of the Court term in late June.

The deliberations among the eight (Justice Kagan did not participate in any of the negotiations) took place over a series of draft opinions, transmitted from computer to computer but also delivered in hard copies by messengers from chamber to chamber as was the long-standing practice.

Individual justices ended up assuming critical roles, among them Sotomayor as agitator, Breyer as broker, and Kennedy as compromiser.

The justices' deliberations are highly secretive and rarely revealed. But in conversations with a majority of justices, some of the negotiations in this case and Sotomayor's role in the final decision became evident.[13]

◆

The protracted negotiations occurred as Sotomayor was promoting publication of her new book, *My Beloved World*, and extolling the virtues of affirmative action in interviews. "I had been admitted to the Ivy League through a special door," she wrote in the book, "and I had more ground than most to make up before I was competing with my classmates on an equal footing. But I worked relentlessly to reach that point, and distinctions such as the Pyne Prize, Phi Beta Kappa, summa cum laude, and a spot on *The Yale Law Journal* were not given out like so many pats on the back to encourage mediocre students."[14]

In related interviews, Sotomayor offered a contrast to Justice Thomas's well-known opposition to affirmative action and its stigma.

With the pending case, Thomas believed that the University of Texas was not only discriminating against white and Asian applicants but also hurting minority students. After the oral arguments, his law clerks gathered statistics that showed that blacks and Hispanics admitted to the university based on race were less prepared than their white and Asian classmates. They found that in the university's entering class of 2009, beyond the separate top 10 percent group, blacks scored at the 52nd percentile of 2009 SAT takers nationwide, while Asians scored at the 93rd percentile. Blacks had a mean GPA of 2.57 and a mean SAT score of 1524 (out of a possible score of 2400); Hispanics had a mean GPA of 2.83 and a mean SAT score of 1794; whites had a mean GPA of 3.04 and a mean SAT score of 1914; and Asians had a mean GPA of 3.07 and a mean SAT score of 1991.[15]

Such statistics made Sotomayor shudder. She rejected the notion that people could be seriously measured by scores. She believed that minorities from disadvantaged situations could catch up with nurturing and academic support on campus.

In an interview related to the promotion of *My Beloved World*, she told NPR reporter Nina Totenberg, "As much as I know Clarence, admire him and have grown to appreciate him, I have never focused on the negative of things. I always look at the positive. And I know one thing: If affirmative action opened the doors for me at Princeton, once I got in, I did the work. I proved myself worthy. So, I don't look at how the door opened."[16]

◆

At the Supreme Court, as the anticipation intensified over how Sotomayor, Thomas, and the other justices were resolving the University of Texas case, the Court took up an equally polarizing dispute over the 1965 Voting Rights Act. Hanging in the balance was a provision, known as Section 5, requiring states and localities with a history of discrimination to obtain federal approval before making any change in their electoral rules.

It was a coincidence that the two cases arrived at the Court at the same time, but together the disputes heightened liberals' fears that the Roberts Court was poised to roll back protections for racial and ethnic minorities.

The iconic Voting Rights Act prohibited poll taxes, literacy tests, and other measures that historically had prevented blacks and Latinos from voting. Democratic president Lyndon B. Johnson had won congressional passage of the law only after the "Bloody Sunday" episode on March 7, 1965, when state troopers clubbed and gassed peaceful civil rights marchers in Selma, Alabama, on the Edmund Pettus Bridge.

Unlike other parts of the Voting Rights Act that targeted intentional discrimination once it happened, Section 5 sought to head off any disenfranchisement of minorities preventively with the preclearance requirement. The provision, historically covering states in the Old South, had been designed to be temporary but had been repeatedly reauthorized by strong bipartisan majorities in Congress. The version of the law before the justices in 2013, signed by President George W. Bush in 2006, covered nine states entirely—Alabama, Alaska, Arizona, Georgia, Louisiana, Mississippi, South Carolina, Texas, and Virginia—and parts of seven others.

That 2006 reauthorization had earlier been tested at the Supreme Court, but the justices punted in the case of *Northwest Austin Municipal Utility District No. 1 v. Holder.*[17] The Supreme Court said that the small water district near Austin that challenged the preclearance rule was eligible for an exemption, so there was no need to access the constitutional validity of the law. Still, in one of the most powerful passages of that 2009 opinion, Chief Justice Roberts declared that "things have changed in the South" and suggested that a majority might be ready to roll back the long-standing protections of Section 5 in the next case.

Alabama officials and the Southern states backing them in the case of *Shelby County v. Holder* tried to establish a record that would make it easy for the Roberts Court to follow through on its suggestion that it was time for the United States to move beyond this racial remedy. They stressed that the huge gap between white and black voter registration in the 1960s had closed and that African American turnout in some places during the 2012 elections was higher than white turnout. The Obama administration and civil rights advocates, alternatively, sought to make it difficult for

the Roberts Court to invalidate the law aimed at Southern states
by building a record that highlighted allegations of bias in such covered places as Texas, Louisiana, and South Carolina.

In his arguments before the justices on behalf of Shelby County
in late February 2013, Bert Rein—again hired by Blum—asserted
that the "preclearance" requirement for any changes to districting
and ballot rules was an unconstitutional relic of an Old South that
no longer existed. Rein contended that the government had been
relying on an outdated formula, tracing to discriminatory polling
practices in the late 1960s and '70s, to restrict the nine states from
making changes without prior approval. U.S. solicitor general Verrilli countered that Congress had compiled a sufficient record to
demonstrate that the decades-old formula continued to target the
places with the most serious problems of voting discrimination.[18]

As with college affirmative action, this was the first time that
Justice Sotomayor was hearing a voting rights dispute on the Supreme Court. Hispanics, along with African Americans, had benefited from the Justice Department's oversight of states with histories
of race discrimination. Rein had not gotten very far along in his argument when Sotomayor and fellow liberal Justice Kagan asked why
a time-honored plank of the Voting Rights Act should be invalidated
in a case from Alabama, a state that had known decades of racial
violence and discrimination.

"Think about this state that you're representing," Justice Kagan
said. "It's about a quarter black, but Alabama has no black statewide
elected officials."

Justice Sotomayor followed up, sharpening the focus on Shelby
County: "Why would we vote in favor of a county whose record is
the epitome of what caused the passage of this law to start with?" In
Shelby County alone, she asserted, Section 5 had prevented "240
discriminatory voting laws" from taking effect over the years. A telling example—though one not mentioned by either side at oral
argument—involved the city of Calera. Over objections of the U.S.
Justice Department, that Shelby County city had drawn a new voting
district map plan that caused the sole African American on the city

council to be voted out of office. After the Justice Department forced Calera to redraw the map, the councilman regained his seat.[19]

Rein did not challenge Sotomayor's numbers, but he said that black voter registration and turnout was "very high" in Alabama. He also stressed that evidence on the ground was irrelevant when officials were lodging such a broad-based challenge to a law.

Justice Kennedy, sitting up in his chair and peering out through rimless glasses, said he was skeptical of a law that singled out the South for special federal regulation decades after the era of Jim Crow. "If Alabama . . . wants to acknowledge the wrongs of its past," he asked Solicitor General Verrilli, defending the federal policy, "is it better off doing that [as an] independent sovereign or . . . under the trusteeship of the United States government?"

Verrilli said that many of the original places Congress targeted because of their deep-seated discrimination still needed oversight. "Of fundamental importance here is that that history remains relevant," he responded to Kennedy. That history of racial bias in America and its remedies created the backdrop for the Alabama voting rights and Texas affirmative action cases.

It would take many more months before the nation saw how the Supreme Court resolved the dilemmas.

After the private vote in the *Fisher v. University of Texas at Austin* case in mid-October, Justice Ginsburg, the most senior of the dissenters, had assigned Sotomayor the task of writing the opinion for their position, favoring the university. Ginsburg knew well Sotomayor's passion on the legal issue and her personal stake. She had heard Sotomayor's stories about the kind of suspicion that greeted her acceptance to Princeton. She knew that Sotomayor had been driven to prove her place at the Ivy League campus and was now proving herself at the Supreme Court.

As Sotomayor drafted and began sending her opinion to colleagues' chambers, they witnessed this intensity. To some, it seemed a dissenting opinion that only Sotomayor, with her Puerto Rican Bronx background, could write. They saw it as the rare instance when she was giving voice to her Latina identity in a legal opinion at the Court. Others compared the dissent to the attention-getting fiery statements that were the trademark of Justice Scalia.

And get attention it did.

Certainly the justices were accustomed to individual differences in cases revolving around race and ethnicity, but in this dispute some were anxious about how Sotomayor's personal defense of affirmative action and indictment of the majority would ultimately play to the public. Justice Breyer was among those who felt strongly that a compromise should be brokered. Breyer had, in effect, adopted a compromise position with Justice O'Connor in the 2003 University of Michigan cases. Breyer, a 1994 Clinton appointee who usually was ready to uphold government racial policies, had voted to endorse the law school program but had joined O'Connor and the conservatives against the automatic benefit for black and Hispanic applicants in the undergraduate program.

Justice Sotomayor was ready to put herself on the line. She knew what affirmative action had meant for her and contended it has continuing value in American society. The details of her opinion might not be public for years, if ever. But those who read it said it was a fierce defense of affirmative action and a direct challenge to conservative justices preparing to undercut it.

Justice Kennedy, to whom the chief justice had assigned the majority opinion, did not close the door to working toward some sort of compromise that would draw as many justices as possible to an opinion. The conservatives themselves were split on how far they would go, and with Thomas advocating complete reversal of *Grutter* based on his view that no classifications tied to race were allowed under the Constitution's guarantee of equality, Kennedy lacked the critical five votes for a single rationale. Kennedy also wanted to lower the temperature of the negotiations, intensified by Sotomayor's dissenting rhetoric.

Stylistically, the two were opposites. Operating best in a buzz of activity, Sotomayor typed furiously on her computer, constantly calling out to aides. Kennedy, who often arrived before dawn, sought a quieter, less cluttered setting. He would often look out his office window, across the Court's marble plaza, to an exquisite view of the Capitol. When he joined the Court in February 1988, he inherited the chambers of Lewis Powell, the centrist conservative who had cast the deciding vote and written the rationale of the 1978 *Bakke* case. That personal history was not lost on Kennedy.

Further, although Kennedy had protested Justice O'Connor's decision for the majority in *Grutter*, he knew it had been the law for a decade and was not ready to reverse it outright. There would be other cases on the issue and time enough to end the racial affirmative action that had proliferated on the nation's campuses.

Justice Scalia, like Thomas, opposed any use of race in admissions, but he saw how the University of Texas dispute could not be used to reverse the University of Michigan decision in *Grutter v. Bollinger*. Lawyer Rein, on behalf of Abigail Fisher, had not directly asked for such a reversal. Rather, Rein had argued that the Court should strike down the University of Texas policy based on the standard of *Grutter*, albeit in a narrow reading of that case.

As the two ideological camps inched toward each other over the weeks, consensus eluded them. They were soon into April, and nearly all the cases from the October–December oral arguments had been resolved.

Tensions were escalating over the Shelby County, Alabama, case, too, but there the votes were clear-cut. There would be no shifting of sentiment or attempts to bridge ideological differences. Voting to invalidate the crucial formula underlying Section 5's preclearance rules were Chief Justice Roberts and Justices Scalia, Kennedy, Thomas, and Alito. Voting to dissent from that view were Justices Ginsburg, Breyer, Sotomayor, and Kagan. Roberts and Ginsburg were writing the lead opinions for the dueling sides. "Our country has changed," Roberts would eventually say in his opinion for the Court, "and while any racial discrimination in voting is too much, Congress must ensure that the legislation it passes to remedy that problem speaks to current conditions."

In her dissent for the liberals, Justice Ginsburg stressed that the states covered by the Voting Rights Act preclearance rule still had the worst voting rights violations nationwide and that the majority's position was turning its back on the vision of slain civil rights leader Martin Luther King, Jr. "The great man who led the march from Selma to Montgomery and there called for the passage of the Voting Rights Act foresaw progress, even in Alabama. 'The arc of the moral universe is long,' he said, but 'it bends toward justice,' if there is a steadfast commitment to see the task through to completion," Ginsburg wrote, "that commitment has been disserved by" the majority's decision.[20]

This case certainly showed the strains over race.

If the heated opinion Sotomayor was drafting in the University of Texas case had made it into the public eye, more fervent conflict would have captured America's attention. It would have marked the first time she revealed, as a Supreme Court justice, her passionate views about race in America. She felt deeply that special measures still were needed to lift blacks, Latinos, and other minorities through higher education. As an initial matter, she preferred phrases such as "race-sensitive admissions policies" to the phrase "affirmative action." She thought it important to explain the nuanced programs universities were then using, as opposed to past policies giving preferential treatment solely on the basis of race. She thought the Court was evading the dilemma of race in America and the reality she knew well, that people were still judged by the color of their skin.

But Sotomayor, who had come on so strongly at the start, became satisfied with Kennedy's retreat in his succession of draft opinions.

Kennedy's draft opinion for the Court now was saying that the University of Texas racial policy should return to lower courts for another review. He was writing that the appeals court's first assessment was too deferential, that the appeals court could not merely take the university's word that race-neutral approaches had failed to provide sufficient diversity in the entering class. He said that a lower court needed to undertake its own inquiry into whether a university could achieve sufficient diversity without using racial classifications and satisfy itself that no workable race-neutral alternatives would produce the same educational benefits of diversity.

Writing for a new majority of seven, Kennedy left intact the central holding of *Grutter.* Sotomayor dropped her dissenting statement. She, along with Breyer, signed the Kennedy opinion, too. Roberts and Alito would have signed Kennedy's stronger statement but agreed to the compromise, as did Scalia. He additionally broke off, however, to write a separate opinion saying that he would have wanted the Court to reconsider *Grutter* but was deterred because challenger Abigail Fisher did not request it. Justice Thomas stuck to his guns and declared that the 2003 precedent should be overturned. "I would overrule *Grutter v. Bollinger,* and hold that a State's use of race in higher education admissions decisions is categorically prohibited by the Equal Protection Clause," he wrote, adding his statement from the 2003 *Grutter* case that "the Constitution abhors classifications based on race because every time the government places citizens on racial registers and makes race relevant to the provisions of burdens or benefits, it demeans us all."[21]

Justice Ginsburg continued to dissent from the majority because she did not think the University of Texas case should be sent back for reconsideration. Even as Ginsburg protested the returning of the case to a lower court, she said that the Kennedy majority "rightly declines to cast off the equal protection framework settled ten years ago in *Grutter.*" She reiterated her sentiment that universities "need not be blind to the lingering effects of an overtly discriminatory past, the legacy of centuries of law-sanctioned inequality." Ginsburg's message to the public: The rules have not changed.

The Supreme Court decision was interpreted by supporters of affirmative action, including President Obama, as accepting the status quo. "The Court preserved the well-established legal principle that colleges and universities have a compelling interest in achieving the educational benefits that flow from a racially and ethnically diverse student body," the Department of Education said in a letter to colleges and universities three months after the ruling. It advised them not to change any of the procedures in place from the 2003 court decision.[22]

Opponents of affirmative action, including lawyer Rein and

activist Blum, countered that the University of Texas ruling required
for the first time that administrators provide extensive data on why
options that did not involve race had fallen short. They and others
predicted that the decision would eventually spell the demise of affirmative action because, as the ruling played out in lower courts,
schools would have the difficult burden of proving that before they
turned to racial classifications, all other alternatives had failed.

Outside observers would quarrel over how much the legal land-
scape had shifted. But it was clear that conservative justices had
retreated, and at least for the immediate future, the University of
Texas policy and national practice of campus affirmative action
would continue.

It had taken compromise and concessions by a number of justices. But it started with the woman who was the first Hispanic and
who would make no apologies for what affirmative action had done
for her.

◆

She would not wield the same influence on her colleagues a year
later. In April 2014, Justice Kennedy won a majority in an equally
contentious but less far-reaching case testing a Michigan state ban
on racial affirmative action, including at public universities.[23]

Now Sotomayor's voice would be heard beyond the Court, and
loudly. She issued a barbed fifty-eight-page dissent to Kennedy's
eighteen-page opinion upholding the Michigan law approved by
voters. For the first time since President Obama appointed her in
2009, she also took the bold step of reading portions of the opinion
from the bench. That occurs when dissenting justices want to draw
special attention to their views. For nearly five years, Sotomayor
had eschewed the practice, saying it seemed overly dramatic for the
judicial setting.

Not this time. For twelve minutes, nearly as long as Kennedy
had taken when he announced the Court's majority views, she condemned the majority stance. She chided her colleagues for ignoring
the needs of people on the margins and pointedly challenged the

contention of Chief Justice Roberts and other conservatives that it was time to look beyond race. Her opinion echoed with her personal story: "Race matters because of the slights, the snickers, the silent judgments that reinforce that most crippling of thoughts: 'I do not belong here.'" She was speaking generally, of course, but the words could have been taken from the text of her speeches, especially to student groups.

She said the 2006 Michigan law forbidding racial criteria placed a heavy burden—"selective barriers"—on just one group. She noted that those seeking other types of preferences in admissions, based on family alumni status, for example, could and did lobby for such measures. In contrast, the only way to obtain race-based affirmative action would be first to win a state constitutional amendment lifting the one approved nearly a decade earlier.

Her opinion, joined only by Justice Ginsburg, immediately drew intense, competing responses that recalled the dual comments to her "wise Latina" remark. Attorney General Eric Holder, who is black and had encouraged people to talk about lingering race discrimination, deemed Sotomayor's dissenting statement "courageous." The conservative National Review called it "legally illiterate and logically indefensible."

Fellow justices were critical, too, notably Chief Justice Roberts, whose views on racial remedies she used as a rhetorical weapon. "The way to stop discrimination on the basis of race is to speak openly and candidly on the subject of race," she said, clearly mocking his view that "the way to stop discrimination on the basis of race is to stop discriminating on the basis of race."

In response, Roberts criticized Sotomayor for "expounding . . . policy preferences." He threw her sentiment about minorities' doubts back at her, rejecting the notion that it was "out of touch" to believe that racial preferences could reinforce feelings among minorities that they do not belong. Clearly irked by the airing of personal strains, he added that it "does more harm than good to question the openness and candor of those on either side of the debate."

Declaring that she could not ignore the ruling's "unfortunate" consequences for minorities trying to improve their lives through education, Sotomayor concluded, "For members of historically marginalized groups . . . the decision can hardly bolster hope for a vision of democracy that preserves for all the right to participate meaningfully and equally in self-government."

TWELVE

Her Divided World

When Sonia Sotomayor left Washington for public appearances to promote her memoir, people lined up hours ahead of time to catch a glimpse or hear a few words from this singular justice. Her book tour, extending from January 2013 into 2014, was extraordinary. No member of the nation's highest court had ever been paid close to the $3 million–plus she had drawn as an advance from Knopf for telling her life story.[1] Nor had any justice attracted the kinds of crowds she did, with their mix of men and women, white, black, and brown, dressed in everything from conservative dark business suits to fruit-colored capri pants.

During her April 2013 visit to San Juan, on the island of her ancestors, people began lining up at 8:00 a.m., more than six hours before Sotomayor was scheduled to appear at the Plaza Las Americas, billed as the Caribbean's largest shopping mall.[2] Carrying copies of her memoir, *My Beloved World*, as it was published in English, and *Mi mundo adorado*, as it was titled in Spanish, they waited near store windows that were decorated for spring, complete with prom dresses and outfits in First Communion white, such as those Soto-mayor wore as a Catholic school girl. By the time she arrived, shortly after 2:30 p.m., people were crowding around the stage where she would speak. Other shoppers leaned over railings on the floor above to get a look at the Latina who had reached the pinnacle of the law.

This Puerto Rican tour—four days of promotional events—came at a particularly important time in the Supreme Court's annual term. The justices were wrestling with cases testing government policies intended to give blacks and Hispanics a lift in college admissions and to protect their voting rights in states that had a history of discrimination. Sotomayor and her eight colleagues would also be resolving their first-ever disputes over same-sex marriage and taking up an emotional custody battle over a baby with Native American roots.[3]

The Court's caseload was not hindering Sotomayor, who had been on a whirlwind of promotional activities since early January. In bookstores and on university campuses from New York to Chicago to Austin to San Diego she was the center of huge events. People came to hear from her, in San Juan and elsewhere, as a person who embodied the American dream far more than as a jurist with certain legal views.

She took full advantage of her popularity, signing hundreds of books at a sitting and selling tens of thousands of copies in the first few weeks of publication. Actress Rita Moreno, a Puerto Rican who was the first Latina to win an Oscar—for her role in the movie *West Side Story*—was the reader for the audio version of *My Beloved World*. In an appearance with Sotomayor in Washington, D.C., featuring the book, Moreno said that she burst into tears when she heard that the first Hispanic had been nominated to the Supreme Court in 2009. Their public conversation in a large theater before a sold-out audience was not the usual judicial fare: Sotomayor revealed that she had no memory of her mother ever hugging her, while Moreno said that her mother had passed down her terrible taste in men.[4]

Sotomayor's appearances in San Juan, just as with Moreno in Washington and elsewhere, offered the kind of atmosphere usually reserved for media celebrities. At the Plaza Las Americas, when it came time to greet her fans, Sotomayor emerged from a closed hallway between a shoe store and clothing shop. Accompanied by island dignitaries, she strode up onto the elevated stage. Spectators whooped and clapped from lines that had formed hours earlier and snaked past a dozen retail shops.

The contrast with the atmosphere at the place where Sotomayor spends most of her days—the mammoth-columned Supreme Court building—was striking. The Court is defined by hierarchies even in the way people line up. On any given day of oral arguments, there are separate, police-monitored lines for lawyers, for news reporters, and for the general public.

At the mall in San Juan, where all gathered together, everyone seemed to have a smartphone or camera to snap photos of the justice. Sotomayor's paparazzi included people decked out in glittery jewelry, students whose parents had allowed them to skip a day of school, and even a maintenance man carting a bright yellow bucket and mops, who stopped to record her appearance.

Sotomayor wore a burnt-orange jacket over a taupe dress, and her usual mass of black curls was combed out. She addressed the crowd in Spanish and said she was thrilled to see so many people. She gestured with her hands, a habit she had tried to control as a member of her high school debate team. But moving as she spoke—moving all the time, really—was her way. She could energize any room, even an enormous shopping mall.

When she began signing books, people greeted her as if she were an old friend, an aunt, or a sister. After an hour the line was still moving but growing longer. Sotomayor left just in time to make an early-evening cocktail reception with local dignitaries at a nearby marina.

The next morning, she drove with an entourage from San Juan to Gurabo, about twenty miles south, and was back at it, talking about her life and signing books. This time her admirers were crowded into the Universidad del Turabo Pedro Rosselló Library. Large pictures of her book jacket—with her face on it—were everywhere. The festivities began with a private reception and luncheon buffet. About two hundred friends, family, and professors—some whom she had known for decades, others she had just collected along the way of this promotional trip—jammed into a suite of small offices. People were more interested in seeing her than in eating lunch.

For this appearance, Sotomayor wore a patterned black, orange, and white dress with a black cardigan. She looked dressed up but more comfortable than the day before—her hair back to its usual curly mass—as she moved effortlessly through the crowd of well-wishers, shaking hands, hugging, posing for pictures. After hobnobbing, sometimes in Spanish, but mostly in English, Sotomayor headed to a large auditorium, where she took questions.

As the main event began, her warmth infused the room. People broke into applause several times as she related the trials of her childhood in the Bronx, her determination to succeed in school, and her early career as a prosecutor and a judge. She spoke mostly in Spanish, but because hers is sometimes fractured, she turned to English when she wanted to make sure she was clear.

No matter the language, the audience was rapt. Hearing her inspirational tales, people wiped tears from their eyes at several points.

Sotomayor regaled them with a favorite case—when she intervened in the Major League Baseball strike of 1994–95—telling the story as if it happened yesterday, not from a judge's perspective, but from that of a rabid fan. She said that her beloved New York Yankees were doing so well they might have made it to the World Series if not for the strike-shortened season. She said she faced Major League Baseball owners who were threatening to destroy the game with their demands related to wages, hours, and other employment conditions. A federal board had accused the owners of engaging in unfair labor practices. "I decided that the government was right," Sotomayor said, simplifying the litigation and judicial order that brought the owners and players back to the bargaining table.

"I became the baseball judge," she declared. It was a label with wide appeal, especially in Puerto Rico, the home of the legendary Roberto Clemente, who played for the Pittsburgh Pirates and was a legend in the Bronx.

When Sotomayor answered questions from students and others in the auditorium, she never went on the defensive. She did not exude cynicism, as other justices sometimes did when they were on the road before crowds of lawyers. She enjoyed using her story to empower others. At times she lowered her voice, as if to say, "We're talking, just you and me. Never mind the large audience."

Although the baseball strike dispute was captivating because of its popular subject, people here had not come to learn about cases or the law. They had come to learn about this Latina who seems to exist to tell others how she made it and assert that she still is confronted by sexist or racist critics who think she is not up to the job.

Sotomayor's mother accompanied her on the 2013 trip to Puerto Rico. In her eighties, Celina still looked elegant, her soft face displaying her beauty. Her manicured nails were painted with rose-colored polish. For this campus event in Gurabo, she wore a black jacket and black thinly striped pants, and favoring accessories more understated than her daughter's jangling silver pieces, she wore small earrings and a silver strand necklace with a tiny jewel in the center. Despite some memory loss and trouble concentrating, she appeared to follow the exchanges as her daughter fielded questions. She smiled broadly at her answers.

It just so happened that no one in this university setting asked—as other audiences had—about parts of *My Beloved World* in which Sotomayor revealed the complicated relationship with her mother: "Mami gone, checked out, the empty apartment. Her back to me, just a log in the bed beside me as a child. Mami, perfectly dressed and made up, like a movie star, the Jacqueline Kennedy of the Bronxdale Houses, refusing to pick me up and wrinkle her spotless outfit. This was the cold image I'd lived with and formed myself in response to, unhappily adopting the aloofness but none of the glamour. I could not free myself from its spell until I could appreciate what formed it and, in its likeness, me."[5] In the book, Sotomayor explained that she came to better understand her mother once she discovered more about her difficult, emotionally bereft childhood.

But there were other touchy subjects, and when Sotomayor was asked about racial divisions in America and beyond, she began speaking in English again. "Today we are segregated in a different way, not easy to dismantle, segregated by wealth," the justice said, adding that she thought it was important to equalize education to end economic disparities. But she also acknowledged long-standing racial, religious, and other cultural tensions. "We still have suspicions about people who are different," she said.

The most emotional moment occurred when a student elaborated on his question with an excerpt from her memoir but kept choking up as he tried to read. The student stopped trying and said he wanted her to sign his copy of her book. "That's initiative," Sotomayor quipped, drawing some chuckles as the student bounded down to the stage. Once at the front of the room with the justice, the young man, in gray jeans and a black T-shirt, knelt next to her as she signed his book. When she finished, she gave him a kiss. Spectators applauded wildly.

◆

It is hard to imagine another justice connecting with a public audience so intimately.

Even before the publication of her bestseller, Sotomayor was a different breed: approachable, human, like the people who came out to greet her. Her book brought her to another level of celebrity and public adulation. She wrote about her "darker experiences" growing up. She wrote that she had a pudgy nose, a mop of hair, and that it would take most of her adult life to feel pulled together. She became an everywoman with everywoman doubts.

Sotomayor dealt with her vulnerabilities directly, even by relating her professional failure as a summer associate at Paul, Weiss, her first major legal job. It was a devastation, she revealed, that haunted her for decades. She seemed to want to make sure her problems were hers to address, not her critics' to broadcast. Her story was motivating: "If I can make it, you can make it."

She said she wanted to offer hope to others. "I know that message can't be recounted often enough for people," she told an audience at Yale Law School in February 2014.[6] She said she also wanted to hold on to her own identity as she was catapulted into the universe of the Supreme Court and national prominence.

Literary reviewers were as struck by her tale as the students and others who flocked to her appearances. "It's an eloquent and affecting testament to the triumph of brains and hard work over circumstance, of a childhood dream realized through extraordinary will and dedication," Michiko Kakutani wrote in *The New York Times*, likening Sotomayor's book to Barack Obama's memoir, *Dreams from My Father*.[7]

In an essay for the *The Atlantic* magazine, Peter Osnos, founder and editor at large of the PublicAffairs publishing house, differentiated Sotomayor's book from Clarence Thomas's account of his life in *My Grandfather's Son*: "In tone and content, Thomas's book reflected his dour persona . . . In contrast, Sotomayor has charmed audiences at signings across the country with a natural warmth and humor, plus shown the patience to sign every copy purchased by turnouts as high as a thousand people at a time."[8] Osnos observed that Sotomayor benefited from her collaboration with Zara Houshmand, an Iranian American poet who helped write the book. Sotomayor said that Houshmand listened to her stories and those of her family and friends to select the most compelling tales.

It was a rare critic who did not embrace the memoir on its own terms. Yet, indicative of how Sotomayor remained a polarizing political figure, some commentators used their reviews of *My Beloved World* to renew complaints about affirmative action or remind readers of Jeffrey Rosen's "case against" her in *The New Republic* at the time of her nomination.[9] Writing in *Reason* magazine, senior editor Damon Root referred to Rosen's interviews with lawyers who griped about Sotomayor's temperament and ability, asserting, "And although the [Rosen] story failed to derail Sotomayor's nomination, it cast a shadow of doubt that continues to follow her on the bench. Sonia Sotomayor does not mention this troubling episode in her new memoir, *My Beloved World*, nor does she do much to dispel any lingering liberal doubts."[10]

But liberals broadly embraced Sotomayor's book and her early record as a justice. On most cases, her vote was on the left, and the attention she called to the plight of criminal defendants was welcome. Many of the "lingering doubts" came from conservatives who simply believed she had gotten where she was only because she was Hispanic.

There was no ignoring the double-edged consequences of her ethnic identity.

That was seen in the final months of President Barack Obama's 2012 reelection campaign. His strategists used Sotomayor to their advantage as the first Hispanic appointee to the Supreme Court, creating a political ad that flashed back to May 26, 2009, when Obama stood beside her in the White House East Room amid gold silk draperies, swag valances, and cut-glass chandeliers. "After completing this exhaustive process," the president says, "I have decided to nominate an inspiring woman who I believe will make a great justice."[11]

With captions in Spanish, the three-minute advertisement mixed Obama's tribute to Sotomayor with the voices of Latina women praising his choice. "My glass ceiling just shattered," says one. "It is very important to have a Latina on the Supreme Court," says another. A Puerto Rican woman refers to her toddler daughter and says, "It means no dream is too big for her to dream."

The ad, unusual for highlighting a president's Court appointment, underscored the value of the Sotomayor choice and offered a reminder that judicial appointments are enduringly political.

How could the president, any candidate really, not try to woo the Hispanic vote?

By late 2012, Hispanics numbered 54 million in the United States, 17 percent of the total population. Hispanics were also reaching milestones that hardly could have been imagined when Sotomayor was young. College enrollment for Hispanic high school students had skyrocketed since her years at Princeton. In 2012, for the first time in the nation's history, a higher percentage of recent Hispanic high school graduates were enrolled in college than whites, 49 percent, compared with 47 percent of white non-Hispanic high school graduates.[12]

President Obama and Vice President Joseph Biden won reelection—with 71 percent of the Hispanic vote. Republican challenger Mitt Romney, a hard-liner on immigration policy, did particularly poorly with this demographic, drawing the lowest percentage for a GOP candidate since Bob Dole in 1996. In the crucial battleground state of Florida, a Pew Hispanic Center study found that the Democratic ticket carried the Hispanic vote by 60 percent, compared with 39 percent for the Republicans. (Hispanics made up 17 percent of the electorate, up from 14 percent in Florida in 2008.) Pew Research attributed Obama's strong showing among Hispanic voters to the state's growing non-Cuban population, notably the Puerto Rican population of central Florida.[13]

After the reelection victory, Vice President Biden asked Justice Sotomayor to administer the oath of office for the January 20, 2013, inaugural. She agreed, but imposed a condition. She needed the event moved up four hours earlier than the traditional noon ceremony. Sotomayor had committed to a book signing in Manhattan that afternoon and wanted to make sure she got to it.

Biden's aides were miffed. The *Los Angeles Times*, the first to report that Biden would not be sworn in with Obama, cheekily observed that Sotomayor would not reveal her plans, that she simply "had somewhere else to be." Court officials would not confirm that Sotomayor's schedule was dictated by the book event posted on the Barnes & Noble website.[14] A writer on the legal blog *Above the Law* remarked, "What was more important to Justice Sonia Sotomayor than swearing in Joe Biden as VP at noon on Sunday? Signing books at Barnes & Noble in New York City. Not so wise Latina."[15]

But Sotomayor's move passed with little public interest or real press scrutiny. Even Vice President Biden accepted the situation matter-of-factly, telling his 120 guests as she rushed off on the morning of the inauguration, "I wanted to explain to you what a wonderful honor it was and how much out of her way the justice had to go. She is due in New York . . . We are going to walk out, you see her car's waiting so she can catch a train I hope I haven't caused her to miss."[16]

When Sotomayor arrived at the Manhattan Barnes & Noble,

she told the two hundred people waiting that she was touched by their enthusiasm. She knew it was her personal story, not legal opinions, that resonated with these audiences, and that may be her enduring legacy. As she addressed the crowd, many of whom had stood in line for hours to see her, she said, "That's an awesome amount of love to feel."[17]

That turned out to be Manhattan on a small scale for Sotomayor.

Almost one year later, on December 31, 2013, she was in Times Square. She had been chosen to lead the sixty-second countdown and pressing of the button to drop the ball commemorating the start of 2014. She was the first Supreme Court justice ever selected for the event, which was witnessed by one million people in Times Square and millions more on television. In the prior two years, the designated special guests had been Lady Gaga and the Radio City Rockettes.[18]

Unlike at an earlier time, when Sotomayor might have been invited to an event because of her ethnicity and appear as the lone Hispanic, she was chosen because of her inspiring life and celebrity. Several other Hispanic entertainers happened to be in the international spotlight that evening. Rául de Molina, the entertainment news host of Univision Networks, also appeared. The Spanish-language Univision was besting such long-standing broadcast networks as ABC and NBC during summer sweeps periods with viewers ages eighteen to forty-nine.[19]

Divisions among cultures in America were fading, and Sotomayor was—as usual—in sync with national change. She no longer was breaking barriers as a Puerto Rican. She was breaking barriers as a justice. A few weeks before the New Year's Eve festivities, she had been a presenter at the nationally televised Kennedy Center Honors. There, she offered the tribute for soprano and international opera star Martina Arroyo. Sotomayor was the first justice to appear at the Honors since the annual show began thirty-six years earlier. The *Washington Post* Style section reported that she received a standing ovation as she emerged onstage wearing a blue gown with a plunging neckline.[20]

As midnight neared on December 31, 2013, a beaming Sotomayor began shouting the countdown, then pressed the ceremonial button to send the glittery ball down. Television screens flashed between Sotomayor and pop star Miley Cyrus.

◆

All the media attention, the public adoration, and the exclusive invitations testified to Sotomayor's place in American life.

When she was asked at the February 2014 Yale Law School forum about her wide travels across the country, she first declared unguardedly, "I wanted to sell books." But then she turned philosophical, saying that she hoped she could "add value . . . to the public's perception of the justices."[21]

As she increased her public profile, her voice became stronger on the Court. The Indian child custody battle, heard in 2013 as Sotomayor was in the thick of her book promotion, demonstrated that. The child had been placed at birth for adoption with a white family but then, at age two, ordered by a South Carolina court to be returned to her father, a member of the Cherokee tribe. It was a case that especially roused Sotomayor, perhaps because of the focus on children, with whom she said she often identifies more than with adults. She wrote in her memoir that she had considered adopting, but concerns about her diabetes stopped her. "There remained the fear that I might not be around long enough to raise a child to adulthood," she said. "Ultimately, the satisfaction of motherhood would be sacrificed."[22]

In the Court case, the baby's biological parents, Dusten Brown and Christina Maldonado, had never married, and Brown, part Cherokee, agreed to relinquish his parental rights rather than pay child support. Maldonado arranged for the Capobiancos, a white couple from South Carolina, to adopt the child, whom they named Veronica.[23] The following year, Brown decided to assert his parental rights, citing the protections of the Indian Child Welfare Act. The 1978 law was intended to stop Indian children from being moved from their tribal surroundings. South Carolina courts ruled for

Brown, emphasizing the federal interest in preserving the tribes' cultural identity.

When the Supreme Court took up the Capobiancos' appeal, the question was whether Brown, as an unwed father lacking legal custody, was a "parent" under the Indian Child Welfare Act. Justice Sotomayor questioned the lawyers in such an intense, confrontational way that Chief Justice Roberts and Justice Scalia, at separate points, implored her to stop interrupting and let the attorney at the lectern answer.[24] In the end, the Court ruled 5–4 in favor of the Capobiancos. Writing for the majority, Justice Alito said that Brown "abandoned the child before birth and never had custody of the child," so he was not covered by the 1978 law.[25]

Sotomayor dissented, with Justices Scalia, Ginsburg, and Kagan, and in part of her opinion she criticized the majority for focusing "on the perceived parental shortcomings" of Brown. "In an ideal world," she wrote, "perhaps all parents would be perfect. They would live up to their parental responsibilities by providing the fullest possible financial and emotional support to their children." Perhaps recalling her own childhood in the Bronx, she continued: "They would never suffer mental health problems, lose their jobs, struggle with substance dependency, or encounter any of the other multitudinous personal crises that can make it difficult to meet these responsibilities . . . But we do not live in such a world."[26]

Alito responded that Sotomayor had offered "a torrent of words" that failed to hide the fact that her interpretation of the law "simply cannot be squared with the statutory text." He said her interpretation of parental custody would lead "even a sperm donor" to be covered by the law.

A few months later Sotomayor found herself writing alone in a case and incurring even more withering criticism. The dispute tested whether a multinational company accused of a role in human rights abuses could be sued in a United States court. It arose from Argentina's "Dirty War" era, 1976–83, and claims by twenty-two Argentinians that Daimler's Argentine subsidiary had collaborated with the government in killings and torture. The legal question was whether the constitutional guarantee of due process of law barred a federal court in California from jurisdiction over Daimler because of the scant connection to the atrocities and perpetrators. Writing for an eight-justice majority, Justice Ginsburg said that the company's link to the United States was insufficient to allow jurisdiction.

Sotomayor agreed that Daimler could not be sued in the case, but she said that Ginsburg's rationale was "unmoored from decades of precedent" and could "produce deep injustice" in other cases involving multinationals. Ginsburg responded that Sotomayor had selectively read the record in the case. "No fair reader" of the key precedent would have interpreted it as Sotomayor did, Ginsburg insisted. Joined by the seven other justices, Ginsburg's complaint about the Sotomayor opinion in the case of *Daimler AG v. Bauman* was notable for its length over several pages of footnotes. Sotomayor simply responded that they were the ones misreading court precedent.[27]

For weeks, Sotomayor had seen drafts of Ginsburg's opinion as it circulated among the justices. She knew she was about to be a public target. But she would have the courage of her convictions—perhaps stubbornly, misguidedly—yet with confidence enough to be the one in an 8–1 vote.

A week before the Daimler opinion was handed down, in January 2014, Sotomayor told an audience of more than a thousand that to bolster her courage, she often thought about the worst thing that could happen when she undertook a challenging endeavor. She would conclude: "You know something . . . so what?"[28]

She was willing to stand out. She always had, anyway. She would not mute her personality, and she was not interested in brokering compromise. Other justices had their antennae up for how to persuade a colleague to their point of view. Breyer telephoned colleagues or wandered into chambers hoping to talk out an issue. Kagan appreciated the spirited back-and-forth that could accompany the drafting of opinions and tried to penetrate the roots of colleagues' reasoning to persuade them.

Sotomayor's former appeals court colleague, Judge Rosemary Pooler, said, "She's less interested in having her antennae up than coming to her own decision." And when she does, "she doesn't think that's up for discussion."[29]

That could not help but raise the question of how effective this luminary in American life would be on the law of the land. She defined herself by being different. As Justice Sotomayor occupied a suite of offices on the third floor, above her colleagues on the second, she had a separate-floor mentality to go with it. She operated in her own world, with the book tour, public speeches, and increasingly with solo dissenting or concurring opinions. Other justices moved toward colleagues. Sandra Day O'Connor, for example, had famously organized group lunches, theater excursions, and other outings to build collegiality and bridges for substantive negotiations.

Sotomayor had learned to be effective in setting herself apart. And now she had no trouble breaking away from colleagues to make uncomfortable assertions, whether regarding the possible injustice of shielding corporations from claims linked to human rights abuses or, as she did a year earlier, the likelihood that Alabama judges were swayed by politics in their death penalty decisions.

Whatever her legacy in the marble confines of the Supreme Court, it seemed bound to be eclipsed by her more public role. Her timing was stunning. At every turn, she was ready for an America that was ready for her. She had arrived on the national stage, at the very top of the United States judiciary, as Hispanics were increasingly visible in all facets of life. She had reached prominence because of what she represented to a nation that still believed in the American dream.

Notes

1. LIFE OF THE PARTY

1. The ceremony marked the first time that the New York City Housing Authority had named a development for a living former resident. Information on the naming and event drawn from interviews and the *New York City Housing Authority Journal* 40, no. 5 (June/July 2010).

2. The program for the event was styled like a Supreme Court case: *Thirty-Eight Law Clerks vs. The Justices of the Supreme Court of the United States*. The annual clerks' party is closed to news media; the invitation and information about the June 2010 event was provided to the author by individual justices and others who attended.

3. Sotomayor is widely regarded as the first Hispanic justice on the United States Supreme Court. Some critics have countered that Justice Benjamin Cardozo, who served from 1932 to 1938 and was a Sephardic Jew with ancestors from Portugal, was the Court's first Hispanic. The term "Hispanic" was not in use during his era, and whether people from Portugal would be labeled Hispanic remains the subject of controversy.

4. Justices Sandra Day O'Connor and Clarence Thomas wrote memoirs as sitting justices, but only after they had served, respectively, twenty-one and sixteen years on the bench.

5. Although this book uses such terms as "Hispanic" and "Latino," the author recognizes that these labels are recent descriptors for people who would identify themselves primarily as, for example, Puerto Rican, Mexican, or Cuban. An October 2013 Pew Research Center study found that most Hispanics had no strong preference between the terms "Hispanic" and "Latino," and among those who expressed a slight preference, "Hispanic" was preferred.

6. Sonia Sotomayor, panelist at "Women in the Judiciary: A Woman's View from the Bench," a Practising Law Institute program broadcast live via satellite on June 9, 1994. Copy of program supplied to author by PLI.

7. Tribe, who was backing Elena Kagan at the time, later told the author he was "totally wrong" in doubting Sotomayor and said she "has contributed splendidly" to the Court.

8. Author interview with Gregory Craig, January 22, 2013.

9. Johnson engineered the vacancy for Marshall by leading Justice Tom Clark to step down and avoid any conflict of interest after Johnson appointed his son Ramsey Clark as attorney general.

10. "Latinos in the United States," Population Reference Bureau, December 2010 Report. The bureau said that while the Hispanic population grew 37 percent between 2000 and 2009, adding nearly 26 million people, the overall U.S. population grew by about 9 percent, rising from 281 million to 307 million.

11. Sonia Sotomayor appearance in Denver, August 26, 2010, before high school and college students, "Diversity and the Legal Profession"; C-SPAN broadcast available at www.c-span.org/video/?295200-1/diversity-legal-profession.

12. Sotomayor, *My Beloved World*, 237–38.

13. Rehnquist said he was inspired by the comic opera *Iolanthe*.

14. Pew Research Center Hispanic Trends Project, October 22, 2013; most Hispanics polled were unable to name the person they considered "the most important Hispanic leader in the country today." The top vote-getters for those who could name someone were Sonia Sotomayor and Marco Rubio, at 5 percent each; others named were Los Angeles mayor Antonio Villaraigosa, at 3 percent, and U.S. representative Luis Gutiérrez of Illinois, at 2 percent. Three-quarters of Latinos living in the United States said that their community needs a national leader.

15. President Obama broke from this pattern in July 2013, when he spoke out about the shooting death in Florida of an unarmed black youth, Trayvon Martin, after his killer was acquitted by a jury. "When Trayvon Martin was first shot, I said that this could have been my son. Another way of saying that is Trayvon Martin could have been me thirty-five years ago."

16. See, e.g., Charlie Savage, "Despite Filibuster Limits, a Door Remains Open to Block Judge Nominees," *New York Times*, November 29, 2013. Savage noted that White House counsel Kathryn Ruemmler said President Obama was seeking "smart and thoughtful" judges who had the "potential to persuade," and she referred to Justice Kagan as a model.

2. "LIFE IS ALL RIGHT IN AMERICA . . . IF YOU'RE ALL WHITE IN AMERICA"

1. See, e.g., Paul Hofmann, "200,000 Watch as Puerto Ricans Parade: 30,000 Join March—Rockefeller and Kennedy Hailed," *New York Times*, June 27, 1966; Martin Gansberg, "Hispanic Parade Attracts 25,000: Rhumba and Cha-Cha Tunes Serenade the Marchers," *New York Times*, June 5, 1967.

2. Lacey Fosburgh, "19 Police Injured at Parade Here: 20 Arrested as Puerto Rican Groups Interrupt March in Protest Over Status," *New York Times*, June 14, 1971.

3. Sonia Sotomayor appearance in Denver, August 26, 2010, "Diversity and the Legal Profession."

4. Ibid.

5. José A. Cabranes, "A Puerto Rican Perspective," in *Minority Opportunities in Law*

for Blacks, Puerto Ricans & Chicanos. edited by Christine Philpot Clark (Law Journal Press, 1974).

6. Edgardo Meléndez Vélez, *"The Puerto Rican Journey* Revisited: Politics and the Study of Puerto Rican Migration," *CENTRO Journal* 17, no. 2 (Fall 2005).

7. "Sugar-Bowl Migrants," *Time,* August 11, 1947.

8. Glazer and Moynihan, *Beyond the Melting Pot,* 87.

9. Celina Baez background drawn from U.S. Census Bureau information, Sotomayor speeches on file with the Senate Judiciary Committee for 2009 nomination, and Sotomayor's *My Beloved World.*

10. Sotomayor, Lehman College Graduation Speech, June 3, 1999, New York; copy in Senate Judiciary Committee 2009 nomination file.

11. Sotomayor, *My Beloved World,* 53.

12. *Hernandez v. Texas,* 347 U.S. 475 (1954).

13. *Hernandez v. Texas.*

14. The 1848 Treaty of Guadalupe Hidalgo, which ended the Mexican-American War, caused large swaths of Mexican territory to become part of the United States and eventually offered Mexicans living there the opportunity to become American citizens.

15. "Zoot Suits" referred to the colorful outfits and broad-brimmed hats in fashion among some young Mexican American men at the time. For a history of such incidents and the exclusion of Mexican Americans, see also Kevin R. Johnson, *"Hernandez v. Texas*: Legacies of Justice and Injustice," UC Davis Law, Legal Studies Research Paper No. 19 (2004).

16. Suro, *Strangers Among Us,* 86.

17. Sonia Sotomayor quoted in *New York City Housing Authority Journal* 40, no. 5 (June/July 2010).

18. Sotomayor, *My Beloved World,* 45.

19. Sotomayor, Smithsonian Associates Evening Lecture, January 8, 2014, George Washington University, Washington, D.C.

20. Sotomayor, "Urban Health Plan" speech, New York, September 21, 2007; copy in Senate Judiciary Committee 2009 nomination file.

21. Sotomayor, *My Beloved World,* 13–14.

22. Joan Biskupic, "Sotomayor Gets Frank on Diabetes; Shares Her Story to Inspire Young Type 1 Patients," *USA Today,* June 22, 2011.

23. Sotomayor, *My Beloved World,* 3.

24. Ibid., 88.

25. *Katzenbach v. Morgan,* 384 U.S. 641 (1966), *Cardona v. Power,* 384 U.S. 672 (1966).

26. *White v. Regester,* 412 U.S. 755 (1973).

27. "Chicago's Proud Puerto Ricans," *Chicago Daily News,* June 5, 1965.

28. See, e.g., "500 Police Keep Watch on N.W. Side," *Chicago Tribune,* June 15, 1966; and "The Cause of the Riot," *Chicago Tribune* editorial, June 15, 1966.

29. "Racial Outbreaks Flare on E. 10th: 30 Held as Puerto Ricans Throw Missiles at Police," *New York Times,* August 31, 1964; Richard J. H. Johnston, "A Calm Settles

over East 10th St.: Policemen and Broken Glass Are Lone Echoes of Fray," *New York Times*, September 1, 1964.

30. Homer Bigart, "Renewed Violence Erupts in 2 Puerto Rican Areas," *New York Times*, July 26, 1967; Peter Kihss, "Puerto Rican Story: A Sensitive People Erupt," *New York Times*, July 26, 1967.

31. Kihss, "Puerto Rican Story."

32. The median number of school years for Puerto Rican students in 1960 was 7.5. Neil J. Smelser, William Julius Wilson, and Faith Mitchell, eds., *America Becoming: Racial Trends and Their Consequences*, vol. 1, National Research Council, Commission on Behavioral and Social Sciences and Education, 2001.

33. Glazer and Moynihan, *The Melting Pot*, 91.

34. Sonia Sotomayer quoted in *New York City Housing Authority Journal* 40, no. 5 (June/July 2010).

35. Author interview with Charles Auffant, May 24, 2011; Auffant became a professor at Rutgers School of Law.

36. Author interview with Theodore Shaw, October 2011.

37. Sotomayor, *My Beloved World*, 106.

38. Ibid., 107.

39. Ibid., 120–121. See also Kathy Kiely, "No Dissent: A Locomotive for Sotomayor '76," *Princeton Alumni Weekly*, June 1, 2011.

40. Sotomayor, *My Beloved World*, 122.

41. Ibid., 119.

42. Sotomayor viewed *12 Angry Men* at a Fordham Law Film Festival in Manhattan on October 17, 2010.

3. "I AM THE PERFECT AFFIRMATIVE ACTION BABY"

1. Sotomayor, *My Beloved World*, 126.

2. Catherine Lawson, "A Touch of Class," *Mademoiselle*, September 1986.

3. Pew Research Center Hispanic Trends Project, August 20, 2012.

4. President Lyndon B. Johnson, Commencement Address at Howard University, June 5, 1965; www.lbjlib.utexas.edu/johnson/archives.hom/speeches.hom/650 604.asp.

5. Ibid.

6. Bowen and Bok, *The Shape of the River*, 6–7.

7. Of the total number of judges President Carter sent to U.S. district courts, 13.9 percent were black and 6.9 percent were Hispanic, compared with President Ford's 5.8 percent black and 1.9 percent Hispanic district court appointees. President Nixon's appointees were 2.8 percent black and 1.1 percent Hispanic. Of President Johnson's total appointments to district court, 3.3 percent were black and 2.5 percent Hispanic. Sheldon Goldman, "Carter's Judicial Appointments: A Lasting Legacy," *Judicature* 64, no. 8 (March 1981).

8. During the Johnson administration 5 percent of his appeals court appointees were black and none was Hispanic.

9. Roy Reed, "Johnson Calls Nominee 'Best Qualified,' and Rights Leaders are Jubilant—Southerners Silent on Confirmation," *New York Times*, June 14, 1967.

10. Carter, *The Confirmation Mess*, 5.

11. Twenty other senators, from the South and North, did not cast a vote. According to the August 20, 1967, *Congressional Record*, some of those twenty missing senators were away on business and said they would have voted for Marshall; www .senate.gov/reference/resources/pdf/240_1967.pdf.

12. See, e.g., Sotomayor, "The Genesis and Needs of an Ethnic Identity," keynote speech to Connecticut Hispanic Bar Association, New Haven, October 24, 1998; copy in Senate Judiciary Committee 2009 nomination file.

13. Sotomayor, *My Beloved World*, 128.

14. Sonia Sotomayor appearance at Cornell University Law School, October 8, 2008; available at www.youtube.com/watch?v=c4hZloq_5S0.

15. Sonia Sotomayor, Smithsonian Associates Evening Lecture, January 8, 2014, George Washington University, Washington, D.C.

16. Sonia Sotomayor, "A Judge's Guide to More Effective Advocacy," keynote speech, 40th National Law Review Conference, March 19, 1994, Condado Plaza Hotel, Puerto Rico.

17. Sonia Sotomayor appearance in Denver, August 26, 2010, "Diversity and the Legal Profession."

18. Peter Winn, "The Education of Sonia Sotomayor," *Washington Post*, July 12, 2009.

19. Sonia Sotomayor letter to the editor, "Anti-Latino Discrimination at Princeton," *Daily Princetonian*, May 10, 1974.

20. "Puerto Ricans Find Bias at Princeton," *New York Times*, April 23, 1974.

21. According to *The Daily Princetonian*, a response from HEW came quickly, as a representative from the Department of Education's civil rights office met with Sotomayor and other Latino students. Episode recounted in Mendy Fisch, "Sotomayor '76 Helped Shape University's Affirmative Action Practices," *Daily Princetonian*, July 16, 2009. Available at http://dailyprincetonian.com/news/2009/07 /sotomayor-76-helped-shape-universitys-affirmative-action-practices/.

22. Ogletree, *All Deliberate Speed*, 41.

23. Ibid., 52. Other black and Latino students, transplanted from small California farming towns or large urban hubs, similarly chafed and adapted in their own ways at elite colleges. Ruben Navarrette, Jr., a Mexican American from the San Joaquin Valley, wrote of his difficult assimilation and alienation at Harvard in *A Darker Shade of Crimson*. He questioned whether the Ivy League schools took only the "cream" of minority applicants, ultimately undermining the goals of affirmative action and generating ethnic infighting.

24. The Pyne Prize is awarded to the "senior who has most clearly manifested excellent scholarship, strength of character and effective leadership." See Emily Aronson,

"Elvin, Valcourt Named Pyne Prize Winners," February 22, 2012; www.princeton.edu/main/news/archive/S32/98/72M47/index.xml?section=topstories. See also Ruth Stevens, "Princeton Alumna, Trustee Confirmed as Supreme Court's First Latina Justice," August 6, 2009; www.princeton.edu/main/news/archive/S24/95/61C10/index.xml?section=topstories.

25. Thomas, *My Grandfather's Son*, 75.

26. Ibid., 75–76.

27. Ibid., 87. Thomas eventually landed a job in the Missouri attorney general's office, headed by Republican John Danforth, who would become a U.S. senator. Danforth would become a crucial advocate of Thomas when he was nominated to the Supreme Court in 1991.

28. Sonia Sotomayor appearance at Cornell University Law School, October 8, 2008.

29. Author interview with Guido Calabresi, September 30, 2013.

30. Sotomayor, *My Beloved World*, 180.

31. "30th Anniversary of Justice O'Connor's Appointment," session with Justices O'Connor, Ginsburg, Sotomayor, and Kagan, Newseum, Washington, D.C., April 11, 2012; available at www.c-span.org/video/?305386-1/30th-anniversary-justice-oconnors-appointment.

32. Text of Cabranes's remarks to the Connecticut Hispanic Bar Association, Hartford, November 1, 2003.

33. Sonia Sotomayor, "José Cabranes Intro," Puerto Rican Bar Association dinner honoring Cabranes, undated, circa 1996; copy in Senate Judiciary Committee 2009 nomination file.

34. Sotomayor, *My Beloved World*, 188; Stuart Auerbach, "Law Firm Apologizes to Yale Student," *Washington Post*, December 16, 1978.

35. Sotomayor, *My Beloved World*, 188–89.

36. Auerbach, "Law Firm Apologizes to Yale Student."

37. Author interviews with Carmen Shepard, February 7 and 9, 2011.

38. Sotomayor, *My Beloved World*, 183.

39. Zeke Miller, "At Yale, Sotomayor Was Sharp but Not Outspoken," *Yale Daily News*, May 31, 2009; available at http://yaledailynews.com/blog/2009/05/31/at-yale-sotomayor-was-sharp-but-not-outspoken.

40. Sonia Sotomayor appearance in Denver, August 26, 2010, "Diversity and the Legal Profession."

41. Facts of case drawn from *University of California Regents v. Bakke*, 438 U.S. 265 (1978). See also Don Speich, "Former UC Davis Official Backed 'Reverse Bias' Suit: Ex-Admissions Aide Says He Thought Special Minority Enrollment Program Was Unconstitutional," *Los Angeles Times*, February 4, 1977.

42. David S. Saxon, "UC's Minorities Plan Serves Public Needs," *Los Angeles Times*, January 23, 1977.

43. Powell opinion in *Regents of the University of California v. Bakke*.

44. Marshall dissenting opinion in *Regents of the University of California v. Bakke*.

45. The University of California at Davis subsequently enrolled Allan Bakke, and he graduated from the medical school in 1982.

46. Sotomayor, panelist at "Women in the Judiciary: A Woman's View from the Bench," 1994.

47. Sotomayor, *My Beloved World*, 192.

48. Ibid., 253–54.

49. Morgenthau continually faced complaints that his office was not doing enough to bring in minority prosecutors. When a claim arose in 1990, he said, "When I became District Attorney in 1975, there were 11 minority assistant district attorneys. As of this class . . . in August, there are 98 or 99, a tremendous increase." He also told the *Times* that he had "an affirmative hiring policy in this office, which is reflected in our statistics, and I have every intention of continuing that." Nadine Brozan, "Group of Blacks Sees Hiring Bias By Morgenthau," *New York Times*, August 2, 1990. See also M. A. Farber, "As He Seeks a 4th Term, Morgenthau Confronts First Sustained Criticism," *New York Times*, June 17, 1985.

50. Jonathan Barzilay, "The D.A.'s Right Arms," *New York Times*, November 27, 1983.

51. Sotomayor appearance at Cornell University Law School, October 8, 2008.

52. Benjamin Weiser and William K. Rashbaum, "Sotomayor Is Recalled as a Driven Rookie Prosecutor," *New York Times*, June 7, 2009; Robert Morgenthau testimony before the Senate Judiciary Committee, July 16, 2009.

53. Barzilay, "The D.A.'s Right Arms."

54. Noonan, who would earn his Ph.D. and a J.D., became a lawyer specializing in patents and other intellectual property. When Sotomayor was nominated to be a justice in May 2009, the New York *Daily News* quoted Noonan saying, "She'll be a great judge." Michael Saul, "Never Lost Touch with Her Roots," New York *Daily News*, May 27, 2009.

55. 1986 interview "Sonia Sotomayor: Then and Now," *Good Morning America*, ABC News, uploaded July 18, 2009, available at www.youtube.com/watch ?v=i6eikaV9IuE.

56. Sotomayor, *My Beloved World*, 238.

57. Ibid., 261.

58. It was founded by three officials of Mayor Lindsay's administration who had witnessed the social and legal problems affecting Puerto Ricans: Jorge Batista, Victor Marrero, and Cesar Perales.

59. Sotomayor, *My Beloved World*, 218.

4. CHANCE AND CONNECTIONS

1. Leonard Garment, a former counselor to Republican president Richard Nixon and longtime Moynihan friend, suggested the judicial screening committee, according to Richard K. Eaton, "The Third Branch," in *Daniel Patrick Moynihan*, edited by Robert A. Katzmann.

2. Ibid. Noted in November 5, 1992, Moynihan news release cited by Eaton.

3. Transcript of Induction Proceedings for Judge Sonia Sotomayor, U.S. Court of Appeals for the Second Circuit, New York, November 6, 1998.

4. Author interview with Judah Gribetz, January 27, 2012.

5. Author interview with Robert Peck, January 5, 2012.

6. Glazer and Moynihan, *Beyond the Melting Pot*, xlvi.

7. Author interview with Robert Peck, January 5, 2012.

8. Author interview with Judah Gribetz, January 27, 2012.

9. Wayne King, "Now, No Hispanic Candidates for Federal Bench in New York," *New York Times*, February 15, 1991.

10. Hodgson, *The Gentleman from New York*, 9.

11. Linda Charlton, "21 Rights Leaders Rebut Moynihan; Assert 'Benign Neglect' Idea Is 'Symptomatic of Effort to Wipe Out Gains,'" *New York Times*, March 6, 1970.

12. James Traub, "Daniel Patrick Moynihan, Liberal? Conservative? Or Just Pat?" *New York Times*, September 16, 1990.

13. Moynihan to King, March 4, 1991, Moynihan Papers, Library of Congress. See also Wayne King, "3 Recommended for U.S. Court; One Is Hispanic," *New York Times*, March 2, 1991.

14. Moynihan to Danforth, October 4, 1991, Moynihan Papers, Library of Congress.

15. "Debriefing After Justice Interviews"; Joe Gale notes from Sotomayor meeting, April 15, 1991, Moynihan Papers, Library of Congress.

16. Sotomayor to Gale, March 1, 1991, Moynihan Papers, Library of Congress.

17. "Impact of the Criminal Justice System on Hispanics," by John Carro; copy in Moynihan Papers, Library of Congress.

18. Both Carro and Martínez were suggested by Latino organizations in the mid-1990s, when Bill Clinton was in office.

19. Carro to Moynihan, Janaury 25, 1991, Moynihan Papers, Library of Congress.

20. Moynihan to Carro, February 4, 1991, Moynihan Papers, Library of Congress.

21. Jeff Peck was a cousin of Robert Peck, Moynihan's chief of staff.

22. Gale to Moynihan, June 7, 1991, Moynihan Papers, Library of Congress.

23. Joan Biskupic, "Bush Lags in Appointments to the Federal Judiciary," *Congressional Quarterly Weekly Report*, January 6, 1990.

24. Ruth Marcus, "Plain-Spoken Marshall Spars with Reporters," *Washington Post*, June 29, 1991.

25. Marshall denounced the conservative majority for turning back constitutional rights, particularly those protecting defendants, and predicted that "tomorrow's victims [of adverse Court rulings] may be minorities, women or the indigent." Marshall accused the five-justice majority that prevailed in the death penalty case *Payne v. Tennessee* of being ready to "squander the authority and legitimacy of this court as a protector of the powerless." *Payne v. Tennessee*, 501 U.S. 808 (1991).

26. Karen Tumulty, "Marshall Says Bush Should Not Use Race as 'Excuse' for Picking Wrong Successor," *Los Angeles Times*, June 29, 1991.

27. Author interview with Dick Thornburgh, April 18, 2011. The suggestion in news articles of Cabranes as a Bush possibility, however, helped lay the ground for

liberals' suspicions of Cabranes when Democratic president Bill Clinton began considering Supreme Court candidates two years later.

28. Gray was a longtime friend of Thomas's who would insist decades later that one of George H. W. Bush's greatest legacies was the appointment of Thomas.

29. Ann Devroy and Sharon LaFraniere, "Danforth's Backing Was Key to President's Choice of Thomas," *Washington Post*, July 3, 1991; Michael Wines, "Bush Says List for Marshall Successor Is Short," *New York Times*, June 29, 1991.

30. Author interview with Dick Thornburgh, April 18, 2011.

31. John E. Yang and Sharon LaFraniere, "Bush Picks Thomas for Supreme Court: Appeals Court Judge Served as EEOC Chairman in Reagan Administration," *Washington Post*, July 2, 1991.

32. President George H. W. Bush news conference, July 1, 1991; available at www .presidency.ucsb.edu/ws/?pid=29651.

33. Thomas, *My Grandfather's Son*, 216.

34. John Lewis, "He's Forgotten Where He's From," *Los Angeles Times*, August 12, 1991.

35. Andrew Rosenthal, "The Thomas Nomination; White House Role in Thomas Defense," *New York Times*, October 14, 1991; Anthony Lewis, "Abroad at Home; Slash and Burn," *New York Times*, October 18, 1991; "Thomas Role Questioned," *Washington Post*, October 22, 1991.

36. Author interview with Robert Peck, January 5, 2012.

37. Moynihan to Sulzberger, August 8, 1991, Moynihan Papers, Library of Congress.

38. Batts and Trager were not nominated or confirmed until Democrat Bill Clinton took office in 1993.

39. Gray to Bush, November 27, 1991, George H. W. Bush Presidential Archive.

40. Testimony of Kim J. Askew and American Bar Association report to the Senate Judiciary Committee, July 16, 2009.

41. Committee hearings for district court nominees were generally low-key, routine events, which is why three candidates could testify in a single sitting.

42. Transcript of Senate Judiciary Committee hearing, June 4, 1992, for Sonia Sotomayor and other U.S. district court nominees; available at www.loc.gov/law/find /nominations/sotomayor/shrg105-205pt9.pdf.

43. President Obama, May 26, 2009; www.whitehouse.gov/the_press_office/Re marks-by-the-President-in-Nominating-Judge-Sonia-Sotomayor-to-the-United -States-Supreme-Court.

44. Sotomayor, panelist at "Women in the Judiciary: A Woman's View from the Bench," a Practising Law Institute program broadcast live via satellite on June 9, 1994. Copy of program supplied to author by PLI.

5. A PRESIDENT AND POLITICS

1. Biskupic, *Sandra Day O'Connor*, 71–72.

2. John P. Schmal, "Electing the President: The Latino Electorate (1960–2000)," *La Prensa San Diego*, April 30, 2004, http://laprensa-sandiego.org/archive/april30

-04/elect.htm. See also Roper Center Public Opinion Research Archives, U.S. Elections, How Groups Voted in 1992, www.ropercenter.uconn.edu/elections /how_groups_voted/voted_92.html.

3. Hutchinson, *The Man Who Once Was Whizzer White*, 277–281.

4. Byron R. White letter to President Clinton, March 19, 1993.

5. Paul M. Barrett and David Rogers, "Senate Support for Zoe Baird Is Precarious," *Wall Street Journal*, January 22, 1993 (describing Baird's employing of undocumented workers in her household); Adam Nagourney, "Clinton Missteps Again," *USA Today*, February 8, 1993 (detailing Wood's alleged failure to disclose to the White House that she had hired undocumented workers).

6. Clinton later said that her positions conflicted with his opposition to quotas and a "cumulative voting" approach that intended to inflate the chances of minority candidates to win office. Clinton, *My Life*, 523.

7. Stephanopoulos, *All Too Human*, 166–67.

8. Dolores S. Atencio, "The Making of an American Justice: The HNBA's Quest for the First Hispanic Supreme Court Justice," *Hispanic National Bar Association Journal of Law and Policy* 2, issue 1 (Summer 2010).

9. Ibid.

10. Author interview with Carlos Ortiz, September 16, 2010. See also Atencio, "The Making of an American Justice."

11. Richard Berke, "Judge in Boston Is Called Likely for High Court," *New York Times*, June 11, 1993.

12. Author interview with Bernard Nussbaum, February 10, 2012.

13. She said women's access to abortion would have been better grounded in Fourteenth Amendment equality rights. "The sweep and detail of the opinion stimulated the mobilization of a right-to-life movement and an attendant reaction in Congress and state legislatures," Ginsburg wrote in the law review article. "In place of the trend 'toward liberalization of abortion statutes' noted in *Roe*, legislatures adopted measures aimed at minimizing the impact of the 1973 rulings, including notification and consent requirements, prescriptions for the protection of fetal life, and bans on public expenditures for poor women's abortions." From "Some Thoughts on Autonomy and Equality in Relation to *Roe v. Wade*," *North Carolina Law Review* 63, no. 2 (January 1985).

14. Stephen Labaton, "The Man Behind the High Court Nominee," *New York Times*, June 17, 1993.

15. Weisman, *Daniel Patrick Moynihan*, 605–606.

16. Blackmun dissenting opinion in *Callins v. Collins*, 510 U.S. 1141 (1994).

17. Author interview with Harold Koh, September 11, 2013.

18. *Ibanez v. Florida Department of Business and Professional Regulation* was argued on April 19, 1994.

19. Author interview with Justice Ruth Bader Ginsburg, June 29, 2011; author confirmed with Justice Antonin Scalia, August 1, 2012.

20. Ibanez won her case. The Supreme Court ruled on June 13, 1994, that she had a First Amendment commercial-speech right to use CPA and CFP in her legal credentials. The justices overturned a Florida state court ruling that would have allowed her to be reprimanded by the Florida Board of Accountancy for "false, deceptive, and misleading" advertising because she was not practicing as an accountant. *Ibanez v. Florida Department of Business and Professional Regulation*, 512 U.S. 136 (1994).

21. Biskupic, *American Original*, 110.

22. After his confirmation, Blackmun bristled at news media reports that dubbed him and Burger the "Minnesota Twins." Blackmun steadily moved to the left, notably with his opinion for the majority in *Roe v. Wade*, declaring that women had a right to end a pregnancy before the fetus became viable—that is, could live outside the womb.

23. Mark Pazniokas, "Lawyers Praise Cabranes' Intellect," Hartford *Courant*, April 17, 1994.

24. Price, *Judge Richard S. Arnold*, 332.

25. See, e.g., Michael Wines, "Bush Says List for Marshall Successor Is Short," *New York Times*, June 29, 1991.

26. Author interview with Adelfa Callejo, April 2, 2011. Callejo also voiced regard for Sotomayor's effort to move up on the federal bench, saying, "She impressed me as someone who set goals and set timetables to achieve those goals."

27. Ruth Marcus, "Ideal Supreme Court Candidate May Exist Only in Clinton's Mind," *Washington Post*, April 19, 1994.

28. Neil A. Lewis, "No Apparent Front-Runner to Fill Supreme Court Seat," *New York Times*, April 28, 1994.

29. For context on differences among groups, see, for exmple, Bergad and Klein, *Hispanics in the United States: A Demographic, Social, and Economic History, 1980–2005*.

30. David Lauter, "Latino Groups Seek United Push for High Court Hopeful," *Los Angeles Times*, April 14, 1994.

31. Antonia Hernández letter to President Bill Clinton, April 24, 1994.

32. Author interview with Bernard Nussbaum, February 10, 2012.

33. Clinton, *My Life*, 592.

34. Neil A. Lewis, "As Political Terrain Shifts, Breyer Lands on His Feet," *New York Times*, May 15, 1994; John H. Cushman Jr., "For Babbitt, a Horizon of Hills and Valleys," *New York Times*, May 14, 1994.

35. Clinton, *My Life*, 592.

36. Joan Biskupic, "Mitchell, Cabranes Said to Top High Court List; Senate Majority Leader, Hispanic Judge Offer Clinton Choices on Opposite Ends of Spectrum," *Washington Post*, April 8, 1994.

37. After Clinton opted to nominate Calabresi over Cabranes in early 1994 for the Second Circuit, Connecticut senator Lieberman began working with White

House counsel Nussbaum to ensure that the next vacancy would go to Cabranes, even though, through an informal long-standing deal among senators, the next opening would be for a New Yorker. New York senator Moynihan eventually agreed with the plan. Dick Eaton memorandum to Senator Moynihan entitled "Cabranes Nomination Chronology," July 16, 1998, Moynihan Papers; see also David Lightman, "2 Appellate Seats Sought for Calabresi, Cabranes," *Hartford Courant*, January 27, 1994.

38. "Clinton Names Cabranes to Federal Appeals Court," *Wall Street Journal*, May 25, 1994.

39. Atencio, "The Making of an American Justice."

40. Brian Baron, "President Clinton Defers Again: As Another Supreme Court Nomination Slips By, Leaders Admit the Effort Lacked a United Front," *Hispanic-Business*, July 1994.

41. Ibid.

42. Pew Hispanic Center analysis of national exit poll data 1980–2012.

43. Lewis, "As Political Terrain Shifts, Breyer Lands on His Feet."

44. Transcript of Induction Proceedings for Judge Sonia Sotomayor, U.S. Court of Appeals for the Second Circuit, New York, November 6, 1998.

45. Ibid. See also, for example, May 12, 1998, letter from Xavier Romeu in White House file for mass mailing on behalf of numerous bar associations touting Sotomayor's "strong bi-partisan support" and "exceptional legal career," and July 9, 1998, letter from Gloria E. Markus, assistant to Romeu, to Sarah Wilson, associate counsel to the president, detailing solicited letters from constituents from New York and Connecticut on behalf of Sotomayor; William Clinton Presidential Library.

46. "Hearings Before the Committee on the Judiciary, United States Senate"; transcript available at www.loc.gov/law/find/nominations/sotomayor/shrg105-205pt2.pdf.

47. Jan Hoffman, "A Breakthrough Judge: What She Always Wanted," *New York Times*, September 25, 1992.

48. Sonia Sotomayor response to Jeff Sessions, September 30, 1997, "Hearings Before the Committee on the Judiciary, United States Senate," transcript available at www.loc.gov/law/find/nominations/sotomayor/shrg105-205pt2.pdf.

49. "The Souter Strategy," *Wall Street Journal*, June 8, 1998.

50. Markus letter to Wilson, July 9, 1998, and separate fact sheet with the headline "The Following Are in Response to Some of the Unfounded Statements Found in the Wall Street Journal: Facts About Judge Sonia Sotomayor's Record"; William Clinton Presidential Library.

51. Transcript of Induction Proceedings for Judge Sonia Sotomayor, U.S. Court of Appeals for the Second Circuit, New York, November 6, 1998.

52. On her Senate Judiciary Committee questionnaire for the Second Circuit judgeship, Sotomayor had written, "Engaged to be married to Peter White, President of Commercial Residential and Industrial Construction Corporation." *The New York Times* reported at the time of her nomination, "Less than two years later, she gave a party at their newly renovated apartment for his 50th birthday. And

not long after that, their relationship ended. He returned to Westchester County, bought a small boat and married a woman who was an acquaintance of the judge and 14 years her junior." Michael Powell, Russ Buettner, and Serge F. Kovaleski, "To Get to Sotomayor's Core, Start in New York," *New York Times*, July 9, 2009.

53. Author interview with Carlos Ortiz, November 19, 2010.

6. THE RIGHT HISPANIC

1. The national civil rights group changed its name to LatinoJustice PRLDEF in 2008. Its first letter to senators referring to Estrada's lack of involvement with the Hispanic community and "ultra-conservative views" was written on June 11, 2001, a month after his nomination.

2. Ortiz was general counsel of a large food manufacturer and distributor. Figueroa, president of PRLDEF at the time, was a former assistant Connecticut attorney general and member of the Connecticut General Assembly. Romano, who had been a top-ranking prosecutor in the U.S. attorney's office in the Southern District of New York, became a partner in a large New York firm. Sotomayor wrote in her 2013 memoir that Romano had been among those who gave her name to Senator Moynihan's search committee.

3. Dahlia Lithwick, "Miguel, Ma Belle: The Racial Ugliness Under the Miguel Estrada Nomination," *Slate*, February 27, 2003.

4. Estrada response to Senator Herb Kohl, September 26, 2002, Senate Judiciary Committee hearing on the nomination of Miguel Estrada to the U.S. Court of Appeals for the District of Columbia Circuit.

5. Juan Figueroa to Patrick Leahy, June 11, 2001.

6. All quotations from the transcript of the Senate Judiciary Committee hearing on Miguel Estrada's nomination, September 26, 2002. Author attended the hearing; transcript available through the U.S. Government Printing Office.

7. PRLDEF report originally issued in September 2002, reissued January 27, 2003.

8. Obama, *Audacity of Hope*, 79.

9. "Talking Points re D.C. Circuit," from John Roberts file in archives of President George H. W. Bush; made available to reporters in 2005 when Roberts was chosen for the U.S. Supreme Court.

10. "The Hispanic Population: Census 2000 Brief," U.S. Census Bureau report issued in May 2001. The report noted that an additional 3.8 million Hispanics were counted in the Commonwealth of Puerto Rico.

11. Kagan, nominated by Clinton but denied a hearing by the Senate, became a Supreme Court justice in 2010.

12. Ronald Klain to Senator Patrick Leahy, January 16, 2002.

13. Charles E. Schumer, "Judging by Ideology," *New York Times*, June 26, 2001.

14. Jack Newfield, "The Right's Judicial Juggernaut," *The Nation*, October 7, 2002.

15. They were the Mexican American Legal Defense and Educational Fund, the National Association of Latino Elected and Appointed Officials, the National

Council of La Raza, the National Puerto Rican Coalition, and the Puerto Rican Legal Defense and Education Fund. May 1, 2002, letter to Leahy, signed by leaders of the five groups.

16. PRLDEF report originally issued in September 2002, reissued January 27, 2003.

17. California La Raza Lawyers Association and Mexican American Legal Defense and Educational Fund (MALDEF) letter and report to the Senate Judiciary Committee, September 24, 2002.

18. Estrada testimony, Senate Judiciary Committee hearing.

19. Darryl Fears, "For Hispanic Groups, a Divide on Estrada: Political, Geographic Fault Lines Exposed," *Washington Post*, February 20, 2003; Lithwick, "Miguel, Ma Belle."

20. Bill Miller, "Appeals Court Nominees Share Conservative Roots: Records of Roberts and Estrada Are Being Studied Closely," *Washington Post*, May 23, 2001.

21. Letter of former U.S. solicitors general to Leahy, June 24, 2002.

22. Newfield, "The Right's Judicial Juggernaut."

23. Hatch statement, Senate Judiciary Committee hearing.

24. Senator Dianne Feinstein, February 13, 2003, *Senate Congressional Record*, S2373–S2374.

25. Senator Patrick Leahy, February 10, 2003, *Senate Congressional Record*, S2072.

26. Neil A. Lewis, "Impasse on Judicial Pick Defies Quick Resolution," *New York Times*, March 30, 2003.

27. David Firestone, "Frist Forsakes Deal Making to Focus on Party Principles," *New York Times*, March 13, 2003.

28. Ibid.

29. Joan Biskupic, "Democrats: 'We Will Not Relent on Filibuster,'" *USA Today*, February 14, 2003.

30. Antonia Hernández, "Latino Would Set Back Latinos," *Los Angeles Times*, February 5, 2003.

31. Linda Chavez, "Hispanic Like Me?: Racial Games, Racial Tags—the Way the Left Plays," *National Review*, March 10, 2003.

32. Miguel Estrada to President George W. Bush, September 4, 2003. His wife had a series of health problems, and in November 2004, a year after Estrada withdrew his name, she died of an accidental overdose of sleeping pills.

33. Carlos D. Conde, "The Saga of Miguel Estrada," *Hispanic Outlook in Higher Education*, June 30, 2003.

34. In an October 7, 2005, interview with MSNBC's Tucker Carlson, Robert Bork said Miers had "no experience with constitutional law whatever" and termed her nomination a "slap in the face" to conservatives.

35. *Dorsey v. United States*, 567 U.S. ___ (2012).

36. Lindsey Graham, July 13, 2009, "Confirmation Hearing on the Nomination of Hon. Sonia Sotomayor, To Be an Associate Justice of the Supreme Court of the United States," before the Senate Judiciary Committee, July 13–16, 2009, Washington, D.C. Author attended the hearings; transcript available through multiple sources, including U.S. Government Printing Office.

37. Lindsey Graham, Tom Coburn, Elena Kagan testimony, June 29 and 30, 2010, "The Nomination of Elena Kagan To Be an Associate Justice of the Supreme Court of the United States," before the Senate Judiciary Committee, Washington, D.C. Author attended the hearings; transcript available through multiple sources, including U.S. Government Printing Office.

7. THE WISE LATINA

1. The speech was reprinted in "A Latina Judge's Voice," *Berkeley La Raza Law Journal* 13, no. 88 (2002).
2. Radio host Rush Limbaugh called Sotomayor a "reverse racist." See also Gingrich's comment in Jonathan Weisman and Naftali Bendavid, "Battle Over Sotomayor Heats Up," *Wall Street Journal*, May 28, 2009.
3. Sotomayor articulated her general support for a kind of "legal realism" in a 1996 lecture at Suffolk University Law School in Boston when she said, "Lawyers do themselves a disservice by acceding to the public myth that law can be certain and stable." Sonia Sotomayor and Nicole A. Gordon, "Returning Majesty to the Law and Politics: A Modern Approach," *Suffolk University Law Review*, 1996.
4. For context on strife arising from Hispanics in the labor force and ballot initiatives against affirmative action, see Fraga et al., *Latino Lives in America*, 3.
5. Sotomayor, "A Latina Judge's Voice."
6. Author interview with Rachel Moran, August 21, 2013.
7. Justices Sandra Day O'Connor and Ruth Bader Ginsburg cited Coyne. See Jennifer M. Fitzenberger, "Obituary: M. Jeanne Coyne, Second Woman on State Supreme Court," Minneapolis *Star Tribune*, August 6, 1998.
8. Sotomayor, "Women in the Judiciary," Panel Presentation, the 40th National Conference of Law Reviews, March 17, 1994, Condado Plaza Hotel, Puerto Rico; copy of speech in Senate Judiciary Committee 2009 nomination file.
9. *Almanac of the Federal Judiciary*, vol. 2 (2001) and vol. 2 (2009).
10. American Bar Association report submitted in testimony to the Senate Judiciary Committee by Kim Askew, chairman of the ABA Standing Committee on the Federal Judiciary, July 16, 2009.
11. Sonia Sotomayor appearance at Cornell University Law School, October 8, 2008.
12. Sonia Sotomayor statement, July 14, 2009, "Confirmation Hearing on the Nomination of Hon. Sonia Sotomayor, To Be an Associate Justice of the Supreme Court of the United States," before the Senate Judiciary Committee, July 13–16, 2009, Washington, D.C. Author attended the hearings; transcript available through multiple sources including U.S. Government Printing Office.
13. Jeff Sessions statement, July 14, 2009, "Confirmation Hearing on the Nomination of Hon. Sonia Sotomayor, To Be an Associate Justice of the Supreme Court of the United States."
14. "On Sonia Sotomayor: Words from 'Wise Latinas,'" *Los Angeles Times*, July 17, 2009.

8. RACE AND THE *RICCI* CASE

1. William Kaempffer, "U.S. Court Tosses Out Case Over City Jobs," *New Haven Register*; appeared online at nhregsiter.com, February 15, 2008.
2. Author interview with Karen Torre, August 5, 2013.
3. Neither Cabranes nor Sotomayor would discuss their respective roles in the *Ricci* case.
4. The disparate-impact doctrine was not explicitly written into Title VII at the start. The Supreme Court recognized the doctrine in *Griggs v. Duke Power Co.*, 401 U.S. 424 (1971), then went on to alternately expand and contract disparate-impact theory, leading Congress to codify disparate-impact remedies in the Civil Rights Act of 1991.
5. *Parents Involved v. Seattle School District No. 1*, 551 U.S. 701, 748 (2007).
6. Ginsburg dissenting opinion in *Ricci v. DeStefano*, 557 U.S. 557 (2009).
7. *Ricci v. DeStefano*, 554 F.Supp.2d 142 (D. Conn. 2006), district court opinion, September 28, 2006.
8. Frank Ricci and Benjamin Vargas statements, July 16, 2009, "Confirmation Hearing on the Nomination of Hon. Sonia Sotomayor, To Be an Associate Justice of the Supreme Court of the United States," before the Senate Judiciary Committee, July 13–16, 2009, Washington, D.C. Author attended the hearings; transcript available through multiple sources including U.S. Government Printing Office.
9. *Ricci v. DeStefano*, 554 F.Supp. 2d 142 (D.Conn. 2006).
10. Sotomayor, *My Beloved World*, 283.
11. Oral arguments in *Ricci v. DeStefano*, U.S. Court of Appeals for the Second Circuit, December 9, 2007; available at www.c-span.org/video/?287320-1/-ricci-v-destefano -court-appeals-oral-argument.
12. Author interview with Judge Rosemary Pooler, February 6, 2014.
13. A Congressional Research Service June 19, 2009, report stated: "Perhaps the most consistent characteristics of Judge Sotomayor's approach as an appellate judge has been an adherence to the doctrine of *stare decisis*, i.e., the upholding of past judicial precedents. Other characteristics appear to include what many would describe as a careful application of particular facts at issue in a case and a dislike for situations in which the court might be seen as overstepping its judicial role." When the American Bar Association issued a report on her record on July 16, 2009, it concluded, "Her opinions are well-reasoned, well-organized, meticulously researched, easily understandable, and demonstrate a profound command of the law, even when sophisticated and complicated factual and legal issues are presented."
14. American Bar Association report submitted in testimony to the Senate Judiciary Committee by Kim Askew, chairman of the ABA Standing Committee on the Federal Judiciary, July 16, 2009.
15. *Silverman v. Major League Baseball Players Relations Committee*, 880 F.Supp. 246 (1995).
16. Larry Milson, "Fans Flock to Spring Training Game as All Is Forgiven," *The*

Globe and Mail, April 14, 1995; Greg B. Smith, "Heavy Hitter on Bench," New York *Daily News*, April 1, 1995.

17. Sonia Sotomayor, panelist at "Women in the Judiciary: A Woman's View from the Bench," a Practising Law Institute program broadcast live via satellite on June 9, 1994. Copy of program supplied to author by PLI.

18. Sotomayor's comments at a Duke University School of Law event were made with some levity: "All of the legal defense funds out there, they are looking for people with court of appeals experience because the court of appeals is where policy is made. And I know this is on tape and I should never say that because we don't make law. I know. I'm not promoting it. I'm not advocating it." Available at www.youtube.com/watch?v=OfC99LrrM2Q.

19. *Ricci v. DeStefano*, No. 06-4996-cv, February 15, 2008. 264 Fed.Appx. 106 (2d Cir. 2008).

20. Lawyer Torre, representing the firefighters, did not notice when the Second Circuit clerk placed a hold on the issuance of the mandate in the case, effectively blocking the Sotomayor panel's order from taking effect. She was plowing ahead with her petition to the Supreme Court.

21. *Ricci v. DeStefano*, 530 F.3d 88; Second Circuit judges' order and opinions issued June 9, 12, and 13, 2008.

22. *Northwest Austin Municipal Utility District No. 1 v. Holder*, 557 U.S. 193 (2009). The case involved the "bailout" provision of the Voting Rights Act. In the end, the Supreme Court ruled that the utility district was entitled to be considered for the bailout provision. Lawyer Coleman died in a plane crash in 2010. Chuck Lindell, "Plane Crash Kills Noted Lawyer," *Austin American-Statesman*, November 25, 2010.

23. *Ricci v. DeStefano*, Nos. 07-1428 and 07-328, brief for the United States as amicus curiae supporting vacatur and remand, February 2009.

24. Author attended oral arguments in *Ricci v. DeStefano* on April 22, 2009; transcript on Supreme Court website at www.supremecourt.gov/oral_arguments/argument_transcripts/07-1428.pdf.

25. Ibid.

26. *Ricci v. DeStefano*, 557 U.S. 557 (2009). In a concurring opinion, Justice Scalia noted that the Court did not reach the question "Whether, or to what extent, are the disparate-impact provisions of Title VII of the Civil Rights Act of 1964 consistent with the Constitution's guarantee of equal protection?"

27. Sotomayor statement, July 14, 2009. "Confirmation Hearing on the Nomination of Hon. Sonia Sotomayor, To Be an Associate Justice of the Supreme Court of the United States."

28. Ibid.

29. Author interview with Gregory Craig, January 22, 2013.

30. Frank Ricci statement, July 16, 2009, "Confirmation Hearing on the Nomination of Hon. Sonia Sotomayor, To Be an Associate Justice of the Supreme Court of the United States."

9. THE PRESIDENT'S CHOICE

1. Author interview with Gregory Craig, January 22 and October 4, 2013. Craig spoke on the record. Other Obama officials filled in details of the nomination process but declined to speak on the record.

2. Obama, *Audacity of Hope*, 84–86.

3. Ibid., 79.

4. Pew Research Center Hispanic Trends Project, November 5, 2008.

5. John O'Connor died from complications of Alzheimer's disease on November 11, 2009.

6. Joan Biskupic, "Ginsburg Plans to Stay on High Court for Years, Despite Cancer," *USA Today*, March 5, 2009.

7. Joan Biskupic, "Ginsburg: Court Needs Another Woman," *USA Today*, May 5, 2009.

8. Sotomayor, *My Beloved World*, 237–38.

9. Author interview with Carlos Ortiz, November 19, 2010.

10. Ibid.

11. Sotomayor's fellow judges on the Second Circuit made clear early and often that they believed she would be an excellent candidate for a Supreme Court opening. Judge Robert Katzmann, whom Sotomayor said she regarded as a brother, said he tried to boost her chances of selection at a separate meeting with Craig, in December 2008, before the Obama administration was in the White House.

12. Author interview with Judge Guido Calabresi, September 30, 2013.

13. Author interview with Gregory Craig, January 22, 2013.

14. Assessments in the *Almanac of the Federal Judiciary*, vol. 2, 2009.

15. Author interview with Barrington Parker, April 17, 2014.

16. Edwin Meese, Leonard Leo, Edward Whelan, and Wendy Long to Senate Judiciary Committee Republicans, January 22, 2009.

17. *Hinrichs v. Bosma*, 2005 WL 3544300, *7 (S.D. Ind. 2005).

18. Transcript of President Obama's remarks on Justice Souter, May 1, 2009. www .whitehouse.gov/blog/2009/05/01/presidents-remarks-justice-souter.

19. Sotomayor Senate questionnaire and supplemental materials submitted to Senate Judiciary Committee, June 2009.

20. Diane P. Wood, "Madison Lecture: Our 18th Century Constitution in the 21st Century World," *New York University Law Review* 80, no. 1079 (2005): 1107.

21. Tribe letter to Obama, May 4, 2009. Made public by Edward Whelan, "Tribe to Obama: Sotomayor Is 'Not Nearly as Smart as She Seems to Think She Is,'" *National Review Online*, October 28, 2010; available at www.nationalreview .com/bench-memos/251301/tribe-obama-sotomayor-not-nearly-smart-she -seems-think-she-ed-whelan. Letter pdf at www.eppc.org/docLib/20101028 _tribeletter.pdf.

22. Charlie Savage, "Leaked: Obama Mentor's Blunt Advice on Court Choices," *New York Times* website, October 28, 2010; additional comments from Tribe in e-mail to author, April 16, 2014.

23. Jeffrey Rosen, "The Case Against Sotomayor," *The New Republic* online edition, May 4, 2009.

24. Adam Serwer, "What's Jeffrey Rosen's Beef with Sonia Sotomayor?" *American Prospect*, May 4, 2009; Rebecca Traister, "Her Honor: Domineering and Dumb," *Salon.com*, May 4, 2009.

25. Traister, "Her Honor."

26. James Warren, "Sonia Sotomayor on Dating, Deciding, and Being the Newest Supreme Court Justice," *The Atlantic*, March 7, 2011; available at www.theatlan tic.com/politics/archive/2011/03/sonia-sotomayor-on-dating-deciding-and-being -the-newest-supreme-court-justice/72168/.

27. Sonia Sotomayor, Smithsonian Associates Evening Lecture, January 8, 2014, George Washington University, Washington, D.C.

28. Alter, *The Promise*, 292–93.

29. Sotomayor interview, C-SPAN, September 16, 2009.

30. Transcript of President Obama's and Judge Sotomayor's remarks on May 26, 2009; provided by the White House Office of the Press Secretary.

31. Ibid.

32. Dana Milbank, "But Will She Suit Up with the Washington Nine?" *Washington Post*, May 27, 2009.

33. Eli Saslow, "Sotomayor Nomination Unites Hispanics," *Washington Post*, May 27, 2009.

34. Author interview with Ronald Klain, July 26, 2012.

10. STANDING OUT

1. Justice O'Connor was a conservative centrist who navigated the middle of the Court and resisted being called a "feminist" and being identified with such causes as abortion rights. Justice Thomas separated himself from the African American identity Justice Marshall fostered. In a 2001 appearance before the conservative Washington-based American Enterprise Institute, Thomas noted that early in his career he was regarded as a heretic for questioning the value of affirmative action, welfare, and school busing. "It became clear in rather short order that on the very difficult issues such as race there was no real debate or honest discussion," he said. "Those who raised questions that suggested doubt about popular policies were subjected to intimidation. Debate was not permitted. Orthodoxy was enforced. When whites questioned the conventional wisdom on these issues, it was considered bad form; when blacks did so, it was treason."

2. See, e.g., "The Genesis and Needs of an Ethnic Identity," keynote speech October 24, 1998, at Connecticut Hispanic Bar Association dinner, New Haven; copy in Senate Judiciary Committee 2009 nomination file.

3. Sonia Sotomayor appearance in Denver, August 26, 2010, "Diversity and the Legal Profession."

4. In 1993, when Ginsburg first became a justice, she took a third-floor suite, too, for the airy atmosphere and to ensure more room for her staff. She later moved down to the second floor, where most of the other justices had chambers.

5. Sotomayor interview, C-SPAN, September 16, 2009.

6. David Saltonstall, "Justice Sonia Looking for Law Not Love; Still Humbled by Appointment," New York *Daily News*, December 19, 2009.

7. Sonia Sotomayor, Smithsonian Associates Evening Lecture, January 8, 2014, George Washington University, Washington, D.C.

8. Sotomayor, *My Beloved World*, 20.

9. Latoya Peterson, "Towards a More Perfect Nation: Sotomayor Navigates a Race, Gender, and Class Minefield in Pursuit of Justice," *Jezebel*, January 5, 2010.

10. Joan Biskupic, "Sotomayor Gets Frank on Diabetes: Shares her Story to Inspire Young Type 1 Patients," *USA Today*, June 22, 2011.

11. Sotomayor interview, C-SPAN, September 16, 2009.

12. Sandra Guzman, "Her Honor: A Portrait of Justice Sonia Sotomayor," *Latina*, December/January 2009.

13. Ibid.

14. Author attended oral arguments in *Schwarzenegger v. Plata* on November 30, 2010; transcript on Supreme Court website at www.supremecourt.gov/oral_argu ments/argument_transcripts/09-1233.pdf.

15. Sotomayor interview, C-SPAN, September 16, 2009.

16. Supreme Court justices would not speak for the record about Justice Sotomayor. None of the differences revealed to the author rose to the magnitude of the real personality clashes among justices that occurred notably in the early 1900s, when individuals refused to speak to each other.

17. Justice Stevens told the author in an October 1, 2010, interview that his stumbles in the public announcement of the *Citizens United* opinion helped lead to his decision that it was time to retire; he remained an active speaker and writer for years after he stepped down.

18. *Citizens United v. Federal Election Commission*, 588 U.S. 310 (2010).

19. President Obama's January 27, 2010, remarks about the potential for foreign con tributions was widely seen as an exaggeration. See, e.g., PolitiFact.com at www .politifact.com/truth-o-meter/statements/2010/jan/27/barack-obama/obama-says -supreme-court-ruling-allows-foreign-com/.

20. Joan Biskupic, "Tensions Rise Between Supreme Court, Politicians," *USA Today*, January 24, 2011.

21. Sotomayor, July 14, 2009, "Confirmation Hearing on the Nomination of Hon. Sonia Sotomayor, To Be an Associate Justice of the Supreme Court of the United States."

22. *Mohawk Industries, Inc. v. Carpenter*, 558 U.S. 100 (2009).

23. "Justice Sonia Sotomayor '79 Delivers the James A. Thomas Lecture at YLS," report of February 4, 2014. www.law.yale.edu/news/17931.htm.

24. *Arizona v. United States*, 567 U.S. ___ (2012).

25. *Arizona v. United States*, No. 11-182, April 25, 2012, www.supremecourt.gov/oral
_arguments/argument_transcripts/11-182.pdf.

26. Sonia Sotomayor appearance in Denver, August 26, 2010, "Diversity and the Legal
Profession."

27. Sandra Day O'Connor, "Thurgood Marshall: The Influence of a Raconteur,"
Stanford Law Review 44 (1992): 1217.

28. Sotomayor has stressed her interest in criminal procedure in numerous public
appearances, including her lecture at the Yale Law School, New Haven, February 3, 2014; available at http://vimeo.com/85872053.

29. *Berghuis v. Thompkins*, 560 U.S. 370 (2010).

30. Ibid., Sotomayor dissenting.

31. Sotomayor dissented from several Supreme Court rejections of prisoner appeals
in her early years, including *Pitre v. Cain*, 562 U.S. ___(2010); *Gamache v. California*, 562 U.S. ___ (2010); and *Williams v. Hobbs*, 562 U.S. ___ (2010).

32. *Pitre v. Cain*.

33. *Calhoun v. United States*, 568 U.S. ___ (2013), Sotomayor statement respecting
the denial of certiorari.

34. *Woodward v. Alabama*, 571 U.S. ___ (2013), Sotomayor dissenting.

35. *Cullen v. Pinholster*, 538 U.S. ___ (2011), Thomas majority opinion and Sotomayor dissenting statement.

36. *Perry v. New Hampshire*, 565 U.S. ___ (2012), Sotomayor dissenting.

37. *Perry v. New Hampshire*, Ginsburg opinion for the majority.

38. *United States v. Jones*, 565 U.S. ___ (2012).

39. See, e.g., Dean Robert Post at Sotomayor lecture, Yale Law School, New Haven,
February 3, 2014; available at http://vimeo.com/85872053.

40. Kagan's most attention-getting early opinions on behalf of the liberals came in
ideologically charged cases, and in dissent. In an Arizona campaign finance dispute, for example, she wrote that although the conservative majority said it had
found the "smoking guns" at the center of the dispute, "the only smoke here is the
majority's, and it is the kind that goes with mirrors." The majority, in an opinion by
Roberts, had invalidated a state law that gave extra funds to political candidates
who used the public-finance system rather than rely on wealthy private backers.

41. Jay Kernis, "The 10 Most Intriguing People of 2009," *CNN.com*, December 28,
2009; www.cnn.com/2009/OPINION/12/28/kernis.10.most.intriguing/index.html.

42. "Sonia Sotomayor to Publish Memoir," http://knopfdoubleday.com/2010/07/12
/sonia-sotomayor-to-publish-memoir.

11. EQUALITY AND IDENTITY

1. Senator Arlen Specter, a longtime Republican, switched his affiliation to the
Democratic Party in April 2009, three months before the hearings.

2. Arlen Specter statement, July 16, 2009, "Confirmation Hearing on the Nomination of Hon. Sonia Sotomayor, To Be an Associate Justice of the Supreme Court of the United States," before the Senate Judiciary Committee, July 13–16, 2009, Washington, D.C. Author attended the hearings; transcript available through multiple sources including U.S. Government Printing Office.

3. When questioned about her role in the case, Justice Sotomayor declined to provide any information; a majority of her colleagues, however, related parts of the behind-the-scene events to the author. None of what transpired has previously been made public.

4. Joan Biskupic, "Analysis: U.S. Battle Over Ballots Averted, but Not Forever," November 7, 2012, Reuters; www.reuters.com/article/2012/11/07/us-usa-campaign -voting-rights-idUSBRE8A62C520121107.

5. *Regents of the University of California v. Bakke.*

6. *Grutter v. Bollinger,* 539 U.S. 306 (2003) and *Gratz v. Bollinger,* 539 U.S. 244 (2003).

7. *League of United Latin American Citizens v. Perry,* 548 U.S. 399 (2006) and *Ricci v. DeStefano,* 557 U.S. 557 (2009).

8. *Parents Involved in Community Schools v. Seattle School District No. 1,* 551 U.S. 701 (2007).

9. Breyer was joined in his written dissenting opinion in *Parents Involved* by Justices Stevens, Souter, and Ginsburg.

10. Joan Biskupic, "Special Report: Behind U.S. Race Cases, a Little-Known Recruiter," Reuters, December 4, 2012. www.reuters.com/article/2012/12/04/us-usa-court -casemaker-idUSBRE8B30V220121204.

11. Details of claim found in *Abigail Noel Fisher v. State of Texas,* U.S. District Court for the Western District of Texas, amended complaint, April 17, 2008.

12. Author attended oral arguments in *Fisher v. University of Texas at Austin* on October 10, 2012; transcript on Supreme Court website at www.supremecourt.gov /oral_arguments/argument_transcripts/11-345.pdf.

13. Individual justices from both sides of the ideological divide revealed elements of the discussion and the evolution of draft opinions on the condition that information not be attributed to them. Not all of the justices would speak about the case, and Sotomayor herself declined to disclose private negotiations. Internal court documents are kept secret, so a full understanding of the give-and-take remained elusive. It was plain, however, that the case that was argued in October 2012 and seemed headed in one direction took a major turn because of Sotomayor. When asked by the author to describe the attitude Sotomayor had expressed in her draft opinion on the University of Texas program, justices intimated that it would be revealed in the then-pending Michigan affirmative action case. On April 22, 2014, when *Schuette v. Coalition to Defend Affirmative Action* was handed down, Sotomayor's strong feelings indeed were on display.

14. Sotomayor, *My Beloved World,* 191.

15. Justice Thomas included these numbers and other statistics in his concurring statement in the *Fisher* case, citing an amicus curiae brief from Richard Sander et al.

16. "A Justice Deliberates: Sotomayor on Love, Health and Family," interview with Nina Totenberg, NPR, January 12, 2013.

17. *Northwest Austin Municipal Utility District No. 1 v. Holder*, 557 U.S. 193 (2009); Edward Blum, who bankrolled the *Fisher* and *Shelby County* cases, helped with the financing of this lawsuit, too.

18. Author attended oral arguments in *Shelby County v. Holder* on February 27, 2013. Transcript on Supreme Court website at www.supremecourt.gov/oral_arguments/argument_transcripts/12-96_7648.pdf.

19. Joan Biskupic, "Insight: From Alabama, an Epic Challenge to Voting Rights," Reuters, June 4, 2012; available at www.reuters.com/article/2012/06/04/us-usacourt-votingrights-idUSBRE85304M20120604.

20. *Shelby County v. Holder*, 570 U.S. ___ (2013).

21. *Fisher v. University of Texas at Austin*, 570 U.S. ___ (2013).

22. September 27, 2013, letter to universities from Catherine E. Lhamon, assistant secretary, Department of Education Office for Civil Rights, and Jocelyn Samuels, acting assistant attorney general, Department of Justice Civil Rights Division. Their Q-and-A fact sheet is available at www2.ed.gov/about/offices/list/ocr/docs/dcl-qa-201309.pdf.

23. *Schuette v. Coalition to Defend Affirmative Action*, No. 12-682, April 22, 2014.

12. HER DIVIDED WORLD

1. Financial disclosure forms on file at the Administrative Office of the U.S. Courts showed that Sotomayor earned advances from Knopf of $1.175 million in 2010 and $1.925 million in 2012.

2. Author followed Justice Sotomayor on portions of her four-day book tour to Puerto Rico, April 1–4, 2013.

3. Sotomayor was in the five-justice majority that invalidated a Defense of Marriage Act provision that barred federal benefits for legally married same-sex couples. She separately dissented in a California case when the Court ruled that a state senator lacked legal standing to defend Proposition 8. She was the only justice who aligned in both with key vote Kennedy. *United States v. Windsor* and *Hollingsworth v. Perry*.

4. Amy Argetsinger, "Sonia Sotomayor and Rita Moreno Discuss Men, Moms, Love, Life," *Washington Post*, March 12, 2013.

5. Sotomayor, *My Beloved World*, 280.

6. Sotomayor lecture, Yale Law School, New Haven, February 3, 2014; available at http://vimeo.com/85872053.

7. Michiko Kakutani, "The Bronx, the Bench and the Life in Between," *New York Times*, January 21, 2013.

8. Peter Osnos, "How Sonia Sotomayor's Memoir Outsold Clarence Thomas's," *The Atlantic*, February 12, 2013; available online at www.theatlantic.com/national/archive/2013/02/how-sonia-sotomayors-memoir-outsold-clarence-thomass/273064/.

9. See, for example, Florence King, "Where She's Coming From," *National Review/ Digital*, April 22, 2013; Damon Root, "Sonia Sotomayor's Disappointing Memoir," *Reason.com*, January 15, 2013.

10. Root, "Sonia Sotomayor's Disappointing Memoir."

11. President Barack Obama Campaign Video, produced on three-year anniversary of the May 26, 2009, nomination announcement of Sonia Sotomayor to succeed retiring justice David Souter.

12. Mark Hugo Lopez, "Among Recent High School Grads, Hispanic College Enrollment Rate Surpasses That of Whites," Pew Research Center, September 4, 2013.

13. Pew Hispanic Center analysis of national exit poll data 1980–2012.

14. David G. Savage and Michael A. Memoli, "Sotomayor Scheduling Conflict Leads to Biden's Early Swearing-in," *Los Angeles Times*, January 18, 2013.

15. Staci Zaretsky, Morning Docket, *Above the Law* blog, January 22, 2013; http://abovethelaw.com/2013/01/morning-docket-01-22-13/.

16. "Hurry Up Mr. Vice President, I Have a Train to Catch," Reuters, January 20, 2013; www.reuters.com/article/2013/01/20/us-usa-inauguration-sotomayor-idUSB RE90J0I520130120.

17. Ibid.

18. Emma G. Fitzsimmons, "Sotomayor to Lead Countdown to New Year in Times Square," *New York Times*, December 29, 2013.

19. Mark Hugo Lopez, "What Univision's Milestone Says About U.S. Demographics," Pew Research Center, July 29, 2013.

20. "Sonia Sotomayor's Dress and Other Revelations . . . ," *Washington Post*, December 13, 2013.

21. Sotomayor lecture, Yale Law School, New Haven, February 3, 2014.

22. Sotomayor, *My Beloved World*, 232.

23. *Adoptive Couple v. Baby Girl*, 570 U.S. ___ (2013).

24. Author attended oral arguments in *Adoptive Couple v. Baby Girl* on April 16, 2013. Transcript on Supreme Court website at www.supremecourt.gov/oral_arguments/argument_transcripts/12-399_53k8.pdf. Before attorney Lisa Blatt, who represented the Capobiancos, could utter a complete sentence, Sotomayor interrupted with protracted questioning, the core of which was: "Is it your position that because that father's not a custodian, he has no protections whatsoever under [key parts of the law]?" Blatt tried to answer, but Sotomayor cut her off six times, amending the question as she interrupted. Chief Justice Roberts said, "Could I hear her answer, please?" Sotomayor's intensity did not ease when lawyer Paul Clement began to argue on behalf of baby Veronica in a legal guardian role. Sotomayor interrupted him, asking questions related to the "best interest of the child" standard, a legal calculus used in most states to help determine which parent receives custody of the child. When Clement tried to answer, Sotomayor cut him off twice. When she interrupted Clement a third time, Scalia interjected, telling Clement to "Please finish. Let's finish."

25. *Adoptive Couple v. Baby Girl*, Alito decision for the majority.

26. *Adoptive Couple v. Baby Girl*, Sotomayor dissent. Regarding the law, she highlighted Congress's goal of trying to prevent Indian children from ending up in homes with no connection to the tribe.

27. *Daimler AG v. Bauman*, 571 U.S. ___ (2014).

28. Sonia Sotomayor, Smithsonian Associates Evening Lecture, January 8, 2014, George Washington University, Washington, D.C.

29. Author interview with Judge Rosemary Pooler, February 6, 2014.

Selected Bibliography

ARCHIVES

George H. W. Bush Presidential Library

William Clinton Presidential Library

Senator Daniel Patrick Moynihan Papers, Library of Congress

Puerto Rican Legal Defense and Education Fund Collection, Hunter College, New York

Senate Judiciary Committee collections of questionnaires, transcripts, and other materials on nominees Sonia Sotomayor in 2009, to the Supreme Court, and in 1998 to the U.S. Court of Appeals for the Second Circuit; José Cabranes in 1994, to the U.S. Court of Appeals for the Second Circuit; Miguel Estrada in 2003, to the U.S. Court of Appeals for the District of Columbia Circuit; and Elena Kagan in 2010, to the Supreme Court

NEWSPAPERS, MAGAZINES, JOURNALS, AND PRESS AGENCIES

Associated Press, *Atlantic, Berkeley La Raza Law Journal, Boston Globe,* CENTRO *Journal, Chicago Tribune, Christian Science Monitor, Congressional Quarterly Weekly Report, Daily Princetonian, Foreign Policy, Hartford Courant, Hispanic-Business, Hispanic National Bar Association Journal of Law and Policy, Hispanic Outlook in Higher Education, Judicature, La Prensa San Diego, Latina, Los Angeles Times, Nation, National Journal, National Review, New Haven Register, New Republic, Newsweek,* New York *Daily News, New Yorker, New York Review of Books, New York Times, Politico,* Reuters, *Salon, Slate, Time,* USA Today, *Wall Street Journal, Washington Post, Yale Daily News*

BOOKS

Alter, Jonathan. *The Promise: President Obama, Year One.* New York: Simon & Schuster, 2011.

Aparicio, Frances R. *Listening to Salsa: Gender, Latin Popular Music, and Puerto Rican Cultures.* Middletown, Conn.: Wesleyan University Press, 1998.

Baker, Peter. *Days of Fire: Bush and Cheney in the White House.* New York: Doubleday, 2013.

Balz, Dan. *Collision 2012: Obama vs. Romney and the Future of Elections in America.* New York: Viking, 2013.

Bergad, Laird W., and Herbert S. Klein, *Hispanics in the United States: A Demographic, Social, and Economic History, 1980–2005.* New York: Cambridge University Press, 2010.

Biskupic, Joan. *American Original: The Life and Constitution of Supreme Court Justice Antonin Scalia.* New York: Sarah Crichton Books/Farrar, Straus and Giroux, 2009.

———. *Sandra Day O'Connor: How the First Woman on the Supreme Court Became Its Most Influential Justice.* New York: Ecco/HarperCollins, 2005.

Bowen, William G., and Derek Bok. *The Shape of the River: Long-Term Consequences of Considering Race in College and University Admissions.* Princeton, N.J.: Princeton University Press, 1998.

Bronner, Ethan. *Battle for Justice: How the Bork Nomination Shook America.* New York: Union Square Press, 2007.

Carter, Stephen L. *The Confirmation Mess: Cleaning Up the Federal Appointments Process.* New York: Basic Books, 1994.

Clinton, Bill. *My Life.* New York: Alfred A. Knopf, 2004.

Coyle, Marcia. *The Roberts Court: The Struggle for the Constitution.* New York: Simon & Schuster, 2013.

De Genova, Nicholas, and Ana Y. Ramos-Zayos. *Latino Crossings: Mexicans, Puerto Ricans, and the Politics of Race and Citizenship.* New York: Routledge, 2003.

Eisgruber, Christopher L. *The Next Justice: Repairing the Supreme Court Appointments Process.* Princeton, N.J.: Princeton University Press, 2007.

Fraga, Luis Ricardo, et al. *Latino Lives in America: Making It Home.* Philadelphia: Temple University Press, 2010.

Glazer, Nathan, and Daniel P. Moynihan. *Beyond the Melting Pot: The Negroes, Puerto Ricans, Jews, Italians, and Irish of New York City.* 2nd ed. Cambridge, Mass.: MIT Press, 1970.

Gonzalez, Juan. *Harvest of Empire: A History of Latinos in America.* New York: Penguin Books, 2000.

Greenburg, Jan Crawford. *Supreme Conflict: The Inside Struggle for Control of the United States Supreme Court.* New York: Penguin Press, 2007.

Greenhouse, Linda. *Becoming Justice Blackmun: Harry Blackmun's Supreme Court Journey.* New York: Times Books, 2005.

Helyar, John. *Lords of the Realm: The Real History of Baseball.* New York: Ballantine, 1994.

Hodgson, Godfrey. *The Gentleman from New York: Daniel Patrick Moynihan.* New York: Houghton Mifflin Harcourt, 2000.

Hutchinson, Dennis J. *The Man Who Once Was Whizzer White: Portrait of Justice Byron R. White.* New York: The Free Press, 1998.

Ifill, Gwen. *The Breakthrough: Politics and Race in the Age of Obama.* New York: Doubleday, 2009.

Jeffries, John C., Jr. *Justice Lewis F. Powell, Jr. and the Era of Judicial Balance.* New York: Scribner, 1994.

Jennings, Kenneth M. *Swings and Misses: Moribund Labor Relations in Professional Baseball.* Westport, Conn.: Praeger, 1997.

Katzmann, Robert A., ed. *Daniel Patrick Moynihan: The Intellectual in Public Life.* Washington, D.C.: Woodrow Wilson Center Press, 1998.

Klarman, Michael J. *From Jim Crow to Civil Rights: The Supreme Court and the Struggle for Racial Equality.* New York: Oxford University Press, 2004.

Lewis, Oscar. *La Vida: A Puerto Rican Family in the Culture of Poverty—San Juan and New York.* New York: Vintage Books, 1965.

Navarrette, Ruben, Jr. *A Darker Shade of Crimson: Odyssey of a Harvard Chicano.* New York: Bantam Books, 1993.

Obama, Barack. *The Audacity of Hope: Thoughts on Reclaiming the American Dream.* New York: Crown, 2006.

Ogletree, Charles J., Jr. *All Deliberate Speed: Reflections on the First Half Century of "Brown v. Board of Education."* New York: W. W. Norton, 2005.

Price, Polly J. *Judge Richard S. Arnold: A Legacy of Justice on the Federal Bench.* Amherst, N.Y.: Prometheus Books, 2009.

Remnick, David. *The Bridge: The Life and Rise of Barack Obama.* New York: Alfred A. Knopf, 2010.

Smelser, Neil J., William Julius Wilson, and Faith Mitchell, eds. *America Becoming: Racial Trends and Their Consequences,* vol. 1. National Research Council, Commission on Behavioral and Social Sciences and Education. Washington, D.C.: National Academy Press, 2001.

Soltero, Carlos R. *Latinos and American Law: Landmark Supreme Court Cases.* Austin: University of Texas Press, 2006.

Sotomayor, Sonia. *My Beloved World.* New York: Alfred A. Knopf, 2013.

Stephanopoulos, George. *All Too Human: A Political Education.* Boston: Little, Brown, 1999.

Strum, Philippa. *"Mendez v. Westminster": School Desegregation and Mexican-American Rights.* Lawrence: University of Kansas Press, 2010.

Suárez-Orozco, Marcelo M., and Mariela M. Paez, eds. *Latinos: Remaking America.* Berkeley: University of California Press, 2002.

Suro, Roberto. *Strangers Among Us: How Latino Immigration Is Transforming America.* New York: Alfred A. Knopf, 1998.

Thomas, Clarence. *My Grandfather's Son: A Memoir.* New York: Harper, 2007.

Thomas, Lorrin. *Puerto Rican Citizen: History and Political Identity in Twentieth-Century New York City.* Chicago: University of Chicago Press, 2010.

Thornburgh, Dick. *Where the Evidence Leads: An Autobiography*. Pittsburgh: University of Pittsburgh Press, 2003.

Toobin, Jeffrey. *The Oath: The Obama White House and the Supreme Court*. New York: Doubleday, 2012.

Tushnet, Mark. *In the Balance: Law and Politics on the Roberts Court*. New York: W. W. Norton, 2013.

Valencia, Reynaldo Anaya, Sonia R. Garcia, Henry Flores, and José Roberto Juárez, Jr. *Mexican Americans and the Law*. Tucson: University of Arizona Press, 2004.

Weisman, Steven R., ed. *Daniel Patrick Moynihan: A Portrait in Letters of an American Visionary*. New York: Public Affairs, 2010.

Williams, Juan. *Thurgood Marshall: American Revolutionary*. New York: Random House, 1998.

Wittes, Benjamin. *Confirmation Wars: Preserving Independent Courts in Angry Times*. Stanford, Calif.: Hoover Institution, 2006.

Acknowledgments

This book began a year after Sonia Sotomayor joined the Supreme Court, as an exploration of her rise in the judiciary and the progress of Latinos in America. The project grew more exciting with her early moves on the bench and beyond the Court. Yet none of the story would have ended up between these covers if I had not been supported by dear friends and colleagues.

Some of them have been with me for more than a decade on these book projects, talking out ideas, reading draft chapters, offering their wisdom. At the top of that list is Elder Witt, a former Supreme Court journalist who provided guidance early and often on this one. Others who especially enhanced this book were Douglas Armstrong, Dick Carelli, Jim Drinkard, Pam Fessler, Judith Gaskell, Liz Hayes, Robin Meszoly, Phyllis Richman, and Andrea Weiswasser.

Mark Hugo Lopez, Becky Rivera, Ishmael Rivera, and Roberto Suro offered insights along the way about Hispanic politics and culture. Lopez, director of the Pew Research Center's Hispanic Trends Project, was boundless with his time in this regard.

Erwin Chemerinsky, dean of the law school at the University of California–Irvine and a longtime friend, deserves special mention. He knows the law, he knows the Court, he knows this justice. He is also unmatched in his generosity, taking the time to provide substantive knowledge and personal encouragement no matter the hour on the California coast. Toni Locy, with whom I worked at *The*

Washington Post and *USA Today*, must be singled out, too. As I was nearing a crucial deadline at the end of 2013 and thinking I'd never make it, she stepped in with her trademark energy and assisted especially on the final chapters.

For the third time, the Woodrow Wilson International Center for Scholars offered me research help on a book project. Alice Bosley, a WWIC research fellow in summer 2011, was first-rate, as was Edward Lawrence, my researcher on the Antonin Scalia biography who returned to help me in 2013. My thanks go especially to Lee Hamilton, Jane Harman, and Mike Van Dusen. The Wilson Center makes books possible.

In my daily journalism, I have been guided by a series of remarkable editors, including Fred Barbash, with whom I worked at *The Washington Post* in the 1990s and at Reuters more recently. Fred's reporting on the Court in the 1980s remains a model. At *USA Today*, my home when this book began, three editors at the time, Lee Horwich, David Lindsey, and Rachel Smolkin, were especially encouraging of this project. Now at Reuters, I have the lucky fate that nearly everyone up my editing chain is not only passionate about journalism but also holds a law degree and is intrigued by all things judicial: from Howard Goller and Amy Stevens, with whom I work most closely, to Dayan Candappa, editor for the Americas, and Steve Adler, editor in chief. I am above all grateful to Howard, who turned his sharp editor's eye to the final draft.

Others in the Reuters Washington bureau whose friendship and professionalism have sustained me along the way include Marilyn Thompson, our bureau chief, who I was fortunate enough to know first as an editor in the 1990s, and colleagues Caren Bohan, Kevin Drawbaugh, Ros Krasny, Katherina Lemus, Jack Shafer, and John Shiffman.

For twenty-five years, I have been part of a top-flight press corps at the Supreme Court. Two in our ranks were exceptionally generous in reading chapters and helping me explore ideas: Garrett Epps and Adam Liptak. Their thoughts made this a stronger book. Others who lent advice include Bob Barnes, Marcia Coyle, Tony Mauro,

David Savage, Mark Sherman, Nina Totenberg, and Pete Williams. I have special appreciation for Lawrence Hurley, my partner covering the Supreme Court for Reuters.

At the Court, Public Information Officer Kathy Arberg and deputy Patricia McCabe Estrada were as professional as ever in arranging interviews and answering research questions. Court photographer Steve Petteway, with his usual creativity and cheer, helped round up the best photos.

I am grateful to Justice Sotomayor for her time and candor. This book was not "authorized," and she was writing her autobiography for most of the time this project was under way. Yet she allowed me numerous visits to clarify and elucidate her life and views. Anchored by Theresa Bartenope, her staff was unfailingly obliging as I pursued information and trailed after the justice on her appearances, including to Puerto Rico.

My agents, Gail Ross and Howard Yoon, gave smart, steady advice. Without Howard's support, especially, this book simply might not have been completed on time.

Finally, but essentially: Sarah Crichton, editor extraordinaire at Farrar, Straus and Giroux. Her ideas are fresh, her editing inspired, her humor sustaining. The super-efficient Marsha Sasmor joined Sarah as an editorial assistant just as this book was landing. I could not imagine finishing it without her.

My family likes these books most when they are done. In the intervening months (years), I am too preoccupied, postpone vacations, and fill our house with toppling stacks of research. Yet everyone I love seems to hang in there with me, generating appreciation as high as those stacks. My mother, Mary Jane Biskupic, remains a creative influence, as does the memory of my late father, Vince Biskupic. My husband, Clay, and daughter, Elizabeth, put up with the worst yet offer the most. My dedication page never changes.

Index

A NOTE ABOUT THE AUTHOR

Joan Biskupic has covered the U.S. Supreme Court for more than twenty years and is the author of several books, including *American Original: The Life and Constitution of Supreme Court Justice Antonin Scalia* and *Sandra Day O'Connor: How the First Woman on the Supreme Court Became Its Most Influential Justice.* Biskupic is an editor in charge for legal affairs at Reuters News. Before joining Reuters in 2012, she was the Supreme Court correspondent for *The Washington Post* and for *USA Today.* A graduate of Georgetown Law, she is a regular panelist on PBS's *Washington Week* with Gwen Ifill. She lives in Washington, D.C., with her husband and daughter.